Lecture Notes in Computer Science 1167

Edited by G. Goos, J. Hartmanis and J. van Leeuwen

Advisory Board: W. Brauer D. Gries J. Stoer

Springer
Berlin
Heidelberg
New York
Barcelona
Budapest
Hong Kong
London
Milan
Paris
Santa Clara
Singapore
Tokyo

Ian Sommerville (Ed.)

Software Configuration Management

ICSE'96 SCM-6 Workshop
Berlin, Germany, March 25-26, 1996
Selected Papers

Springer

Series Editors

Gerhard Goos, Karlsruhe University, Germany

Juris Hartmanis, Cornell University, NY, USA

Jan van Leeuwen, Utrecht University, The Netherlands

Volume Editor

Ian Sommerville
Computing Department, Lancaster University
Lancaster LA1 4YR, UK
E-mail: is@comp.lancs.ac.uk

Cataloging-in-Publication data applied for

Die Deutsche Bibliothek - CIP-Einheitsaufnahme

Software configuration management : selected papers / ICSE 96
SCM-6 Workshop, Berlin, Germany, March 25 - 26, 1996. Ian
Sommerville (ed.). - Berlin ; Heidelberg ; New York ;
Barcelona ; Budapest ; Hong Kong ; London ; Milan ; Paris ;
Santa Clara ; Singapore ; Tokyo : Springer, 1996
  (Lecture notes in computer science ; Vol. 1167)
  ISBN 3-540-61964-X
NE: Sommerville, Ian [Hrsg.]; ICSE <18, 1996, Berlin>; SCM <6, 1996,
  Berlin>; GT

CR Subject Classification (1991): D.2, K.6

ISSN 0302-9743
ISBN 3-540-61964-X Springer-Verlag Berlin Heidelberg New York

Typesetting: Camera-ready by author
SPIN 10549195   06/3142 – 5 4 3 2 1 0   Printed on acid-free paper

Table of Contents

CM Challenges for the 21st Century

Selected Position Papers

Program Committee

Program Chair

Ian Sommerville, Lancaster University (UK)

Program Committee Members

Reidar Conradi, NTNU (Norway)

Walter Tichy, Univ. of Karlsruhe (Germany)

Jacky Estublier, LSR (France)

Susan Dart, Dart Technology Strategies (USA)

Stu Feldman, IBM (USA)

Introduction

Ian Sommerville

Computing Dept., Lancaster University, LANCASTER LA1 4YR, UK.
E-mail: is@comp.lancs.ac.uk

The sixth international workshop on software configuration management was held in Berlin in March 1996, in conjunction with the 18th International Conference on Software Engineering (ICSE 18). There were a total of 49 attendees from industry, research laboratories and universities. The workshop was supplemented by demonstrations of SCM tools by Continuus Software Corporation and of a client-server system, implemented by the University of Karlsruhe, for WWW-based revision control. These proceedings include all full papers which were accepted for the workshop and a selection of the position papers which were submitted by attendees.

The workshop was organised in six sessions:

1. Versioning models and experiences

2. Version space management

3. CM databases and workspaces

4. Distributed configuration management

5. Industrial experiences with CM systems

6. CM challenges for the 21st century

The key objective of the workshop was to initiate a dialogue between practitioners in industry with software configuration management (SCM) problems and researchers developing new SCM technology. It was recognised that there is an urgent need for effective technology transfer in this area. We felt that the workshop could be a catalyst for this. In this respect, the workshop was a success. Research-based presentations showed an awareness of industrial needs and there were several good industrial presentations which reported positive experiences with introducing SCM and SCM technology.

1 Versioning models and experiences

The opening presentation of the workshop was made by Andreas Zeller of the Technical University of Braunschweig, Germany who described a system called ICE - an Incremental Configuration Environment. ICE is based on a formalism called feature logic which is used to denote sets and operations and to deduce consistency. Features are akin to attributes and are used to characterise versions, components and configurations. An experimental system has been built around this and incorporated into a featured file system which can serve as a basis for a set of configuration management tools.

The provision of configuration support in a collaborative program editing system was the topic of the second presentation by Boris Magnusson of Lund University, Sweden. As well as control over system versions, an important objective of the work was to provide collaboration awareness so that users editing a program were aware of other concurrent editing activities on different versions. Ultimately, it is planned to provide a window onto these other users so that synchronous collaboration is possible. The work so far has focused on providing a framework for version support and viewing mechanisms to represent version information to users.

The third presentation by James Hunt of the University of Karlsruhe, Germany entitled 'An Empirical Study of Delta Algorithms' was something completely different. Hunt and his colleagues Kiem-Phong Vo and Walter Tichy had carried out an empirical comparison of several delta algorithms which are used to compute the differences or deltas between versions. They used 2 complete versions of the gnu gcc and gnu emacs software as an experimental vehicle. They compared the Unix diff algorithm with newer bdiff and vdelta algorithms and found that these newer algorithms gave far superior performance. They also found that when diff was used to compute deltas on uuencoded binary code it was particularly inefficient and sometimes resulted in deltas larger than the original files. Their conclusion was that you should throw away diff as a basis for computing deltas and move to one of the newer algorithms which have been developed.

Finally, in this session, Chris Seiwald from P3 software presented an industrial perspective. He described his work in developing a practical and easily comprehensible method of representing variants i.e. the alternative implementations of a configuration item. Rather than manage these as a version tree, the identification of a variant is moved to the name of the configuration item leaving the version namespace as a linear set of revisions. Therefore, the name applies to each branch of the version tree rather than to a single file.

This approach has been implemented in a commercial software product called P3. The key advantages of this system is that it presents a simple model to developers and allows them to build and maintain a product in an environment which is customised to their needs.

2 Version space management

David Tilbrook from qef Advanced Software, USA also described a commercial SCM product (qef) which is being developed by his company. Early versions of the system have already been used by a number of large companies. qef addresses the same problem as the widely-used Unix utility make. Make can be thought of a relatively simple tool which is driven by a complex script constructed by end-users. This is an error-prone process. qef's approach is more abstract and hence less prone to user error. It uses simple user commands which drive a set of more complex tools. The sequence of operations consists of constructing the parameter/configuration database (using a tool called lclvrs), processing a user script, which refers to this database, to generate a sequence of build instructions and, finally, interpreting these to build the system. Tilbrook claimed that system building using qef was much simper, more consistent and more efficient than with make.

Bernard Westfechtel reported on work carried out with Reidar Conradi at the Norwegian University of Technology and Science where he surveyed different approaches to configuring versioned software products. Westfechtel identified two complementary approaches which are used by different tools:

1. Version-oriented modelling where the configuration is described in terms of explicit versions of components. Version rules, in conjunction with attributes and history information, are used to select versions.

2. Change-oriented models which describe configurations in terms of changes to some base version. No explicit reference to component versions are used and a change description may reference multiple components.

Westfechtel compared commercially available SCM tools using this classification (the paper is a very useful listing of available tools). His conclusion was that both approaches have particular strengths and we need further research to investigate how they may be integrated.

The following presentation by Bjoern Munch from Telenor, R&D, Norway complemented Westfechel's talk in that it gave a more detailed description of research in change-oriented versioning. Based on the CoV system which supported version selection by querying a database by defining a set of options used to select product versions, Munch had addressed problems of the usability of this system. users did not know which options to select and which option combinations were appropriate. He developed two tools namely VRMAN for creating and manipulating version rules and COVST for version selection. The overall system makes it easier to navigate through the set of available options, minimises the number of options which must be selected avoids user errors and prevents accidental changes to versions.

3 Discussion

The first day's discussion was sparked off by the last presentation on change-oriented versioning and change-oriented and version-oriented views of configurations. It was suggested that the change-oriented approach is most appropriate for process management (i.e. how are change requests dealt with and implemented) but it was difficult to ensure that changes were managed individually rather than as part of the normal system evolution process. There was a natural tendency to mix change implementation and other development processes.

There was general agreement that end-users of applications were not interested in a version model but were interested in the changes made to previous versions and, at a more abstract level, in the features offered by different versions of a system.

These different views were seen as appropriate to different stakeholders in the SCM process:

1. The feature view (logical/functional changes) was appropriate to managers and quality assurance people.

2. The change view (the actual change set) was appropriate to quality assurance people and to end-users of the system who request changes (e.g. bug fixes)

3. The version/file view was appropriate to developers responsible for implementing system changes.

Other issues which were touched on during the discussion included the problems of usability as identified in Seiwald's talk, the interaction between SCM systems and the embedded SCM which exists in a number of products such as Lotus Notes) and the challenges posed to the SCM-community by the moves towards end-user development on PC-based systems. We recognised that approaches to SCM which were used in large projects could not be simply transferred to end-user development environments. However, we only agreed that these were problems; we didn't come up with any answers!

4   CM databases and workspaces

The second day of the workshop was opened by a presentation from Jacky Estublier from LSR, Grenoble, France who discussed workspace management in software engineering environments. Estublier made the point that effective workspace management was required to support teams working on shared artefacts. A work space manager was required to identify the data to be worked on, to provide the data where it was needed in a distribute environment and to represent the data in the form required by tools or people using that data. Effective solutions in this area need input from SCM, CSCW, databases and process management research.

The solution which has been implemented in the Adele environment provides tailorable collaboration policies which define how artefacts in the workspaces of people using the system may be shared. A synchronize command is provided to invoke these policies and synchronize the user workspaces as defined. A library of basic collaboration policies has been defined. The workspace manager has been implemented using database triggers with the objective of providing a mechanism for cooperative process support integrated with the database.

Dewayne Perry from AT&T Bell Labs, Lucent Technology, USA talked mostly about an approach for maintaining consistency across configurations but also explained some of the recent changes in AT & T's organisation. In telecommunication systems, the features of the system such as call forwarding are implemented using a number of components in the design hierarchy. These components therefore have shared dependencies, the topic covered by the presentation. Conventional CM provides some support for managing dependencies between design entities but not the orthogonal dependencies between features and components. Perry has developed a formalism to support reasoning about the consequences of substituting one component for another in the system design. This requires special interfaces to be introduced and component interface specifications to be formally defined using his formalism. Perry explained how reasoning about shared dependencies was therefore possible. This helps to address the shared dependency problem but, during the discussion which followed the talk, Perry agreed that it would be difficult to transfer this technology to practical use.

5   Distributed configuration management

Herman Rao from AT&T Research, USA described a system called GRADIENT which addressed the problems of supporting distributed R&D and, in particular, helped manage configurations in multi-site development. This system has been developed by Rao and his colleagues Dave Belanger and David Korn.

The cooperating R&D sites were in the eastern USA and Taiwan so they had to cope with a 12 hour time difference and had only a relatively low bandwidth communication link between the sites. Their solution was based on replicated repositories of versioned objects which could be treated as either files (delivering their contents) or as directories (delivering the object versions). These were implemented using deltas from a base object and only deltas were transferred between sites. The system was implemented to make it appear to users that they were working in the Unix file system and only two new commands were required. Rao emphasised the importance of simplicity and usability and how this contributed to the acceptance of the system by developers.

Stefan Hänßgen with his colleagues James Hunt, Walter Tichy, and Jurgen Reuter from the University of Karlsruhe, Germany described a WWW-based system to support version management. This was a client server system with a server managing the system versions and clients implemented on top of the Netscape browser. The advantage of this system was global connectivity, platform independence and rapid development of clients. The revision server dynamically created html pages and transmitted them to clients. Files to be checked out were requested and delivered to the client system. Check-in was managed by developing a helper application which communicated directly with the server for file transfer.

The final presentation in this session was given by Josephine Micallef of Bellcore, USA who worked with Geoff Clemm from Atria software to develop Asgard, a system for activity-based configuration management. The system provides support for change tracking, version selection and team work.

In the classification proposed by Westfechtel, Asgard is a change-oriented system. It has been built on top of the ClearCase SCM tools from Atria Software. Using Asgard, developers specify the source versions to be used by defining a baseline and a list of activities where an activity is a cluster of versions produced in some development task. Version selection in the case of ambiguities is a manual process. Activities may have nested sub-activities to model task decomposition. A new baseline may be created and the activities used to create that baseline are removed from the workspace activity list.

6 Industrial experiences with CM systems

Jorma Taramaa from VTT Electronics, Finland described work he had done with Antti Auer as part of the LEIVO project, a Finnish project concerned with the configuration management of embedded software. They surveyed th configuration management practices of a number of companies involved in embedded software development and found a very wide range of configuration management maturity in these companies. The SCM practices varied from virtually no configuration management or very informal, ad hoc practices to comprehensive product management.

To introduce SCM into an organisation and to promote continual improvement of SCM processes and procedures, Taramaa and Auer proposed an incremental SCM introduction model. At the base of this model were simple practices such as elementary version control; in the middle of the model were automated and process-oriented configuration management and at the summit were application management and massive software reuse. In introducing SCM, Taramaa emphasised the importance of understanding the current SCM practices in a company, the domain of applications and the role of software developers in product technologies.

Jacqueline Floch from SINTEF, Norway presented work done by Björn Gulla and Joe Gorman which discussed experiences with the use of a configuration language in describing the product configurations of telecommunications products. This language, called PCL (Proteus Configuration Language), was used in conjunction with the SDL method to specify the structure of communication systems. This system model (922 lines of code compared to a 1262 linemakefile) was then used as a basis for system building. PCL allows families of systems to be modelled, provides integrated tool descriptions, facilities to represent variability in system families and to link logical and physical system models. PCL has an associated set of tools to create and edit system models, to remove variability from model descriptions, to build systems and to reverse engineer system models from file system configurations.

Their practical experience with PCL was positive and its facilities to provide a complete hardware and software system model were appreciated. The PCL model of a 70KLOC system was 922 lines of code compared with 1262 lines in the makefile. However, the loose integration between the SDL tools and the PCL tools caused problems in maintaining model consistency and the lack of maturity of the PCL toolset was also a significant hindrance to model development.

Sissel Kolvik from Stentofon, Norway gave an excellent talk on the practicalities of introducing configuration management into a small company developing systems products. The objective of the work, carried out as part of the Norwegian SISU project, was to introduce CM for all managed entities i.e. software, hardware components, hardware designs, documentation, etc. She made the points that the principal problems faced were not technical but were organisational . Their was a need for SCM champions who must be prepared to introduce configuration management in an incremental way. They must be both patient (as results take time) and stubborn (as the results will eventually appear). All stakeholders from senior management to hardware and software engineers must be convinced that there is value for them in introducing new processes with configuration management.

7 CM challenges for the 21st century

This session was originally intended to focus on technical issues which CM researchers might address in the development of SCM solutions for the 21st century. However, it seemed that the key challenges which we face are technology transfer challenges to ensure that effective SCM support is deployed and used in large and small organisations.

Taek Lee gave an interesting complementary talk to Sissel Kolvik where he described work he has done with his colleagues Peggy Thomas and Vivienne Lowen in introducing CM into the Xerox organisation. This was done in the context of a project called Odysssey, a system of 450KLOC being developed by about 45 people. The transition to configuration management was done in the context of Xerox's objective of quality improvement and their aim to become a CMM Level 2 organisation.

The key requirements were to support concurrent system development across releases and different Unix systems and to develop a solution which was standard, portable, reliable and dynamically generated dependencies. Lee emphasised the importance of good process definition and briefly described the configuration management process which he and his colleagues have developed. This is based on a standard directory structure, widely available tools (Imake and Gnu make) plus a specially written Electronic Filing Assistant which is used to inform team members by E-mail of all new checkins. Significant productivity gains have been observed after introducing the system.

Susan Dart from Continuus Software Corporation described the best practice for choosing and deploying an SCM solution. A number of high quality tools are now available and these can contribute significantly to improving software development processes. Dart suggested that companies could either have an enterprise-wide SCM solution i.e. a single solution for all development teams or a project-based approach where solutions were introduced incrementally on a project by project basis. While this latter approach is quicker and easier, it can lead to piecemeal solutions with different tools used in different parts of an organisation.

Introducing an SCM solution involves procurement of the systems and the deployment of the systems in an organisation. Under procurement, organisations must budget for all elements of the solution (not just tool costs but also training, customisation, consultancy, etc.), tool evaluation and selection and preparing for system deployment. Deployment involves using a focused deployment team which uses a risk-based adoption methodology to design and (where possible) automate SCM processes. Key lessons learned were the need to allow enough time for procurement and deployment, to work with vendors and to ensure that all users see some gain from the new configuration management systems.

8 Discussion

Based on the presentations on experiences in introducing SCM into organisations, the open discussion started with organisational issues and the problems of introducing CM. One of the previous speakers had made the point that the tools were only 10% of the problem (or the solution) and that the other 90% were organisational. This met with fairly general agreement. Under this heading, there was a wide-ranging discussion where the need for metrics to strengthen the case for configuration management was discussed. There were opposing views on the introduction of SCM - should it be a top-down management crusade or should it be introduced by guerrilla tactics by small innovative groups? Top-down introduction would be helped if there was some kind of investment model for configuration management; bottom-up introduction needs cheap tools.

The general discussion on how to introduce SCM and the capital investments required led to a wide-ranging discussion on tool pricing. There was a widespread feeling that good quality tools were so expensive that, in many organisations, it was difficult to justify their costs irrespective of the facilities which they provide. The notion of a 'ClearCase-lite' was proposed which was a lower cost, lower functionality system that organisations could invest in and expand as their SCM maturity increased. There was much support for this although vendor representatives made the case that, because of their marketing costs, this was unlikely to generate sufficient income for development.

In summary, we concluded that:

1. Configuration management is concerned with version modelling and product modelling in a database or repository. Process modelling and support is important.

2. There is a need for the SCM community to interact with people working in other areas such as databases, process modelling and technologies and CSCW.

3. Research issues include user interfaces for SCM, tool architectures and ways to measure the efffectiveness of software configuration management.

Smooth Operations with Square Operators —
The Version Set Model in ICE

Andreas Zeller*

Technische Universität Braunschweig
Abteilung Softwaretechnologie
D-38092 Braunschweig
zeller@acm.org

Abstract Implementing software configuration management (SCM) in an organization raises various integration problems. We present the *Incremental Configuration Environment* (ICE), a novel SCM system providing smooth integration with both the software process and the development environment. ICE is based on the *version set model*, where versions, components, and configurations are grouped into sets according to their features, using *feature logic* as a formal base to denote sets and operations and to deduce consistency. Version sets generalize well-known SCM concepts such as components, repositories, workspaces, or configurations and allow for flexibility in combining these concepts. For integration in software development environments, ICE provides a *featured file system* (FFS), where version sets are represented as files and directories. In the FFS, arbitrary programs can incrementally access and explore version sets. Using the well-known C preprocessor (CPP) representation, users can view and edit multiple versions simultaneously, while still only the differences between version sets are stored. Facilities for multi-version merging or deductive program construction care for effective work coordination and automatic reuse of derived objects.

Key words: Software configuration management, Version control, File systems management, Deduction and theorem proving, Knowledge representation formalisms and methods, Feature logic

1   Introduction

Implementing software configuration management (SCM) in an organization raises various integration problems. Each SCM system realizes a specific SCM model. For an organization, adopting a specific SCM model through the purchase of an SCM system means to adapt the software process such that the model fits in. Moreover, adopting a SCM model is a long-term commitment as the current SCM models do not integrate well with each other. Other integration problems occur in the software development environment, where existing tools must be extended to access SCM items.

In this paper, we present the *Incremental Configuration Environment* (ICE), a novel SCM system providing integration with both the software process and the development

* This work is funded by the Deutsche Forschungsgemeinschaft, grants Sn11/1-2 and Sn11/2-2.

environment. ICE is based on the *version set model*, a logic-based SCM model realizing an integrated uniform approach to SCM tasks like variant control, revision control, workspace management or software builds. Through version sets, ICE allows for flexibility in realizing the desired SCM process. For integration with the development environment, ICE provides a *featured file system* (FFS), where version sets are represented as files and directories and where arbitrary programs can incrementally access and explore version sets.

ICE has a strong formal foundation. In ICE, all SCM tasks are described through operations on *version sets*. Version sets are sets of objects (typically software components), characterized by a *feature term*—a boolean expression over *(feature: value)*-attributions denoting common and individual version properties, following the SCM convention to characterize objects by their attributes. Using *feature logic*, intersection, union, and complement operations on version sets are realized in order to express and generalize the semantics of SCM models.

2 Basic Notions of Feature Logic

We begin with a short overview of feature logic. Feature terms and feature logic have originally been developed for semantic analysis of natural language [19, 37]. Later, they were used as a general mechanism for knowledge representation [4, 31] and as a basis for logic programming [18, 38]. Throughout this paper, we will concentrate on an intuitive understanding, based on the formal semantics described by Smolka [39]; a full description of feature logic is contained in [47].

In feature logic, *feature terms* denote sets of objects characterized by certain features. In their simplest form, feature terms consist of a conjunction of *(feature: value)*-pairs, called *slots*, where each feature represents an attribute of an object. Feature values may be literals, variables, and (nested) feature terms; PROLOG-like first-order terms may also be used. As an example, consider the following feature term T, which expresses linguistic properties of a piece of natural language:

$$T = \begin{bmatrix} tense: present, \\ predicate: [verb: sing, agent: X, what: Y], \\ subject: [X, num: sg, person: third], \\ object: Y \end{bmatrix}$$

This term says that the language fragment is in present tense, third person singular, that the agent of the predicate is equal to the subject etc.: T is a representation of the sentence template "X sings Y".

The syntax of feature terms is given in table 1, where a denotes a literal (e.g. numbers, strings, and atomic constants), V denotes a variable, f and g denote features, and S and T denote feature terms. complement operations. If $S = [f: X]$ and $T = [g: Y]$, then $S \sqcap T = [f: X, g: Y]$, which is read as "$f$ has value X and g has value Y". Similarly, $S \sqcup T = \{f: X, g: Y\}$, which is read as "$f$ has value X or g has value Y". Feature values may be feature terms as well; in this paper, we restrict ourselves to simple equivalences like $f: \{X, Y\} = \{f: X, f: Y\}$, which is read "$f$ has value X or Y". For implications, we write $S \rightarrow T$ instead of the equivalent $\sim S \sqcup T$. Feature terms form

Notation	Name	Interpretation
a	Literal	
V	Variable	
$\top$ (also [])	Top	Ignorance
$\bot$ (also {})	Bottom	Inconsistency
$f:S$	Selection	The value of f is S
$f:\top$	Existence	f is defined
$f\uparrow$	Divergence	f is undefined
$f\downarrow g$	Agreement	f and g have the same value
$f\uparrow g$	Disagreement	f and g have different values
$S\sqcap T$ (also $[S,T]$)	Intersection	Both S and T hold
$S\sqcup T$ (also $\{S,T\}$)	Union	S or T holds
$\sim S$	Complement	S does not hold
$S\to T$	Implication	If S holds, then T holds
$S\sqsupseteq T$	Subsumption	S subsumes T; T implies S

Table 1. The syntax of feature terms

a boolean algebra; boolean transformations like distribution, de Morgan's law etc. hold for feature terms as well.

Sometimes it is necessary to specify that a feature exists (i.e. is defined, but without giving any value), or that a feature does not exist in a feature term. This is written $f:\top$ resp. $\sim f:\top$ (abbreviated as $f\uparrow$). The possibility to specify complements greatly increases the expressive power of the logic. For example, the term $\sim[compiler\!:gcc]$ denotes all objects whose feature *compiler* is either undefined or has another value than *gcc*. The term $[compiler\!:\sim gcc]$ denotes all objects whose feature *compiler* is defined, but with a value other than *gcc*.

A feature term can be interpreted as a representation of the infinite set of all ground terms T' which are *subsumed* by the original term T (that is, $T\sqsupseteq T'$). Subsumed terms are obtained by substituting variables or adding more features. Hence, feature terms always allow for further specialization, like classes in object-oriented models. For instance, $\top\sqsupseteq[fruit\!:apple]\sqsupseteq[fruit\!:apple,color\!:green]\sqsupseteq$ $[fruit\!:apple,color\!:green,wormy\!:no]$, and so on.

Feature logic also provides a simple consistency notion. As feature logic assumes that each feature can have only one value, the term $[os\!:dos,os\!:unix]$ is equivalent to $\bot$, the empty set; such terms are called *inconsistent*. Through *feature unification* [39], a constraint-solving technique, one can determine consistency of arbitrary feature terms. For terms without unions and complements, feature unification works similar to classical unification of first-order terms; the only difference is that subterms are not identified by position (as in PROLOG), but by feature name. Adding unions forces unification to compute a (finite) union of unifiers as well, whereas complements are usually handled by constraint solving (similar to negation as failure).

3 Versions and Version Sets

We now give a summary of the version set model, following [47]. To model version sets, each version of a component k is tagged with a term $K' = [object\!:k]\sqcap K$, where k

is some unique component identifier, and K is a feature term describing the features of the specific version. K and K' may be interpreted as boolean expressions denoting the features of k; formally, each K' is a singleton set containing the version K of the object k. The component itself is identified by K, where K is the union of all sets K' (or, using boolean interpretation, the logical "or" of all version features). So, if we have a component k in n versions $V_1, V_2, \ldots, V_n$, the version set K is determined as

$$K = V_1 \sqcup V_2 \sqcup \cdots \sqcup V_n = \bigsqcup_{i=1}^{n} V_i \ .$$

Features F of the component itself (as $[object: k]$) are the same across all versions, and hence can be factored out through

$$(F \sqcap V_1) \sqcup (F \sqcap V_2) = F \sqcap (V_1 \sqcup V_2) \ .$$

As a simple example, consider the *tty* component of the EMACS editor. The EMACS editor comes in two major variants: one called GNU EMACS that is maintained by the Free Software Foundation (FSF), and one called XEMACS that stems from a collaboration of Lucid, Inc. with Sun Microsystems, Inc. and the University of Illinois. Until its latest revision, XEMACS ran on the X window system only and had no teletype (TTY) support; the *tty* component did not work. The *tty* component thus comes in three versions:

$$tty_1 = [object: tty, author: fsf, tty\text{-}support: true]$$
$$tty_2 = [object: tty, author: lucid, tty\text{-}support: false]$$
$$tty_3 = [object: tty, author: lucid, tty\text{-}support: true]$$

The version set denoting all versions of *tty* is

$$tty = tty_1 \sqcup tty_2 \sqcup tty_3$$
$$= \big[object: tty, \{[author: fsf, tty\text{-}support: true],$$
$$[author: lucid, tty\text{-}support: \{true, false\}]\}\big]$$

To access a specific version in a version set T, we intersect T with a *selection term* S specifying the desired features. For any selection term S and a set of versions T, we can identify the versions satisfying S by determining $T' = T \sqcap S$—that is, the set of versions that are in S as well as in T. If $T' = \bot$, or if T' does not denote any existing version, selection fails. In the above example, selecting $S = [tty\text{-}support: true]$ from the *tty* component results in $tty \sqcap S = (tty_1 \sqcup tty_2 \sqcup tty_3) \sqcap S = (tty_1 \sqcap S) \sqcup (tty_2 \sqcap S) \sqcup (tty_3 \sqcap S) = tty_1 \sqcup \bot \sqcup tty_3 = [object: tty, author: \{fsf, lucid\}, tty\text{-}support: true]$. The tty_2 version is excluded, because the *tty-support* feature may have only one value; therefore, $tty_2 \sqcap S = \bot$ holds.

The version set resulting from a selection need not be singleton. In our example, a second selection is required to choose the final version by specifying the author as either *fsf* or *lucid*.

4 Systems and Configurations

When versions and components are composed to configurations, the configurations inherit the features of the components. For instance, any configuration containing the tty_2 component will have the feature [*tty-support*: *false*]. Obviously, configuration features are obtained by intersection of the component features. However, not all component features need be common: features like *author* or *status* might be different across components, *object* features differ by definition. The idea is to make such features dependent on the current object, using implications like [*object*: *tty*] → [*author*: *richard*] to ensure that whenever the *tty* object is selected, Richard's version is returned.

To construct such implications, we define a special *aggregation operator*. The operator "$⊞_I$" is similar to "$⊓$", but has a special handling of independent features: instead of unifying them, it makes them dependent on the specific component; *object* features are stripped altogether. Let $I = \{f_1: \top, f_2: \top, \ldots, f_n: \top\}$ be a feature term denoting independent features. Let S and T denote components with

$$S = [object: s] \sqcap S' \sqcap S'' \quad and \quad T = [object: t] \sqcap T' \sqcap T'' \ ,$$

such that S'', $T'' \sqsubseteq I$ denote the independent features, and S', $T' \not\sqsubseteq I$ denote ordinary features. The *aggregation* of S and T, written $S ⊞_I T$, is then defined as

$$S ⊞_I T = S' \sqcap T' \sqcap \big([object: s] \to S''\big) \sqcap \big([object: t] \to T''\big) \ .$$

We shall now demonstrate the use of the aggregation operator. Beside *tty*, let us assume we have a second component *display* = $display_1 \sqcup display_2$ coming in an X window version

$$display_1 = [object: display, author: fsf, display\text{-}model: x]$$

and a TTY version

$$display_2 = [object: display, author: fsf, display\text{-}model: tty, tty\text{-}support: true] \ .$$

Using "$⊞_I$" with $I \sqsupseteq \{object: \top, author: \top\}$ containing the independent features, $tty_2 ⊞_I$ $display_1$ is

$$\big[[object: display] \to [author: fsf], [object: tty] \to [author: lucid],$$
$$display\text{-}model: x, tty\text{-}support: false\big] \ ,$$

that is, a term selecting the *fsf* version from the *display* component and the *lucid* version from the *tty* component, and correctly describing the remaining common features. Formally, if we have a configuration C composed of n components $K_1, K_2, \ldots, K_n$ with $K_i \sqsubseteq [object: k_i]$, and a term I denoting the independent features, the configuration C is identified by

$$C = [object: k_1 \sqcup k_2 \sqcup \cdots \sqcup k_n] \sqcap \boxed{+}_I{}^{n}_{i=1} K_i \ ,$$

that is, *object* features are united, independent features are made dependent on the respective component, and all other features are unified.[2] From a configuration C, we

---

[2] In [46], we used simple intersection for configurations, ignoring independent features.

may again select arbitrary subsets, just like versions are selected from ordinary version sets. Each version set C contains only configurations which are consistent respective to their features. For instance, we cannot compose a configuration from $display_2$ and tty_2, since their *tty-support* features differ; formally, $display_2 \sqcap_I tty_2 = \perp$.

5 Revisions and Workspaces

The version set model was born out of the need to determine consistency in aggregates of program variants identified by features. By assigning appropriate features, our model can easily accommodate other SCM concepts like revisions and workspaces.

In our model, revisions are distinguished whether a change (or *delta*) has been applied, or not—which is represented by existence or non-existence of a *delta feature* standing for the change application. Let δ_i be the change leading up to a revision R_i. To every R_i revision except the originating R_0, we assign a delta feature $[\delta_i: \top]$. Each revision R_i also inherits the delta features of all revisions it is based upon, such that a revision R_2 based on revision R_1 has the features $[\delta_1: \top, \delta_2: \top]$—that is, revision R_2 is the result of the δ_1 and δ_2 changes applied to revision R_0. For convenience, we shall use the abbreviations $\Delta_i = [\delta_i: \top]$ and $\nabla_i = \sim\Delta_i = [\delta_i\uparrow]$ in the remainder of this paper.

As shown in figure 1, each new revision forms a subset of the originating version set, resulting in a subsumption lattice. Revisions are selected by specifying included and excluded changes, denoting paths in the lattice. For instance, in figure 1, revision R_3 is selected by including δ_3 and excluding δ_4; the selection term is $\Delta_3 \sqcap \nabla_4 = [\delta_3: \top, \delta_4\uparrow]$.

Workspaces are areas where users can make changes independent of other users. To model workspaces, we assign individual features like *user* or *team* denoting individual variants. Changes are confined to a workspace by applying them to the individual workspace variants only. When user Jamie performs a change in his workspace $W = [user: jamie]$, only the W variants are touched; user Richard in his workspace $W' = [user: richard]$ will not see any of Jamie's changes, since $W' \sqsubseteq \sim W$.

Revisions and workspaces are specified and selected just the way variants are, by intersection with a selection term S, where S may contain other features as well. For instance, $S = [\Delta_5, os: unix]$ selects a UNIX variant where the change δ_5 has been applied; $S = \{\nabla_3, user: jamie\}$ selects all versions either in Jamie's workspace or where the change δ_3 has not been applied. To select specific or current revisions, implications like $[[r_3: \top] \rightarrow [\Delta_3, \nabla_4], [current: \top] \rightarrow [r_3: \top]]$ can be added to the features of the revision set R, such that the current revision can be selected via $R \sqcap [current: \top] = R_3$. More details on implications, revisions and workspaces can be found in [45] and [47].

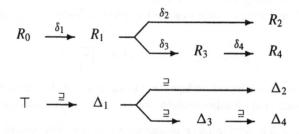

Figure 1. A revision history and its version sets

6 Unified Version Selection

In practice, it may prove useful to support additional selection schemes. Some SCM systems select component versions through a set of configuration rules, using PROLOG-like syntax as in SHAPE [24, 28] or pattern matching rules as in CLEARCASE [25]. The basic idea is that the first matching rule is applied. An alternate scheme is realized in preference clauses [23], where each configuration rule refines the results of the previous one, until an unambiguous version is selected. The semantics of such more complex selection schemes can be described on top of feature logic, using *preference operators:*

$$S_1 \text{ and-then } S_2 = \begin{cases} S_1 & \text{if } S_1 \text{ is unambiguous (that is, } |S_1| = 1), \\ S_1 \sqcap S_2 & \text{otherwise} \end{cases}$$

$$S_1 \text{ or-else } S_2 = \begin{cases} S_1 & \text{if } S_1 \neq \perp, \\ S_2 & \text{otherwise} \end{cases}$$

with the equivalences $T \sqcap (S_1 \text{ and-then } S_2) = (T \sqcap S_1 \text{ and-then } T \sqcap S_2)$ and $T \sqcap (S_1 \text{ or-else } S_2) = (T \sqcap S_1 \text{ or-else } T \sqcap S_2)$. Using "and-then" and "or-else", we can express *preferences* in our selection terms. For instance, $S = ([current: \top] \text{ or-else } [fixed: true])$ first selects the current version, and, if there is none, a "fixed" version; $S = ([\Delta_2, \nabla_3] \text{ and-then } [os: unix])$ selects revision 2 and, should this choice be ambiguous, the UNIX variant.

Even without ad-hoc extensions like preference operators or additional constraints, using feature logic for both identification and selection of components subsumes all common identification and selection schemes as found in SCM systems.

- One model is to identify versions with a conjunction of attributes and to select them using boolean expressions over these attributes, as in ADELE [8], the Context Model [32], EPOS [26], JASON [43], or SHAPE [24, 28]; such attribute conjunctions and attribute expressions can immediately be translated into equivalent feature terms.
- Another model is to name edges in the revision history, as in CLEARCASE, and to select versions through a disjunction of name patterns. This can be modeled by assigning each component version the names on its history path as features and again using feature terms for selection; preference operators may be of great use here.
- A third version selection model is found in the C preprocessor (CPP) [17] and frequently used to enhance existing SCM systems with variant control. In CPP, versions are identified with boolean attribute expressions and selected using a conjunction of attributes; the modeling is obvious again.

All three versioning models can be handled efficiently [47]. In fact, it can be shown that the SCM concepts of all four major SCM models [9] can be realized and integrated within the version set model [45].

7 Storage and Retrieval of Version Sets

To find out how far integration of SCM concepts can go, we have developed an SCM system called ICE for *Incremental Configuration Environment*, which realizes the version set model. The first question to be answered was how to represent version sets efficiently.

In SCM, one basically finds two approaches for efficient storage of multiple component versions. The first approach, used in RCS [40], for instance, is to store the latest version together with the differences (or *deltas*) to earlier versions. Upon retrieval of an earlier version, all deltas leading up to that version are applied; retrieval of the latest version is also the fastest. Such an approach is unsuitable for the version set model, since there is no concept of a single "latest" version; instead, several long-term and short-term variants may exist in parallel.

The second approach is more suitable, since it does not rely on a single base revision. The lines of all versions are all stored within a single text, where each line is flagged with the version(s) it actually belongs to. Such an approach is used in SCCS [35]; its most popular realization is the C preprocessor (CPP): Code pieces relevant for certain versions only are enclosed in *#if C* ... *#endif* pairs, where *C* expresses the condition under which the code piece is to be included.

In ICE, we have chosen the CPP representation for storing version sets [46]. The main advantage of the CPP representation is that feature terms can be represented as boolean CPP expressions (and vice versa), expressing feature names as CPP symbols. This allows end users to view and edit several versions at once, using a familiar and well-understood representation. In table 2, we give some examples catching the transformation spirit.[3]

We will now show how to realize read/write access on version sets represented as CPP files. Read access is realized through selection of version subsets. Given a traditional CPP file F representing all source code versions, and a feature term S for selection of a version subset, the CPP file representing the selected subset can be computed as follows. For each code piece, the feature term representation C of its governing CPP expression is unified with the selection term S. If $C \sqcap S = \bot$, the code piece is removed from F. If $C \sqcap S = S$, the *#if* directive is removed, because S implies C or $S \sqsubseteq C$. More generally, if $C = A \sqcap B$ and $B \sqcap S = S$ (or if $C = A \sqcup B$ and $B \sqcap S = \bot$), B can be omitted. These simplifications are similar in spirit to *partial evaluation*. The new (smaller) CPP file can be characterized by S and is written $F[S]$ (obviously, $F = F[\top]$).

Writing back a changed version set is realized through uniting it with its unchanged complement. Whenever a version subset $F[S]$ has changed, the containing CPP file F is reconstructed by uniting $F[S]$ and $F[\sim S]$. Generally, the union of CPP files $F[S]$

Feature term	CPP expression	Feature term	CPP expression
[GCC: 2]	GCC $\equiv$ 2	[GCC: 2, GNUG: 2]	GCC $\equiv$ 2 $\wedge$ GNUG $\equiv$ 2
[OS: *unix*]	OS $\equiv$ *unix*	[LANG: {*c, pascal*}]	LANG $\equiv$ *c* $\vee$ LANG $\equiv$ *pascal*
[DEBUG: ~0]	DEBUG	[SIN: ~*proc*]	SIN $\not\equiv$ *proc*
~[OPTIMIZE: ~0]	¬OPTIMIZE	~[SIN: *proc*]	¬(SIN $\equiv$ *proc*)
[δ_1: $\top$]	*defined*(δ_1)	[HOST $\downarrow$ TARGET]	HOST $\equiv$ TARGET
[$\delta_2\uparrow$]	¬*defined*(δ_2)	[HOST $\uparrow$ TARGET]	HOST $\not\equiv$ TARGET

Table 2. Translating feature terms into CPP constraints

---

[3] For better readability, the C tokens ==, !=, &&, | |, and ! are represented as $\equiv$, $\not\equiv$, $\wedge$, $\vee$, and ¬, respectively.

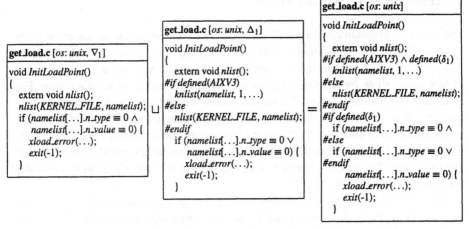

Figure 2. Version sets represented as CPP files

and $F[T]$ can be computed through $F[S] \sqcup F[T] = F[S \sqcup T]$. ICE builds a compact representation of $F[S \sqcup T]$ using a DIFF algorithm [29] with special handling of CPP directives. In the resulting file $F[S \sqcup T]$, parts occurring only in $F[S]$ or $F[T]$ are governed by $S \sqcap \sim T$ or $\sim S \sqcap T$, respectively; common parts are governed by $S \sqcup T$. When a version set is written, we have $T = \sim S$: Parts occurring only in $F[S]$ or $F[\sim S]$ are governed by S or $\sim S$, respectively; common parts are governed by $\top$.

Let us illustrate read and write access by an example. Figure 2 shows the constrained CPP file *get_load.c* taken from *xload*, a tool displaying the system load for several architectures. On the left, we see two version subsets of *get_load.c*[*os: unix*], namely a version without the δ_1 change, $R_0 = get\_load.c[os: unix, \nabla_1]$, and a modified version, $R_1 = get\_load.c[os: unix, \Delta_1]$; the change δ_1 introduces a AIXV3 variant and fixes a logical expression below applying to all versions. To incorporate both version sets R_0 and R_1 in the single CPP file *get_load.c*[*os: unix*], ICE must reconstruct the original version set by reuniting the version subsets according to the rules above. Indeed, figure 2 demonstrates that

$$get\_load.c[os: unix, \nabla_1] \sqcup get\_load.c[os: unix, \Delta_1]$$
$$= get\_load.c\big[[os: unix, \Delta_1] \sqcup [os: unix, \nabla_1]\big]$$
$$= get\_load.c[os: unix] \ ,$$

where the DIFF algorithm creates a compact representation for the generated version set *get_load.c*[*os: unix*].

Figure 2 can also be read from right to left, showing the decomposition of the version set *get_load.c*[*os: unix*] into two subsets. These subsets R_0 and R_1 are obtained from *get_load.c*[*os: unix*] by simplification of the CPP expressions respective to the selection terms ∇_1 or Δ_1. Selecting Δ_1 yields the version set *get_load.c*[*os: unix*][Δ_1] = *get_load.c*[*os: unix*, Δ_1] from which further subsets [AIXV3: $\top$] or [AIXV3↑] can be selected to view or modify individual variants. We see that feature terms, introduced as a syntactic device for the description of version sets, now have a precise semantics in terms of CPP files.

8 Transparent Version Set Access

The common denominator for nearly all software development environments is a file system. While early SCM tools like RCS or SCCS require explicit copying of source components from a file system to a version repository and vice versa, more advanced SCM systems allow for transparent repository access through a *virtual file system*. For instance, in CLEARCASE, the color variant of component *zbuf.c* can be accessed under the name *zbuf.c@@/color*. Various technical approaches are possible, from providing specialized system libraries [24, 28] over adapted network file system (NFS) servers [1, 7] and file-to-database mappers [8] to specific device drivers integrated in the operating system kernel [25]; generic approaches independent from a specific SCM system have also been developed [14].

The main disadvantages of all these systems are *lack of orthogonality* and *lack of incrementality*. By lack of orthogonality, we mean that only parts of the file system are versioned: for instance, files can be accessed in arbitrary versions, while directories cannot [24] or vice versa [7], or through entirely different concepts [25]. Lack of incrementality means that only fully specified versions (called *bound* or *generic* configurations) can be handled; there is no way of operate on several versions (or *abstract* configurations or *configuration templates*) as single items—with the notable exception of *all* versions, which can be handled through the repository.[4]

For ICE, we have thus chosen an alternate approach, realized in the *featured file system* (FFS). First, we use the version set model to provide uniform and orthogonal access to revisions, variants, and workspaces. Second, besides versioned files, we support *versioned directories*, switching incrementally between working environments through changes in directory versions. Third, we allow *abstract configurations*, representing non-singleton version sets as directories containing the individual versions and allowing for incremental exploration of the configuration space.

The FFS stores text files as version sets using the CPP representation. For binary files, we have implemented a slightly different representation, where CPP directives are not enclosed in newline characters, but in square brackets instead, determining and flagging differences anywhere in the file; the current implementation obtains satisfying results by running the DIFF algorithm on blocks delimited by null bytes.

After entering the FFS, all files occurring in multiple versions can be accessed by appending a version specification to the file name—using our notation above, except that the FFS requires CPP expressions. The FFS provides transparent access to arbitrary version sets; opening the virtual file *tty.c[user ≡ jamie]* gives access to the version set *[user: jamie]* from the file *tty.c*.

To express that a file be existent in some configuration only, we use the CPP *#error* directive. The *#error* directive stands for a non-existent file: each *#error* directive in F governed by a feature term S indicates that $F[S]$ is non-existent. Hence, removing a file $F[S]$ augments F with an *#error* directive governed by S, such that only $F[\sim S]$ is accessible. As an example, consider the creation of a file *printer.c[data: postscript]*.

---

[4] The only other SCM system where abstract configurations can be manipulated as individual items is the EPOS system [15, 30], where changes to individual versions can be propagated to abstract configurations (called *ambitions*).

After creation, *printer.c* will contain the lines *#if ¬(data ≡ postscript)* ... *#error* ... *#endif*—any attempt to read *printer.c*[¬(data ≡ postscript)] will fail.

An alternate interpretation of "a file F exists in some specific configuration S only" is "the features of F are $\sim S$". Hence, removal can be used to set and manipulate the features of a file F: To set the features of a file F to S, remove $F[\sim S]$—or, more intuitive, rename F to $F[S]$.

9 A Versioned File System

Besides versioned files, the FFS provides *versioned directories*, covering state and changes of the entire file system—that is, the whole configuration universe. Basically, a versioned directory is stored and accessed like ordinary versioned files are, using a CPP-like format. A directory entry enclosed in *#if C* ... *#endif* is visible only if C is a subset of the selection term S, or $C \sqsubseteq S$. If Jamie creates a new file *color-tty.c* in his workspace [*user:jamie*], the *color-tty.c* entry in the current directory "." is enclosed in a CPP directive *#if user ≡ jamie* ... *#endif*; in Richard's workspace, that is, the . [*user: richard*] directory version, *color-tty.c* is non-existent.

If a versioned directory $D[T]$ is part of the current path, the directory version T affects all contents of the directory, including subdirectories and all files contained therein; any file version $F[S]$ in $D[T]$ will be implicitly read as $F[S \sqcap T]$. Hence, opening a directory . [*os ≡ unix*] selects the UNIX variants of all files and subdirectories; all changes applied in a . [*user ≡ richard*] directory or below affects Richard's workspace only.

By changing the current directory, users can switch between workspaces and versions. Entering *cd* . [$\delta_3 \wedge os \not\equiv dos$] makes sure all subsequent changes apply to the R_3 revision in the non-DOS variants only. As illustrated in figure 3, such directory changes may be also be performed incrementally, subsequently narrowing the configuration space as more and more features are specified.

The features of a directory are set like the features of individual files, by removing the complement. Removing the directory version . [*tested↑*] makes the current directory and all contained items available in the [*tested*: T] version only. This is convenient for setting the features of all files in one directory or file system subset.

Besides accepting version specifications as parts of the file path, all other features of file systems still apply. The ".." directory refers to the second last component from the current path; that is, *testdir/[user ≢ jamie]/..* is equivalent to *testdir*. File modes, times, and access restrictions are versioned as well; symbolic links may be used to create aliases for long version specifications.

By storing all workspaces and versions in one single file system, the FFS exploits a maximum of commonality between all versions. Each workspace, variant, or revision is an individual view on the configuration space. In contrast to file systems organizing workspaces through copy-on-write techniques [14, 7], the FFS realizes one single access method for all versioning concepts and does not impose any hierarchy on how version sets are to be combined or accessed. Abstract configurations containing non-singleton version sets can be refined by adding further version specifications, forming an inheritance hierarchy in a matter similar to Wiebe's object-oriented SCM [43].

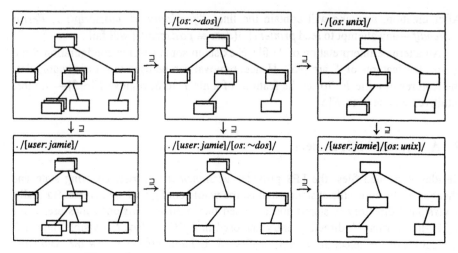

Figure 3. Narrowing the configuration space in the FFS

10 Exploring the Configuration Space

To show which version sets actually exist, we have developed a specialized file/configuration browser in ICE. The SKATE browser, shown in figure 4, enhances a usual file system browser with the ability to visualize and explore the configuration space. For each possible feature, we generate a menu listing the possible feature values. The subsumption lattice formed by the version sets is shown as a graph, visualizing revision histories and variant/workspace hierarchies. Through these menus, the user can specify a (possibly incomplete) configuration. As discussed in [46], SKATE ensures consistency by making items insensitive that would result in an inconsistent or non-existent configuration, allowing for incremental exploration of the possible configurations.

In order to make such configuration browsing available in other applications as well, the FFS server adds *virtual directory entries* listing possible version specifications in the same way the SKATE browser builds its feature menus. To avoid combinatorical explosion, we restrict ourselves to listing simple feature/value combinations and their negation. Listing a directory where users Richard, Chuck, and Jamie maintain individual workspaces results in six additional entries [*user* ≡ *richard*], [*user* ≡ *chuck*], [*user* ≡ *jamie*], [¬(*user* ≡ *richard*)], [¬(*user* ≡ *chuck*)] and [¬(*user* ≡ *jamie*)]. Listing the contents of the [¬(*user* ≡ *chuck*)] version set shows the current directory, but without Chuck's individual changes and four additional entries referring to Richard's and Jamie's workspaces. Through subsequent refinement through conjunction of the listed version specifications, users can explore which further version sets exist and how they interrelate. Besides the listed versions, arbitrary feature expressions (especially disjunctions) are still possible.

Another problem arises if we open a non-singleton version set. Using the scenario above, what happens if we open the file *tty.c* in the workspace [¬(*user* ≡ *chuck*)]? If *tty.c* is the same across all versions, the version set is singleton: we can open and modify

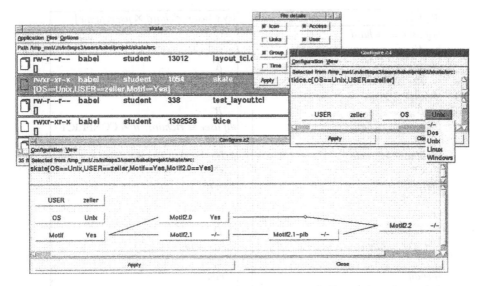

Figure 4. Using the SKATE browser to navigate through files and configurations

tty.c just as we like. If Richard's and Jamie's versions differ, it may be inappropriate to present the internal CPP representation to the user—or worse, to feed it to some program expecting a single version.

The FFS server addresses this problem by representing non-singleton version sets as *directories* of which individual version specifications can again be selected as virtual entries. The non-singleton *tty.c* appears as a directory of which the versions *tty.c/[user ≡ richard]*—which is equivalent to *tty.c[user ≡ richard]*—and *tty.c/[user ≡ jamie]* can be selected; again, the available configurations are presented to the user.

Having *tty.c* as file now and as a directory later may seem confusing at first glance. In practice, the individual workspace should be sufficiently specified that only singleton version sets remain—a directory path containing *[current]* may select the "most current" revision, for instance.

If the path name contains a [], the version set as a whole in CPP representation is returned. Instead of exploring the configuration space of *get_load.c*, we can open *get_load.c/[os ≡ unix]/[]* and thus view and edit all UNIX versions at once. Besides being convenient for developers, this feature is a must for programs that recursively descend the directory tree; such programs would otherwise suffer from the combinatorical explosion of possible configurations if they traversed all possible configurations through virtual directories.

11 Multi-Version Merging

In software development, it is important that the multitude of versions generated is eventually reduced to a tiny set of versions actually shipped out. For this purpose, parallel changes on components must be *merged*. The basic textual merging algorithm, as realized in the UNIX tool DIFF3, merges textual files only; much more sophisti-

tty.c []	tty.c [*user: richard* ⋈ *user: jamie*]
#if user ≡ richard	
A'	
#else	A'
A	
#endif	
B	B
#if user ≡ richard	#if user ≡ richard // ⋈ CONFLICT
C'	C'
#elif user ≡ jamie	#else
C''	C''
#else	#endif
C	
#endif	
D	D
#if user ≡ jamie ∧ os ≡ unix	#if os ≡ unix
E	E
#endif	#endif

Figure 5. Merging of version sets

cated merging algorithms have been developed for specific domains, especially programs [3, 42, 44].

The CPP representation used in ICE inspired a simple textual merging algorithm that merges an arbitrary number of versions. Let T be a version set with $T_1 \sqsubseteq T, T_2 \sqsubseteq T, \dots, T_n \sqsubseteq T$ being n version subsets to be merged. Let us assume that all T_i were created independently from T such that all T_i are pairwise disjoint, i.e. $\forall i, j \in \{1, \dots, n\}(T_i \sqcap T_j = \bot)$ holds.[5]

To generate a merged version from the CPP representation of T, we proceed as follows. The merged version T', denoted as $T' = T_1 \bowtie T_2 \bowtie \cdots \bowtie T_n$, must include code pieces that were added in any T_i and exclude code pieces that were deleted in any T_i. Each code piece governed by a CPP expression C is included if $C \sqsubseteq \bigsqcup_{i=1}^{n} T_i$ holds; in T', the governing expression is simplified (partially evaluated) respective to all T_i. Otherwise, if $\exists i\, (C \sqsubseteq \sim T_i)$ holds, the code piece governed by C was deleted in at least one T_i (and unchanged in all T_j with $j \neq i$) and thus is not included in T'. Everything else stays unchanged.

A minimum distance between parallel changes must be preserved in order to identify merging conflicts. Between any two code pieces governed by C' and C'' both being a subset of different T_i sets, a separating code piece governed by D must reside such that the following holds. Formally, let $T_{i'}$ be the unique element from $\{T_1, \dots, T_n\}$ such that $C' \sqsubseteq T_{i'}$; similarly, $T_{i''}$ is the unique element from $\{T_1, \dots, T_n\}$ such that $C'' \sqsubseteq T_{i''}$. Then, $D \not\sqsubseteq T_{i'} \wedge D \not\sqsubseteq T_{i''}$ must hold. If such a D does not exist, or if the length of D is below a certain minimal distance, C' and C'' are in conflict with each other.

As an example, consider the *tty.c* file in figure 5, where the version subsets $T_1 = $ [*user: richard*] and $T_2 = $ [*user: jamie*] are merged. Code piece A' is included, because

---

[5] Otherwise, replace the non-disjoint pair T_i, T_j by $T_k = T_i \sqcap T_j$.

its governing expression [*user: richard*] is equal to T_1; code piece A is excluded because its governing expression is equal to $\sim T_1$. Code piece C' would be included, as it is in T_1; but as it is immediately followed by C'', whose governing expression is equal to the different T_2 subset, the two changes are in conflict with each other. For convenience, ICE flags this section still being a subset of a T_i with a "$\bowtie$ CONFLICT" comment; only the code piece C can safely be removed as it is a subset of both $\sim T_1$ and $\sim T_2$. At the end, the code piece E is included, since it is separated from the conflict by code piece D; the expression governing E is simplified respective to T_2.

Merged version sets can be accessed transparently by including the appropriate expression in the file path name; directories are merged by merging their entries. For instance, one can create a production version incorporating the current versions of Richard and Jamie by issuing a recursive UNIX copy command

$$cp\ -pr\ .\,[(user \equiv richard \bowtie user \equiv jamie) \wedge current][]\ .\,[production][]$$

Remaining conflicts, if any, can be resolved through an interactive merging tool by determining the differences between .[*production*]/[*user* $\equiv$ *richard*] and .[*production*]/[*user* $\equiv$ *jamie*]—or by searching the .[*production*][] files for "$\bowtie$ CONFLICT" comments.

12 Maintaining Workspaces and Revisions

In ICE, the FFS only realizes the SCM primitive layer; all higher SCM concepts like revisions, currency, and workspaces are realized by accessing and manipulating version sets through the FFS. While this can be done through ordinary f   ystem manipulations, it is more convenient if the higher SCM layers are made explicit through dedicated SCM tools. In ICE, we are currently realizing such a tool suite, called TWICE for "Tasks within ICE", providing elementary support for revision, workspace, and variant control, and demonstrating the integration of SCM concepts.

The SCM setting in TWICE is patterned after the popular *copy-modify-merge* scenario found in the *concurrent versions system* (CVS) [2] and Sun's *network software environment* (NSE) [7]. Each user u accesses the system through his individual workspace identified by [*user* $\equiv$ *u*] and by default works on the current revision only, identified by [*current*]. There is one dedicated virtual user named *project*, whose view (the *project workspace*) reflects the common development state. Users work in parallel in their workspaces, synchronizing with the project workspace by propagating and merging changes.

A new workspace for user Richard is created by copying the project workspace [*user* $\equiv$ *project*] to Richard's individual workspace [*user* $\equiv$ *richard*]. This does not create a physical copy; it only makes the *project* files accessible to Richard as well by changing the features of the top-level directory from $[user: \{project, chuck, jamie, \ldots\}]$ to $[user: \{project, chuck, jamie, richard, \ldots\}]$. To enter his workspace, Richard changes the current directory to [*user* $\equiv$ *richard*]. Richard may now access all project version sets, including all revisions. Usually, he will decide to work on the most recent revision by changing his directory to [*current*]. All changes Richard applies in his workspace

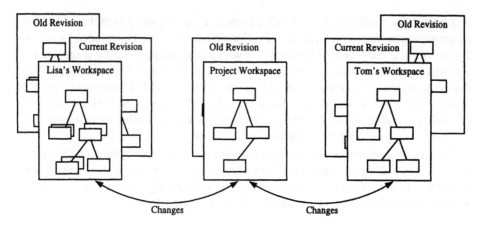

Figure 6. Workspaces maintained by TWICE

are confined to [*user* ≡ *richard*] alone; user Jamie in his workspace [*user* ≡ *jamie*] will not see any of Richard's changes due to the differing *user* features.

TWICE maintains local revision histories for each workspace, as illustrated in figure 6. If Richard wishes to create a new revision of his workspace, TWICE generates a change number δ_i, say δ_{25}, to identify the change and sets up a constraint [(*current* ∧ *user* ≡ *richard*) → δ_{25}] as feature of the top-level directory (by deleting . [¬δ_{25} ∧ *current* ∧ *user* ≡ *richard*]). This constraint ensures that whenever Richard enters the current revision of his workspace, revision R_{25} is returned. Afterwards, TWICE "freezes" the non-current revisions by making all files and directories in . [*user* ≡ *richard* ∧ ¬*current*] read-only. All this is transparent to Richard: he need not change his workspace or current directory. All changes he makes from now on affect the R_{25} revision only, as it is the current revision.

To import recent changes from other workspaces (notably the project workspace), Richard invokes a TWICE command that merges the current revisions of a selected workspace with his workspace, copying the result back to his workspace. To commit his changes to the project workspace, the merge results are written to a new revision of the project workspace instead, which is then made current; occurring conflicts must first be resolved within the individual workspace.

TWICE does not impose any hierarchy on variants, revisions, and workspaces; the access facilities of the FFS are still available. In the individual workspaces, variants can be created and accessed through the FFS, just like workspaces are; similarly, TWICE can be instructed to maintain different currency notions for different variants or to restrict change propagation for certain variants only. TWICE thus demonstrates how SCM concepts can be integrated into a unique SCM protocol on top of the FFS.

13 Deductive Software Builds

Another example of deduction usage is *system construction*. The FFS and TWICE operations are still oriented towards components; there is no notion of configurations or consistency. These issues require a *system model* denoting the components of the software product, the dependencies between source and derived components, and how the product is to be built from these components. This system model is the base for automated construction tools building specific configurations of a software product.

The mother of all software construction tools is the well-known MAKE program [12]. As MAKE has no versioning capabilities, later tools have used version information to identify derived objects [24], to share derived objects in binary pools [6], and to deduce build plans based either on PROLOG [20] or on feature logic [34]. For the purposes of ICE, we are currently realizing a simple extension of MAKE which suffices for subsuming these approaches. The resulting ICE MAKE tool provides automatic identification and reuse of derived components as well as consistency deduction, while no changes to existing MAKE specifications are required.

As an example, consider the MAKE rule

> *tty.o*: *tty.c*
>   *cc −c tty.c*

Let us assume that *tty.c* comes in the three versions tty_1, tty_2, and tty_3, as discussed in section 3. According to the version set model, a derived object can be regarded as aggregate from its source object and the derivation tools (e.g. the compiler); it thus inherits their features. Invoking ICE MAKE to generate the file *tty.o[author ≡ lucid ∧ tty-support ≡ true]* compiles the source file *tty.c[author ≡ lucid ∧ tty-support ≡ true]*; this is done by changing to the virtual subdirectory *. [author ≡ lucid ∧ tty-support ≡ true]* before executing the construction command.

If a derived object is dependent on several source objects, it inherits their unified features according to the aggregation rule. As an example, consider the following ICE MAKE rule involving the *display* component from section 4:

> OBJECTS = *tty.o display.o*
> *emacs*: $(OBJECTS)
>   *cc −o emacs* $(OBJECTS)

Invoking ICE MAKE with target *emacs[tty-support ≡ true]* first selects the appropriate versions from *tty.c* and *display.c*, excluding the $display_1$ version. Since $display_2$ ⊓ $tty_2 = \bot$, ICE MAKE deduces that the tty_2 version is excluded as well. The choice between tty_1 and tty_3 remains; the user can either let ICE MAKE generate all versions (two in this case) or give an unambiguous target by specifying the *author* feature. In case the C compiler *cc* is present in several versions, its version is selected and deduced just like any other component version; the derived *emacs* object inherits the *cc* features as well as the features of other components.

Besides deducing consistency even for incomplete specifications, as in the *emacs* example, ICE MAKE automatically *reuses* derived components built from the same sources, but in other workspaces. For instance, let us assume Richard has already generated a derived object *tty.o* in her workspace *[user ≡ richard]*; Chuck wants do do the same and invokes ICE MAKE with the target *tty.o* in his workspace *[user ≡ chuck]*. By examining the entire version set *tty.o*, ICE MAKE finds out that the version set *tty.o[user ≡ richard]* already exists. Two derived objects must be the same if they were

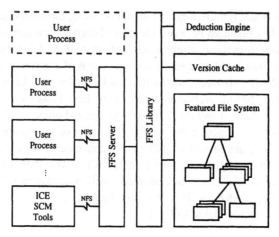

Figure 7. Processes accessing the featured file system

built from the same source objects; ICE MAKE examines the *tty.c* source component and determines that Richard's and Chuck's versions do not differ. ICE MAKE need not invoke construction tools; it copies *tty.o[user ≡ richard]* to *tty.o[user ≡ tom]* instead.

Version reuse is not limited to workspaces; similar time-saving effects take place when derived files are shared across revisions and thus reusable in each new construction run. No change to the MAKE file nor to any construction tool is required.

14   Performance and Complexity

FFS access is realized on top of a modified NFS [36] server. As shown in figure 7, user processes as well as SCM tools access the FFS server through file operations using the NFS protocol. The FFS server accesses files through a FFS library, mapping file operations directly to versioned file accesses. The time required for retrieving a single version from a version set is comparable to a CPP run (excluding expansion of macros and *#include* directives) or a SCCS version retrieval, as long as the version is identified by a simple intersection (conjunction) of features. Further speed-ups are achieved by caching individual versions in a persistent version cache, allowing for fast second-time retrieval.

Writing version sets is more expensive. As stated in section 8, writing to a file $F[S]$—that is, changing $F[S]$ to $F'[S]$—is implemented by generating $F' = F[\sim S] \sqcup F'[S]$. First, the subset $F[\sim S]$ must be generated. The best case is S being a simple conjunction: $\sim S$ then becomes a disjunction of negated primitives, which are checked for consistency one after the other. Second, the DIFF algorithm must be run on $F[\sim S]$ and $F'[S]$, which is moderately expensive. Third, all differing expressions governing common code pieces in $F[\sim S]$ and $F'[S]$ must be united and simplified, which can be a very expensive operation.

This last step is trivial, however, if the governing expressions in $F[S]$ and $F'[S]$ are equal—for instance, because S and the governing expressions do not contain common features. It is also trivial if $F[\sim S]$ or $F'[S]$ do not contain governing expressions—that

Operation	FFS		NFS	RCS
	uncached	cached		
Write file / Check in	122.0s	57.0s	12.5s	58.8s
Read file / Check out	11.2s	1.6s	1.5s	5.8s

Table 3. FFS performance sample

is, a singleton version set was changed. As changing singleton version sets is by far the most common case, and as files are more often read than changed, we found read/write behavior satisfying in practice.

For even better performance, the FFS server keeps version sets in a cache once they are read; written version sets are also kept in the cache until a superset is requested. Second and later version set accesses are served in constant time. In practice, this means that once a workspace is entered, the FFS server has the same performance as an ordinary NFS server. But still, all files common to several workspace are cached only once, showing the space-saving effects of the copy-on-write techniques used in AT&T's n-DFS [14] or Sun's *translucent file system* [7].

Table 3 gives a typical performance sample as measured on a SUN SPARCstation 20. As example operations, we have chosen reading and writing a 4.5 MB file (the present article in PostScript format). For RCS, "reading" means checking out the file from its RCS repository, and "writing" means checking in the file back again after a change.

We see that the FFS write performance is not fully satisfactory, due to deficiencies in the implementation—for instance, the vendor NFS server is multi-threaded, while our FFS server is (yet) single-threaded. The difference between uncached and cached writing of version sets, however, is the time spent in actual work, rather than file transmission. We see that this time ($122s - 57s = 65s$) is similar to the time required by the RCS check in. This does not surprise, as both do the same work: both run DIFF to determine the differences between origin and new revision; afterwards, both create a new version set representation.

Reading version sets shows better performance. The execution times show that reading uncached version sets is comparable with RCS repository access, while reading cached version sets can compete with the original NFS server. Should this still be considered too slow, systems, alternate FFS realizations like dynamic system libraries [14] or virtual device drivers [8] could bypass the NFS bottleneck and show virtually no difference from direct file access.

15 Ambiguity and Deduction

While common SCM operations do not impose complexity problems in the version set model, things get more complex as soon as deduction facilities are needed. If the version specification contains unions (disjunctions), the partial evaluation algorithm must try all possible combinations; if agreements, disagreements, or arithmetic constraints are used as well, a full-fledged feature unification engine [39] is used to solve the constraints. As feature unification is NP-complete, deciding whether $S \sqcap T = \bot$ results in exponential complexity for arbitrary terms S and T. This is a serious problem when having a tool like ICE MAKE deduce derived features and exclude inconsistent configurations from a large number of combinations.

The (preliminary) experience we have had with TWICE also shows how complexity imposes limits on combining versioning concepts. This is especially true for *variance* that may interfere with every other SCM concept. Workspaces that imply certain variants, variants that imply certain revisions, changes that apply to certain variants only, introduce disjunctions into revision constraints and thus make the deduction process overly complex.

Our summary is thus both good news and bad news. The good news is: *Ambiguity at a low scale can be tolerated.* Techniques for keeping ambiguity low are well-known: first, narrowing or disambiguating the configuration space (for instance, by specifying target features in ICE MAKE); second, keeping variance orthogonal to other SCM concepts. These constraints are well known in the SCM world; following them makes ICE behave just as efficient as the original SCM systems.

The bad news is: *Large-scale ambiguity is too complex to be used in practice.* This result imposes tight limits on future integrated SCM models, notably the integration of variance concepts. Research and experience will show how far ambiguity can be tolerated while keeping run-time acceptable.

16 Conclusion

We have shown how the version set model is realized in the incremental configuration environment ICE, providing integration of SCM concepts and integration in common software development environments. In other SCM systems, hard-wired efficiency considerations constrain the resulting SCM process. In ICE, no such a priori constraints exist; all constraints are made explicit and exchangeable. This flexibility makes ICE a framework for integrating today's SCM models as well as developing and evaluating future SCM models and processes.

Still, much work needs to be done, both at the conceptual level as well as on the ICE implementation.

On the conceptual level, we must find out if and how SCM processes might be formalized using the version set model and whether SCM tool behaviour may be verified against the SCM process. In general, there is no true methodology yet how components and versions should be attributed with feature terms; experiences from other attribute-oriented SCM systems [8, 15, 30, 34] or faceted classification [33] might help here.

On the implementation level, like any other fundamental tool, the featured file system suffers the "you want it, you got it" problem—no one checks for compliance with an existing SCM process; damage may follow from misspelled operations. Tools like SKATE and TWICE already help to hide the FFS behind a layer of safe operations. But for full support of high-level SCM tools, the FFS should eventually be extended with synchronization and event notification mechanisms [14].

We believe that the future in SCM in general and SCM systems in particular lies in a clear separation of mechanism and policy, resulting in federated SCM architectures [5]. In the database domain, for example, the mechanism is implemented by standardized databases, on which customized applications are built that realize the individual policy. Through a common SCM mechanism, SCM vendors could concentrate on adapting SCM policy to the software process of their customers, and not vice versa. This can only be done through a common integrating SCM foundation, for which the work has only begun.

ICE is part of the inference-based software development environment NORA[6]. NORA aims at utilizing inference technology in software tools; concepts and preliminary results can be found in [13, 22, 27]

ICE software for UNIX systems and related technical reports can be accessed through the ICE WWW page, http://www.cs.tu-bs.de/softech/ice/, and via FTP from ftp://ftp.ips.cs.tu-bs.de/pub/local/softech/ice/.

Acknowledgments. Many thanks to all who have made ICE possible through contributing to the ICE implementation or by making program sources and tools freely available. Dirk Babel developed the SKATE browser using the *Tcl/Tk* toolkit. Michael Brandes currently realizes ICE MAKE as an extension of GNU MAKE. Lars Düning implemented the CPP representation using GNU DIFF. Andreas Mende contributed attribution and merging facilities and is currently developing TWICE on top of the FFS. Olaf Pfohl built the FFS server on top of a public domain NFS server. Christina Trenkner is integrating solving of arithmetic constraints into the feature unification algorithm, which was originally implemented by Marc Ziehmann. Jens Krinke and Gregor Snelting as well as the anonymous reviewers provided valuable comments on earlier versions of this paper.

Richard Stallman, Chuck Thompson, and Jamie Zawinski are among the principal EMACS authors and maintainers. In reality, they do not share common workspaces.

References

1. Paul Adams and Marvin Solomon. An overview of the CAPITL software development environment. In Jacky Estublier, editor, *Software Configuration Management: selected papers / ICSE SCM-4 and SCM-5 workshops*, number 1005 in Lecture Notes in Computer Science, pages 1–34, Seattle, Washington, October 1995. Springer-Verlag.

2. Brian Berliner. CVS II: Parallelizing software development. In *Proc. of the 1990 Winter USENIX Conference*, Washington, D.C., 1990.

3. David Binkley, Susan Horwitz, and Thoas Reps. Program integration for languages with procedure calls. *ACM Transactions on Software Engineering and Methodology*, 4(1):3–35, January 1995.

4. Ronald. J. Brachman and H. J. Levesque. The tractability of subsumption in frame-based description languages. In *Proc. of the 4th National Conference of the American Association for Artificial Intelligence*, pages 34–37, Austin, Texas, August 1984.

5. A. Brown, S. Dart, P. Feiler, and K. Wallnau. The state of automated configuration management. Technical Report CMU/SEI-ATR-91, Software Engineering Institure, Carnegie Mellon University, Pittsburgh, PA, September 1991.

6. Geoffrey M. Clemm. The Odin specification language. In Jürgen F. H. Winkler, editor, *Proc. of the International Workshop on Software Version and Configuration Control*, pages 145–158, Grassau, January 1988. Teubner Verlag, Stuttgart.

7. William Courington. The Network Software Environment. Technical Report FE 197-0, Sun Microsystems, Inc., February 1989.

---

[6] NORA is a figure in Henrik Ibsen's play "A Dollhouse". Hence, NORA is NO Real Acronym.

8. Jacky Estublier and Rubby Casallas. The Adele configuration manager. In Tichy [41], pages 99–133.
9. Peter H. Feiler. Configuration management models in commercial environments. Technical Report CMU/SEI-91-TR-7, Software Engineering Institure, Carnegie Mellon University, Pittsburgh, PA, March 1991.
10. Peter H. Feiler, editor. *Proc. 3rd International Workshop on Software Configuration Management*, Trondheim, Norway, June 1991. ACM Press.
11. Stuart Feldman, editor. *Proc. 4th International Workshop on Software Configuration Management (Preprint)*, Baltimore, Maryland, May 1993.
12. Stuart I. Feldman. Make—A program for maintaining computer programs. *Software—Practice and Experience*, 9:255–265, April 1979.
13. Bernd Fischer, Matthias Kievernagel, and Gregor Snelting. Deduction-based software component retrieval. In Köhler et al. [21], pages 1–5.
14. Glenn Fowler, David Korn, and Herman Rao. *n*-DFS: The multiple dimensional file system. In Tichy [41], pages 135–154.
15. Bjørn Gulla, Even-André Karlsson, and Dashing Yeh. Change-oriented version descriptions in EPOS. *Software Engineering Journal*, 6(6):378–386, November 1991.
16. Richard Harter. Version management and change control; systematic approaches to keeping track of source code and support files. *Unix World*, 6(6), June 1989.
17. The International Organization for Standardization and The International Electrotechnical Commission. *Programming Languages—C*, December 1990. ISO/IEC International Standard 9899:1990 (E).
18. R. T. Kasper and W. C. Rounds. A logical semantics for feature structures. In *Proc. of the 24th Annual Meeting of the ACL*, pages 257–265, Columbia University, New York, 1986.
19. M. Kay. Functional unification grammar: A formalism for machine translation. In *Proc. 10th International Joint Conference on Artificial Intelligence*, pages 75–78, Stanford, 1984.
20. Thilo Kielmann. Using PROLOG for software system maintenance. In *Proc. of the First International Conference on the Practical Application of PROLOG*, London, UK, April 1992.
21. Jana Köhler, Fausto Giunchiglia, Cordell Green, and Christoph Walther, editors. *Working Notes of the IJCAI-95 Workshop: Formal Approaches to the Reuse of Plans, Proofs, and Programs*, Montréal, August 1995.
22. Maren Krone and Gregor Snelting. On the inference of configuration structures from source code. In *Proc. 16th International Conference on Software Engineering*, pages 49–57, Sorrento, Italy, May 1994. IEEE Computer Society Press.
23. M. Lacroix and P. Lavency. Preferences: Putting more knowledge into queries. In Peter M. Stocker and William Kent, editors, *Proc. of the 13th International Conference on Very Large Data Bases*, pages 217–225, Brighton, 1987.
24. Andreas Lampen and Axel Mahler. An object base for attributed software objects. In *Proc. of the Fall '88 EUUG Conference*, pages 95–105, Cascais, October 1988.
25. David B. Leblang. The CM challenge: Configuration management that works. In Tichy [41], pages 1–37.
26. Anund Lie, Reidar Conradi, Tor M. Didriksen, Even-André Karlsson, Svein O. Hallsteinsen, and Per Holager. Change oriented versioning in a software engineering database. In Walter F. Tichy, editor, *Proc. 2nd International Workshop on Software Configuration Management*, pages 56–65, Princeton, New Jersey, October 1989. ACM Press.
27. Christian Lindig. Concept-based component retrieval. In Köhler et al. [21], pages 21–25.
28. Axel Mahler. Variants: Keeping things together and telling them apart. In Tichy [41], pages 39–69.

29. W. Miller and Eugene Myers. A file comparison program. *Software—Practice and Experience*, 15(11):1025, 1985.

30. Bjørn P. Munch, Jens-Otto Larsen, Bjørn Gulla, Reidar Conradi, and Even Andre Karlsson. Uniform versioning: The change-oriented model. In Feldman [11], pages 188–196.

31. B. Nebel and G. Smolka. Representation and reasoning with attributive descriptions. In K. H. Bläsius, U. Hedstück, and C.-R. Rollinger, editors, *Sorts and Types in Artificial Intelligence*, volume 256 of *Lecture Notes in Artificial Intelligence*, pages 112–139, Eringerfeld, April 1989. Springer-Verlag.

32. Peter Nicklin. Managing multi-variant software configurations. In Feiler [10], pages 53–57.

33. Rubén Prieto-Diaz. Classifying software for reusability. *IEEE Software*, 4(1), January 1987.

34. Anthony Rich and Marvin Solomon. A logic-based approach to system modelling. In Feiler [10], pages 84–93.

35. Marc J. Rochkind. The source code control system. *IEEE Transactions on Software Engineering*, SE-1(4):364–370, December 1975.

36. R. Sandberg, D. Goldberg, S. Kleiman, D. Walsh, and B. Lyon. Design and implementation of the Sun Network filesystem. In *Proc. of the Summer 1985 USENIX conference*, pages 119–130, Portland, Oregon, June 1985.

37. S. Shieber, H. Uszkorzeit, F. Pereira, J. Robinson, and M. Tyson. The formalism and implementation of PATR-II. In J. Bresnan, editor, *Research on Interactive Acquisition and Use of Knowledge*. SRI International, 1983.

38. Gerd Smolka and Hassan Aït-Kaci. Inheritance hierarchies: Semantics and unification. In Claude Kirchner, editor, *Unification*, pages 489–516. Academic Press, London, 1990.

39. Gert Smolka. Feature-constrained logics for unification grammars. *Journal of Logic Programming*, 12:51–87, 1992.

40. Walter F. Tichy. RCS—A system for version control. *Software—Practice and Experience*, 15(7):637–654, July 1985.

41. Walter F. Tichy, editor. *Configuration Management*, volume 2 of *Trends in Software*. John Wiley & Sons, Chichester, England, 1994.

42. Bernhard Westfechtel. Structure-oriented merging of revisions of software documents. In Feiler [10], pages 86–79.

43. Douglas Wiebe. Object-oriented software configuration management. In Feldman [11], pages 241–252.

44. Wuu Yang, Susan Horwitz, and Thomas Reps. A program integration algorithm that accommodates semantics-preserving transformations. *ACM Transactions on Software Engineering and Methodology*, 1(3):310–354, July 1992.

45. Andreas Zeller. A unified version model for configuration management. In Gail Kaiser, editor, *Proc. 3rd ACM SIGSOFT Symposium on the Foundations of Software Engineering*, volume 20 (4) of *ACM Software Engineering Notes*, pages 151–160, Washington, DC, October 1995. ACM Press.

46. Andreas Zeller and Gregor Snelting. Handling version sets through feature logic. In Wilhelm Schäfer and Pere Botella, editors, *Proc. 5th European Software Engineering Conference*, volume 989 of *Lecture Notes in Computer Science*, pages 191–204, Sitges, Spain, September 1995. Springer-Verlag.

47. Andreas Zeller and Gregor Snelting. Unified versioning through feature logic. Computer Science Report 96-01, Technical University of Braunschweig, Germany, February 1996. Submitted for publication.

Fine Grained Version Control of Configurations in COOP/Orm

Boris Magnusson and Ulf Asklund

Dept. of Computer Science, Lund Institute of Technology,
Box 118, S-221 00 Lund, Sweden
E-mail: {Boris I Ulf}@dna.lth.se

Abstract. This paper describes a unified approach to version
control of documents and configurations. Hierarchical structure, which is present in most documents such as programs, is
recognized and utilized in a fine-grained version control system. The same mechanism is used for version control of configurations and extended to handle DAGs as well as trees.
Change propagation within one hierarchical document is automatic while bindings between documents are explicit. The
model is novel because of its integration of version and configuration control, fine-grained version control, and explicit
graphical user interface. It supports teams of distributed users
by offering optimistic check-out with strong support for merging of alternatives.

1 Introduction

Software systems are made up from hierarchical collections of hierarchical documents.
Traditionally, version control has been applied to keep track of the revisions of individual
documents, while configuration management has focused on how to form systems or
sub-systems out of collections of documents [Roe75, SCCS, Tic85, Tic88]. Although this
separation has some benefits in factoring out minimal functionality into single tools it
suffers from the lack of integration. We will here illustrate some of the most severe problems with this approach as we see it, without any ambition of making the list complete.

Document size   There are conflicting demands on the size of the involved documents.
Even a small change to a document creates a new version of the whole document. From
a version control point of view it is a benefit if documents are kept small since the preci-
sion of the information the version control system will give us will get higher.
From the configuration management point of view it is an advantage if the documents are
fewer (and thus larger) since the complexity grows with the number of documents involved and with their versions. The number of meaningless or non-compatible configurations of versions of documents grows exponentially.

Change Size   It is often the case that a change affects only a small part of a document.
Still, the version control and locking scheme is based on the whole document which is
often found as unnecessary coarse.

Related documents   It is often the case that many documents are tightly related and are
in fact version controlled together, but many systems can not represent the connection
between related changes to different documents.

Concurrency control   Lock on check-out, as commonly used by many version control
systems, gets awkward to use when the group of people involved grows. With a locking
system there is a drive for using many small documents since then more people can work

simultaneously without needing to change the same piece of information at the same time. Locking also makes such a system hard to use in a distributed environment.

Configurations Configurations are often only described indirectly through make-files, and although these can be versioned they can not handle structural changes to a configuration since the underlying file system is not versioned.

Awareness It is often hard to find out what documents other developers have changed, and what changes they have made, or even who checked out a particular document. Providing some level of awareness also seems essential in providing flexible work process support.

Some recent systems have identified and addressed some of the problems above. As an example, CVS[Wat,Ced93] can manage collections of files and also allow multiple checkouts, but give only rudimentary help for merge. TeamWare [Team] facilitates distributed development by allowing replicated repositories and facilitating merge of the (SCCS) history files. Again with weak support for merge of the documents themselves. ClearCase [Cla95], on the other hand, has strong support for merge, resolving simple differences automatically and identifying conflicts for human resolution. This through an interface that, according to Ovum [RBI95] sets a new standard for the industry.

To the best of our knowledge no existing configuration management system addresses the problem of awareness.

Version control can be seen as added to current file systems as an afterthought and editors, compilers etc. do not deal with this information. We see version control as essential for any system development and it should therefore be a basic mechanism understood by all processors.

1.1 Our approach

The starting point for this work has been the aim to support teams of programmers working together, providing a collaborative editing environment, an area that combines problems from both CSCW (Computer Supported Cooperative Work) and SE (Software Engineering). Collaboration and sharing information naturally demands a version control system and ambitions to support also synchronous editing [MM93] has led us to support unusually fine-grained versions. We have also taken the position that systems that use a pessimistic, lock on check-out, approach do not scale up to many users in a geographically distributed environment. This has lead us to design our environment on an optimistic approach where developers always can create new versions (forming a new alternative if necessary) and then providing strong support for merging alternatives using an operation-based diffing approach [LvO92]. For configuration management we have taken the position that configurations should be unified as much as possible with other documents and for example also be version controlled with operation-based diffs [MAM93].

Another starting point for this work is the Orm environment [MHM+90] developed in the Mjølner project [KLMM93]. This is a tightly integrated environment built on incremental techniques. Here there are no processors like compilers and linkers visible to the developers, this is merely functionality offered, and managed by the environment. The developer edits and executes. The integrated approach chosen in constructing Orm has also included a storage model for programs in structured form [Gus90]. This storage form has many similarities with engineering databases as described in [Kat90]. The Mjølner/Orm environment includes version and configuration facilities. Compared to what is presented in this paper it is working on a much coarser level and offers a less user friendly interface. Nevertheless it is offering versioned connections between modules and also to 'grammars' defining the language implementation. It is the experience from this environment that have lead to the further development presented in this paper. 'Fine grained version control' as a term was introduced in Orwell [TJ88] meaning version control at the method level rather than at the module or class level in object oriented programming. We use the term in the same meaning, but go further in decreasing grain size. We record each edit operation using 'operation based diffs' in the meaning of [LvO92] and encourage creation of versions more frequently, and thus extend the meaning of fine-grained version control.

Our research has been guided by a goal to explore the possibilities to increase the level of functionality offered to the users. In doing so we have chosen an integrated approach for our prototype environment and put less emphasis on how the parts of the environment integrate with existing systems. As an example we do not put priority in this phase of our work on how to make it possible to use existing editors (such as emacs, which are not version aware) with our system. The situation can be compared with introducing word processors which also represent integrated environments where existing text editors can not be used. Although not everybody have given up tool-based word processing, word processors still represent an important step forward for many users.

The COOP/Orm environment attempts to attack the problems outlined in the introduction with the following techniques:

- Representation of hierarchically structured documents.
- Integrated representation of user data and versioning information.
- Explicit version graph for browsing and comparing versions.
- Versioned bindings between documents.
- Support for parallel development and merge of alternatives.
- Active diffs for on-line awareness of changes by other users.
- Transparent distribution for users at different sites.

This paper is starting with a summary of requirements for an integrated version and configuration system for structured information. A description of the basic functionality and document model in our environment is presented in section 3. In section 4 we describe how configuration management can be introduced, based on this model. In section 5 we evaluate the functionality of our system and compare it with other attempts that go beyond traditional systems. In the following sections we summarize the status of our implementation, future work and our conclusions.

2 Terminology and requirements

We see software documents as highly structured information, preferably managed by an integrated environment. This view is in contrast to the common view of software as plain text files. The following list of requirements on support for versions and configurations has been significantly influenced by Katz work focusing on engineering databases for CAD/CAM systems [Kat90], which also demands support for highly structured information. Our view is similar to the one presented in [Kat90], but not identical, e.g. we see creation of versions as a more lightweight and frequent operation than he does. Katz also points out the need to limit the effects of a change to avoid a too large number of combinations of versions of documents, a problem we address explicitly below.

Terminology:

Information unit - smallest part of a document that is version controlled as one unit. This is typically a procedure (or even smaller: its interface, implementation, and documentation), or a paragraph of text in a structured text document.

Composite unit - hierarchically organized collection of Information units.

Document - semantically meaningful named Composite unit such as a module, a class, or a chapter in a book. A Document includes information about its version history, and all versions of the Information units.

Version - a snapshot of a Document. A Version can never be modified, but new Versions of the Document can be created. A Version has an *Originating Version* from which it is developed (the Originating version of the first Version of a Document is empty).

Variant - a special case of Version where there are several alternative versions developed from the same Originating version.

Delta - the difference between two successive Versions of a Document.

Change propagation - creation of a new version of an Information unit will trigger creation of new Versions of all Composite units including the changed Information unit, and in particular also of the Document it is part of.

Binding - relation between a Version of a Document and specific Versions of other (*Imported*) Documents.

Configuration - set of Versions of Documents related through Bindings.

Requirements on the storage model:

- Support for semantically meaningful named entities.

- Mechanisms to form Composite units out of more primitive parts.

- There should be support for configurations in the limited, tree structured case, since it is very common and offers important simplifications.

- It must be possible to include a Document in several different Configurations, thus the composition mechanism must support a general DAG (directed acyclic graph) structure rather than just Trees.

- From a Version of a Document it must be possible to determine the Version of all included Information units, local to the Document or Imported.

- A Document included in a Configuration through more than one path might as a result be included in more than one Version simultaneously.

- It must be possible to group changes (possibly to different Information units) into the same Delta. This requirement is motivated by the need to limit the number of created Versions and to represent logical changes.

- The model must support distributed development as transparent as possible.

- The model must support users' awareness of what other users are changing or have changed.

A configuration management system must also provide a good user interface and an efficient and compact implementation of the model.

3   The COOP/Orm hierarchical document model

We have chosen to support hierarchically structured documents directly since they are very frequently occurring and simple to represent and handle. Such documents can be seen as a kind of internal configurations where each unit as well as the configuration as .a whole is version controlled together. In figure 1 we see an example of a typical structured document, a program with a class, its operations and documentation. The user interface with nested windows is described in [HM88]. The development history of the document is presented as a graph in a window. This graph can be used to browse the version history of the document, view particular versions of it and compare two versions, either sequential or further apart in time.

Updating a document involves three steps, (1) Selecting an originating version and creating a new version, (2) making a sequence of changes to one or several information units, and finally (3) terminating the update by 'freezing' the new version. Following the 'change propagation' scheme, all change to an information unit will go into the corresponding delta together with new versions of all composite units they are part of. Since a document is a tree structure, seen as repeated composite units, the change propagation ripples up to the top of the tree. As a result of this scheme, selection of a version of a document precisely determines the version of all information units of the document. The changes to a document can include changes to information units as well as to the structure of the document (adding/deleting units).

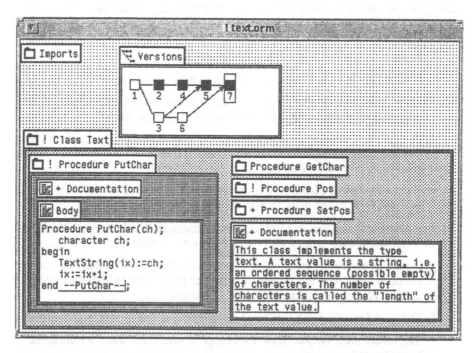

Figure 1   *Hierarchical document with version graph. We see version '7' of the document with marked differences compared with version '2' of the document.*

Version aware editor Hierarchical documents are browsed and edited with a specialized editor which allows the user to directly see the differences between versions of a document, both in terms of changes to an information unit as well as to the configuration itself, such as adding or deleting of units in the configuration. Creating a new version is seen as a comparison with its originating version and changes are highlighted as they are entered.

Explicit version graph An explicit version graph with a graphical user interface allows the user to view and browse the document in terms of its versions. In figure 1 we see the document in version '7'. In the same view we also show all differences relative to version 2. Signs like '+', '!' and '-' marks units that have been added, changed or deleted between the two compared versions. In open units we can see the detailed changes made, here added text is underlined and deleted text is overstroken. The editor is described in more detail in [Ols94]. The version graph also shows that the document has two alternatives, and changes from the alternative have been merged twice (indicated by the two arrows).

Local revision history All the information units in a hierarchical document share the same revision history, but a single unit might be unchanged (or even non-existent) in many of the versions of the document. This information is shown on demand in the 'local version graph' of the unit (an example for the 'Documentation' window of figure 1 is shown in figure 2). Here we can see that this particular unit did not exist in version 1,2,4 (dimmed boxes), thus created in version 3 and equal in some versions (3=5 and 6=7, marked with the double arrows). The user can thus browse the document both in terms of structure and versions at any level of detail at the same time.

Merge of variants Users working on the same document are free to create new versions and variants of the document. The editors offer strong support for merging of variants, suggesting default results and identifying conflicts for the user to solve [Ask94]. During merge changes to the contents of information units as well as changes to the structure can be handled.

Distribution A version of a document is never changed once it is established. The revision history of a document can only be extended with new versions. This means that it is not problematic to replicate a document in a distributed multi-server environment [MA95]. After a communication failure it is possible to synchronize the replicas. Merging of alternatives are done under user control, possibly later, in the same way whether the alternatives have been created in a distributed setting or not.

Awareness The version graph is shared by all users editing or viewing the same document. All creations of new versions of the document is thus immediately visible for all users (who have chosen not to close the version window). The granularity of presented

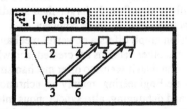

Figure 2 *Local version graph of a single information unit in a hierarchical document. The unit is not present in some versions (1,2,4) of the document, equal in some versions (3=5 and 6=7 respectively) and different when comparing others (e.g. 3 and 6, 5 and 7).*

changes is flexible, so a user can choose to be made aware of single changes as they are made. In [MM93] we have described how the model covers synchronization models from asynchronous to synchronous through the 'Active diffs' technique. This flexible awareness support can be provided also in a distributed situation.

3.1 Discussion

Hierarchical documents are intended to be used for representing relatively tightly dependent information. This might be programs, such as a class or a module with its operations, or a paper with sections and paragraphs. A document can include related information of different type, such as program code, documentation, users' manuals, specifications, test cases, execution results and (as will be discussed further in the next section) bindings to other documents. The explicit representation of the version graph used for simple and fast interaction to view and compare versions helps the user to create a good understanding of the history of a document.

Integrated support for hierarchical representation offers a solution for the document size conflict. On one hand the Information units in a COOP/Orm document can be made relatively small in order to enable users to share small pieces of information and do work in parallel. On the other hand, the size of a COOP/Orm document can be chosen to be relatively large to collect logically related information in one unit.

COOP/Orm also offers a solution to the combination explosion problem since many related changes to the information units can be included in one version update of a document. If each information unit was represented as a single file with a version history of its own there would be a large number of combinations [Tic88], most of which would be inconsistent and uninteresting.

The versions of the document created in our model represent meaningful combinations of versions of the included information units, and the problem with many meaningless configurations is thus avoided. The scheme is not a restriction on the developer since it is always possible to create new variants of a document to include particular combinations of versions of the included information units.

The version control mechanism will register all versions of a document, also so called 'minor-revisions', short lived versions during development of very little interest. In order to counter for a situation where the version graph grows beyond reasonable limits we are considering different mechanisms to collapse (and even remove) in particular long sequences of uninteresting versions of a document.

The underlying representation is using a backwards-delta technique and sharing of information for nodes that have not changed between versions [MAM93]. The use of character based, change oriented, deltas, rather than line based, might turn out to be more compact, in particular for the many small deltas we have to store. Our model also enables sharing of information between alternatives, which might be a significant improvement if there are many alternatives with small differences. There is no reason to believe that this representation form will be significantly larger than standard techniques used by SCCS and RCS, but it might turn out to be more compact.

The explicit shared version graph offers a powerful mechanism for awareness. It is possible to see in real time what other versions are created, and what the changes are. Together with the active diff mechanism it seems to offer mechanisms that covers the modes of interaction used in Software Engineering: mainly asynchronous, but in certain situations, such as initial design and debugging, also synchronous interaction.

The hierarchical document representation offers a mechanism for sharing documents between developers, but from a systems building point of view a document is one unit. In order to share a document between several systems we need also a binding mechanism to create configurations of documents. How to introduce such a mechanism with the document model outlined in this chapter is the main contribution of this paper, presented in the next chapter.

4 Configurations of hierarchical documents

A system can in principle be built as a single hierarchical document, but this would not allow use of a sub-component, such as a library, in several systems. In order to share components or sub-systems between systems, systems are built as a number of components that are then combined to make up complete systems. To provide mechanisms for this situation, a document can in our model contain bindings to other documents. Such a binding is targeted to a specific version of a document. We use the terminology that a document can *import* another document through a *binding*. As with a single hierarchical document, given a specific version of a configuration, it is always determined exactly which version of each imported document is included in the configuration. In figure 3 we can see the content of an 'Imports' window showing all other documents imported. For each document its name and version is shown. This view is called the *global version graph*, since it presents the versions of all documents the current document depends on.

A document can be included in a configuration through several bindings in the same or different configurations. A specific version of a configuration is always importing a specific version of the imported documents. A document that is included into a system through different paths might very well be included in more than one version at the same time.

Documents that contain no external bindings can be seen as a special case, constituting leaf nodes in the DAG of imported documents. Documents which are not further imported are called *systems*, while the intermediate case, documents with both incoming and outgoing bindings, are called *sub-systems*. Apart from the existence of bindings there is no difference between these kinds of documents.

Updating bindings

Changes to external bindings (as well as changes to other units) in a hierarchical document will propagate a version change to the top of the document, establishing a new ver-

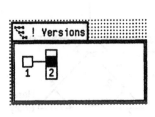
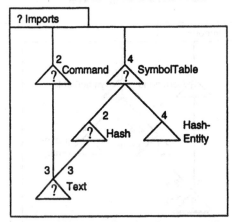

Figure 3 *Imported documents, directly and indirectly, in version '2' of a document. We can see that the document 'Text' is imported in two different ways. The marking, '?', indicates that there is a more modern version of the imported document available.*

sion of the document, as described earlier, but not penetrate through to the, possibly, large number of documents that *import* the document. Changing a binding to import a different, often newer, version of a document is something the developer frequently wants to be in control of. This operation is therefore an active choice (although supported by the user interface) rather than an automatic feature. Rebinding an import to another version of the imported document can be done by editing the external binding, or by editing in the global version graph. In both cases, updating an external binding always means creating a new version of the importing document. In figure 4 we show two steps in re-binding the version of an indirectly imported document. The 'open lid' in the version graph indicates a version under construction. We have decided to use the updated version, '4' of the document 'Text' and as a side-effect we have created new versions also of the intermediate documents. In the left hand situation the graph shows the difference in bindings between two versions of the configuration(2 and 3). The marker '?' marks information units where a newer version of the document is available and markers '!' indicate changed units. Version ranges (like '3-4') are used to show the versions bound to in changed units. Double drawn icons indicate that multiple versions of the document are considered in the current situation.

In the right hand picture of figure 4 the new version, 3, of the configuration is ready and the graph shows the resulting bindings of the document. Note that the developer, in this case, chose to use two different versions of the document 'Text' and the availability of the more modern version is still signaled by the '?' markers which is propagated upwards in the graph.

4.1 Discussion

The COOP/Orm document model extends well to supporting configurations of documents. The requirement to always be able to reconstruct versions of documents in a con-

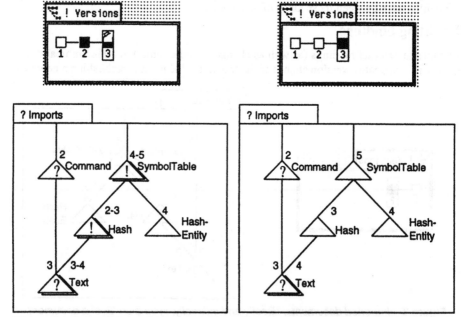

Figure 4 A comparison of versions of a configuration being edited (to the left) and the final result, showing import of a document in multiple versions.

figuration is fulfilled since bindings are to explicit versions of imported documents. In the terminology of [Tic88] our configurations are always 'baselines' and 'generic configurations' are ruled out by the requirement. Generic configurations are, despite the drawback not to fulfill the reconstruction requirement, motivated by the need to, in a flexible way, express selection of versions (like the last stable version) during development. There is also a need to select among the few meaningful combinations of the enormous number of possible configurations generated by combinatorics. The combinatorical explosion is created by the large number of individually versioned documents. Our approach is to try to avoid rather than solve this problem.

In our model information units are grouped together into documents with one and the same version history. There is thus typically fewer (but larger) documents when our model is used. Furthermore, since there is support for grouping of related changes, there will be much fewer versions of this document than the combination of versions of all included information units. These versions represent meaningful combinations of versions since they are created by the developer of the document. These two effects thus greatly reduce the number of combinations that need to be considered.

Attempting to further reduce the number of versions of a document that has to be considered by a developer who imports the document, one can envision techniques based on status of the versions, such as 'released', 'tested' etc. A filtering mechanism could then be used to show only a subset of the existing versions to the users importing the document. Seen from the developers viewpoint, this technique would solve the problem in a similar way as generic configurations, although the binding is done earlier.

A potential problem with our model is the 'snowball' effect that can be triggered when shifting to use a new version of a basic document, used (directly or indirectly) by many documents including the final system. Each of these needs to be extended with a new version in order to make the change take full effect. The binding update mechanism described above, has been designed to make it simple to create these new versions of a large number of documents. The filtering mechanism, outlined above, would help further in automating such regular updates.

We conclude that our model cover the needs addressed by both baselines and generic configurations. Baselines are trivially supported, while an automated re-binding mechanism covers the selection problem. The difference is that the selection is triggered explicitly in our model and as a consequence the requirement to be able to reconstruct systems is fulfilled.

5 Evaluation

The model presented in this paper will be evaluated first of all for the expressiveness and ease of use of the functionality it offers. The efficient implementation of the underlying representation of hierarchical documents has already been reported on in [MAM93]. The model meets the requirements listed above and thus also the requirements in [Kat90] as we interpret them in these circumstances. For further evaluation of the expressiveness we will use the list of questions relevant for software configuration management presented in [Tic88]:

Identification: *Identifying the individual components and configurations is a prerequisite for controlling their evolution. Questions: This program worked yesterday - What happened. I can't reproduce the error in this configuration. I fixed this problem long ago - Why did it reappear? The on-line documentation doesn't match the program. Do we have the latest version?*

Our model is storing all information in a versioned form and clearly supports the demand for identification. A system can always be recreated in any version. Our model also supports interactive presentation of differences between comparable versions and thus helps not only in identifying versions, but also differences both regarding content and structure of documents and configurations. The model supports integrated storage of code and documentation.

Change Tracking: *Change tracking keeps a record of what was done to which component for what reason, at what time and by whom. Questions: Has this problem been fixed? Which bug fixes went into this copy? This seems like an obvious change - Was it tried before? Who is responsible for this modification? Were these independent changes merged?*

Our model immediately answers the questions related to what was done to which components at what time and by whom. Remains to support questions on for what reason. Here we suggest a technique where bug reports are stored as individual documents and used to store bindings to related documents needing update. This is a technique similar to 'projects' in other systems, directly supported by our model. This technique gives a partial answer to the questions, the difficult one is - 'What bug fixes went into this copy'. It could be envisioned to be solved with a search mechanism over such Bug report documents and their external bindings.

Version Selection and Baselining: *Selecting the right versions of components and configurations for testing and baselining can be difficult. Machine support for version selection helps with composing consistent configurations. Questions: How do I configure a test system that contains my temporary fixes to the last baseline, and the released fixes of all other components? Given a list of fixes and enhancements, how do I configure a system that incorporates them? This enhancement won't be ready until the next release - How do I configure it out of the baseline? How exactly does this version differ from the baseline?*

Our model offers explicit choice of modules and versions to include in a configuration (=baseline). Creating versions of configurations as these examples are done interactively and under explicit control by the user. The system can also show differences between versions of configurations, to answer the last question.

Our model is designed to support tracing of the exact version of all components that go into any configuration. Selection of configurations is explicit and manual in our system, but chosen from a much smaller set of meaningful combinations than in a traditional situation. We have also shown how the model could support an automatic selection mechanism.

Software Manufacture: *Putting together a configuration requires numerous steps such as pre-and post-processing, compiling, linking, formatting and regression testing. SCM systems must automate that process and at the same time should be open for adding new processing programs. To reduce redundant work, they must manage a cache of recently generated components. Questions: I just fixed that - Was something not recompiled? How much recompilation will this change cost? Did we deliver an up-to-date binary version to the customer? I wonder whether we applied the processing steps in the right order. How exactly was this configuration produced? Were all regression tests performed on this version?*

These are issues that we regard as the responsibility of the software development environment. The environment we are working with, and where the model we have presented is used, is highly integrated and spares the user the burden of controlling the "manufacturing process" itself. These tasks are done automatically and incrementally as needed.

Managing Simultaneous Update: *Simultaneous update of the same component by several programmers cannot always be prevented. The configuration management system must note such situations and supply tools for merging competing changes later. In so doing helps prevent problems like the following: Why did my change to this module disappear? What happened to my unfinished modules while I was out of town? How do I merge these changes into my version? Do our changes conflict?*

Our version control model is designed to support teams of programmers doing simultaneous updates. The model is that each member is free to create new versions and the system provides support for merging alternatives together using a operation-based diffing approach. Our model in fact goes beyond the requirements here in that it also supports a synchronous editing mode where programmers can see each others work in progress [MM93].

We thus conclude that the functionality needed to provide support for configuration management is covered in our model. We go beyond these requirements when it comes to support for teams of programmers.

5.1 Comparison with other systems

CVS [Wat, Ced93] is a system built on top of RCS and provides a central *repository* which contains *modules*, groups of files, of for instance program sources. The files are hierarchically structured (Unix files and directories). Every file is version controlled and branches as well as merge can be done on a single file.

The idea of module is matched by our hierarchical documents. CVS only uses modules as the configuration structure and not for version control while we use the structure for change propagation, compact storage and advanced presentation of differences. In CVS the revision numbers live a life of their own and it is optional *tags*, symbolic names attached to a certain revision of a file, that support versions of configurations. Thus, even if the structure of the repository is hierarchical the selection of files creating a configuration is not hierarchical. Our change propagation mechanism also enables diffs on configurations, which is not possible in CVS.

Furthermore, our approach supports a finer granularity of version control than CVS does. Our information units are intended for smaller pieces of information than what is usually stored in a single file. Also our model encourages creation of alternatives for development work, the result of which is then merged into the main development line (matched with the *commit* command in CVS). Minor revisions are thus saved in the developer's own alternative enabling a more detailed history log. In this way we support fine grained versions for each developer, without cluttering the main development line with too many versions.

Our integrated architecture also gives a more supportive user interface with graphical presentation of the version graph, and visibility of operation-based diffs (rather than whole source lines).

Teamware is a system designed for use in a distributed setting, supporting a workspace metaphor. Configurations, i.e. directories with files, can be manipulated and copied for independent development and later synchronization. Parallel development is thus supported in the copy-merge style. Merging of workspace copies is supported in that conflicts are detected, i.e. updates that have taken place after the check-out, and have to be merged into the local workspace (and presumably tested) before an update can take place. If exactly the same file has been updated in both places, a three-way merge tool is used to support textual merge of the changes. The effect is that development of a workspace is a linear sequence. Alternative development lines are handled through use of multiple workspaces. Teamware is built on top of SCCS and a workspace includes copies of related SCCS files, which thus are copied and later merged. This enables movement of entire workspaces between file-systems and thus distribution, but with no awareness.

The COOP/Orm Multi-Server architecture enables replication and wide distribution, but also synchronization and awareness as long as there is network connection. Synchronization of SCCS files matches synchronization of replicated Orm documents after a network failure. The workspace model supported by Teamware matches Orm documents with one alternative for each Workspace. Seen this way Teamware insists on a particular merging order between alternatives that could be used also in COOP/Orm, but is not insisted on. In addition Teamware works with the latest version in each workspace, while in COOP/Orm the full development history is always available.

Continuus/CM is a process-driven, client-server system for change and configuration management. The Continuus/CM object management system is built on an inheritance-based type system, with several pre-defined object types. The *directory* and the *project* type represent grouping and configuration respectively, and can be mapped to the COOP/Orm document and configuration. There are, however, some differences. A new version of a *directory* object is only necessary if the set of objects changes (e.g. a new file is added to the directory). I.e., new versions of a file already in a directory can be created within the same directory version. This is in contrast to documents in COOP/Orm, where a change to a leaf unit propagates to be considered a change of the document. The drawback of Continuus solution, as we see it, is that the directory abstraction can not be used for selection of configurations. Instead of selecting a specific version of a directory, every object must be treated individually, which increases the complexity also when the configuration is later viewed. Both systems can compare versions of information units. However, the operation-based deltas used in COOP/Orm and the integration of editor and storage model gives a more fine-grained diff. Additionally, versions of both COOP/Orm documents and configurations can be compared and merged, highlighting the differences. This is, to our knowledge, not possible with directories and projects.

ClearCase is a version-driven configuration management system. It versions file-system objects, including files, directories, and links, of which directories are treated similarly to directories in Continuus/CM discussed above. Configuration control is supported through *views* which is a set of directories and files selected by a set of user-defined rules. Like COOP/Orm, ClearCase makes it easy to create a variant of a file and to reintegrate the work done into other lines of development. The merge is similar to ours, using the 'common ancestor' to find the changes between the common ancestor and each of the versions being merged. Both systems find the parts of the file changed in both branches and highlights them as conflicts. However, when ClearCase merges a file COOP/Orm merges a document, including merge of the document structure at the same time. Our merge is also more fine-grained because we use the operation-based deltas given by the editor instead of comparing files, calculating the differences. This, we think, is the drawback of the transparency approach to integration taken in ClearCase. COOP/Orm also has more comprehensive group awareness, supporting the spectrum from shared version graph to active diffs enabling synchronous work.

CoVer [HH93,Web92] is a hypermedia version server implemented on top of the HyperBase hypermedia engine [SS90]. Versioned objects are represented by *multi-state objects* (mobs), which is a composite holding references to all states of the versioned object it represents. CoVer does not impose a fixed structure on the versions of a versioned object and version selection is based on viewing and browsing versions with respect to values on their attributes or relationships to other objects. General queries are used to find objects of a particular version. If a query returns several versions, they are considered as *alternatives* with respect to the equality characteristic given by the query.

The free format of version control in CoVer is in contrast to our approach where the evolution history is explicit. Versions represents the evolution and alternatives parallel development, i.e. a directed acyclic graph (DAG) structure.

In CoVer a *Task* maintains the (versions of) various objects used and created in the context of performing a job. A Task is implemented as a composite holding references to the objects determining its current state. This approach resembles the AND/OR graphs model presented in [Tic88], where a *mob* matches an OR-node and *Task* composites are AND-nodes. Our configuration mechanism can be used to form a collection for the purpose of performing a job, thus recording and preserving the information on which documents needed updates (and exactly which updates).

6 Implementation

6.1 Operations in the model

In this section we will summarize the functionality of the presented version model in form of the operations which the model supports. The representation of a hierarchical document has three components: revision history, user data, and external bindings.

Revision history
The revision history contains information to represent each revision of the document and their relations. The information is sufficient to create the version graph presented in the user interface. When a new version is created, this information is extended. The information format is a sequence of version pairs representing each arc in the graph.
Operations:

- Read version graph - return information describing the revision history of the document.

- Set focus - change currently viewed version of the document.

- Set compare - change version to which the viewed version is compared.

- Create version - create a new version succeeding from an arbitrary selected (but established) version. If the originating version already has succeeding versions a variant is automatically created. This is an operation that involves a long transaction, it is terminated explicitly and the version is 'frozen'.

- Freeze version - make the version immutable.

- Merge versions - merge two versions creating a third.

User data

The user data constitutes the content of an information unit in one of its versions. The storage format uses backward operation oriented deltas and extensive sharing of common subparts [MAM93].
Operations:

- Read a unit - get the unit information in the version currently in focus. It returns application data for leaf units, and configuration information for branch units.

- Read a unit delta - get the delta information for a unit representing the changes between the focus and compare versions.

- Write a unit - update the unit information of a unit in the version in focus, and at the same time update the delta to its originating version(s).

- Add a unit - the document configuration is expanded with one new unit. Its type can be a composite unit or leaf unit (e.g. text or external binding).

- Delete a unit - delete a unit in the configuration.

The operations, Write, Add and Delete a unit can only be called when a new version is in creation (between the Create and Freeze operations). Add and Delete a unit are actually edit operations on the containing composite unit. The actual content of an information unit depends on the type of the unit. Here we have mentioned the fundamental node types composite and external bindings (as of below), and nodes of type text. The model can, however, handle user data of any type.

External bindings

The external bindings contain the path and version of all external documents this document depends on, or imports. This information is stored and version controlled as part of user data, but considered a special component due to its importance for configuration management.
Operations:

- Read external bindings - return bindings to external document (including version).

- Read binding deltas - return changes to the bindings between the focus and compare versions.

- Create external binding - add an import of a specific version of a document.

- Delete external binding - remove an import of a document.

The operations Create and Delete uses the operation Write unit and can thus only be called during creation of a new version.

6.2 Implementation status

The implementation of the model is carried out as part of a software development system with the ambition to support teams of users working together on shared information. The implementation is organized as a multiple server multiple client architecture. In the first version it supports a semi-structured representation of programs and text. The hierarchical document supports structuring a document as a tree of information units, but each unit can currently only contain unstructured text. A text editor with version control mechanisms provides the means to browse and navigate versioned text.

6.3 Future work

Currently the version graph interface shows all existing versions of a document. This clearly does not scale up to handling systems with a long and complex history. We are therefore working with methods to suppress some of the information in the graph (hiding details like long sequences and older parts) although the user can always 'open' these parts to see all the details as he wish. Similarly, the global version graph shows all included document in a configuration. This does not scale up to large systems with many components. Here we are considering to suppress deeply nested graphs (again allowing the user to explore these parts if he wishes), but still reporting the status of these parts (propagating the '?' markers). Operations are also needed to perform related rebinding operations over a collection of modules in one operation (like switching to use a new release of a popular module without touching all the importing modules one by one).

In future versions we will also provide a versioned editor for abstract syntax trees for integration of the fine-grained version mechanism in the Orm programming environment.

The protocol for server-server communication has been designed but is not yet implemented.

Finally we see the system as an interesting environment for experimenting with process support. The explicit version mechanism is initially motivated for enabling awareness in a cooperative editing environment and a process support system is by nature a CSCW system. We also expect that interactive language development support mechanisms developed in the Mjølner/Orm environment (and available in COOP/Orm when the abstract syntax editor is available) will be useful to develop support for specifying processes.

7 Conclusions

We have presented an integrated model for fine-grained version control and configuration management. The design is exploring a two level approach. A restricted grouping mechanism is supported inside tree structured, hierarchical documents, offering automatic version propagation. Between documents a general binding mechanism is offered with explicit control over version selection of imported documents.

Supporting hierarchical documents have several benefits. At the same time it offers a configuration mechanism for keeping related information together in a tree structure, a fine-grained revision control mechanism, and automatic change propagation. A direct manipulation user interface allows the user to browse a document both according to its structure and its versions presented in a graph. Differences between versions of a document can be interactively constructed and presented both regarding changes to structure and contents.

Through external bindings hierarchical documents can be related in DAG structures, a document can thus be used in many places. In a single hierarchical document, change propagation is automatically generating new versions of containing configurations in the tree structure. Between documents the change of bindings to different versions is explicitly managed by the user, but guided with a graphical user interface. Bindings are always targeted to a particular version of an external document and the bindings are stored as part of the versioned information of a document. As a result it is always possible to recreate all the documents included in a configuration in their correct versions.

The model is initially intended for supporting development in integrated environments, but is also useful in other settings. The model has been developed to support groups of developers sharing information and is offering support for both synchronous and asynchronous modes of editing, parallel development and strong support for merging of variants. The details of these aspects are covered in other papers [MM93, MAM93, Ask94, Mag95].

Acknowledgments

The authors wants to thank all the members of the software development research group at Dept. of Computer Science, Lund Institute of Technology, for stimulating discussions which have contributed substantially to the work presented in this paper. In particular, we want to thank Torsten Olsson who is working on the structured document editor and Görel Hedin for constructive comments on earlier drafts of this paper.

The work presented in this paper was supported in part by NUTEK, the Swedish National Board for Industrial and Technical Development.

References

[Ask94]   Ulf Asklund. Identifying Conflicts During Structural Merge. In Magnusson et al. MHM94.

[Cla95]   Dave St Clair: Continuus/CM vs. ClearCase, URL: http://sunsite.icm.edu.pl/sunworldonline/swol-07-1995/swol-07-cm.html, SunWorld Online, 1995.

[Ced93]   Per Cederqvist. Version Management with CVS. Available from info@signum.se, 1993.

[Gus90]   A. Gustavsson. *Software Configuration Management in an Integrated Environment*. Licentiate thesis, Lund University, Dept. of Computer Science, Lund, Sweden, 1990.

[HH93]   Anja Haake and Jörg M. Haake. Take CoVer: Exploiting Version Support in Cooperative Systems. In *Proceedings of INTERCHI'93*, ACM Press, Amsterdam, The Netherlands, April 24-29 1993. Addison Wesley.

[HM88]   G. Hedin and B. Magnusson. The Mjølner environment: Direct interaction with abstractions. In S. Gjessing and K. Nygaard, editors, *Proceedings of the 2nd European Conference on Object-Oriented Programming (ECOOP'88)*, volume 322 of *Lecture Notes in Computer Science*, pages 41–54, Oslo, August 1988. Springer-Verlag.

[Kat90]   Randy H. Katz. Toward a Unified Framework for Version Modeling in Engineering Databases. *ACM Computing Surveys*, 22(4), December 1990.

[KLMM93]   J.L. Knudsen, M. Löfgren, O.L. Madsen, and B. Magnusson, editors. *Object-Oriented Environments - The Mjølner Approach*. Prentice-Hall, 1993.

[LvO92]   Ernst Lippe and Norbert van Oosterom. Operation-based Merging. In H. Weber, editor, *SIGSOFT'92 Proceedings*, Tyson's Corner, Va., December 1992. ACM. SIGSOFT Software Engineering Notes, 17(5).

[MAM93]   Boris Magnusson, Ulf Asklund, and Sten Minör. Fine-Grained Revision Control for Collaborative Software Development. In *Proceedings of ACM SIGSOFT'93 - Symposium on the Foundations of Software Engineering*, Los Angeles, California, 7-10 December 1993.

[MHM94]   Boris Magnusson, Görel Hedin, and Sten Minör, editors. *Proceedings of the Nordic Workshop on Programming Environment Research*, Lund University of Technology. LU-CS-TR:94-127, Lund, January 1-3 1994.

[MM93]   Sten Minör and Boris Magnusson. A Model for Semi-(a)Synchronous Collaborative Editing. In *Proceedings of the Third European Conference on Computer Supported Cooperative Work*, Milano, Italy, 1993. Kluwer Academic Publishers.

[MA95]   Boris Magnusson and Ulf Asklund: Collaborative Editing - Distributed and replication of shared versioned objects. Presented at the Workshop on Mobility and Replication, held with ECOOP 95, Aarhus, August 1995. Available as: LU-CS-TR:96-162, Dept. of Computer Science, Lund, Sweden.

[Mag95]   Boris Magnusson: Fine-Grained Version Control in COOP/Orm, Presented at the Workshop on Version Control in CSCW, held with ECSCW'95, Stockholm, Sept. 1995. Available as: LU-CS-TR:96-163, Dept. of Computer Science, Lund, Sweden.

[MHM+90]   Boris Magnusson, Görel Hedin, Sten Minör, et al. An Overview of the Mjølner Orm Environment. In J. Bezivin et al., editors, *Proceedings of the 2nd International Conference TOOLS (Technology of Object-Oriented Languages and Systems)*, Paris, June 1990. Angkor.

[Ols94]   Torsten Olsson. Group Awareness Using Fine-Grained Revision Control. In Magnusson et al. MHM94.

[RBI95]   W. Rigg, C. Burrows and P. Ingram: Ovum Evaluates: Configuration Management Tools, Ovum Limited, London, 1995.

[Roe75]   M. J. Roekind. The source code control system. *IEEE Transactions on Software Engineering*, 1(4):364–370, December 1975.

[SCC]   *SCCS - Source Code Control System. UNIX System V programmer's Guide.* Prentice-Hall Inc. pp 59-700.

[SS90]   Helge Schütt and N. Streitz. HyperBase: A Hypermedia Engine Based on a Relational Database Management System. In A. Rizk, N. Streitz, and J. André, editors, *Proceedings of the European Conference on Hypertext (ECHT'90): Hypertext: Concepts, Systems, and Applications*, Cambridge Series on Electronic Publishing, pages 95–108, Versailles, France, November 27-30 1990.

[Team]   TeamWare user's guides, Sun Microsystem, 1994.

[Tic85]   Walter F. Tichy. RCS - a system for revision control. *Software Practice and Experience*, 15(7):634–637, July 1985.

[Tic88]   Walter F. Tichy. Tools for software configuration management. In *Proceedings from International Workshop on Software Version and Configuration Control*, Grassau, Germany, February 1988.

[TJ88]   Dave Thomas and Kent Johnson. Orwell: A Configuration Management System For Team Programming. In N. Meyrowitz, editor, *Proceedings of OOPSLA'88*, San Diego, Ca., September 25-30 1988. ACM. SIGPLAN Notices, 23(11).

[Wat]   Gray Watson. CVS Tutorial. Available from gray.watson@antaire.com.

[Web92]   Anja Weber. CoVer: A Contextual Version Server for Hypertext Applications. In *Proceedings of ECHT'92*, November 30 - December 4 1992.

An Empirical Study of Delta Algorithms

James J. Hunt[1], Kiem-Phong Vo[2] and Walter F. Tichy[1]

[1] University of Karlsruhe, Karlsruhe, Germany
[2] AT&T Research, Murray Hill, NJ

Abstract. Delta algorithms compress data by encoding one file in terms of another. This type of compression is useful in a number of situations: storing multiple versions of data, distributing updates, storing backups, transmitting video sequences, and others. This paper studies the performance parameters of several delta algorithms, using a benchmark of over 1300 pairs of files taken from two successive releases of GNU software. Results indicate that modern delta compression algorithms based on Ziv-Lempel techniques significantly outperform *diff*, a popular but older delta compressor, in terms of compression ratio. The modern compressors also correlate better with the actual difference between files; one of them is even faster than *diff* in both compression and decompression speed.

1 Introduction

Delta algorithms, i.e., algorithms that compute differences between two files or strings, have a number of uses when multiple versions of data objects must be stored, transmitted, or processed. Differencing compression is an essential ingredient of most software configuration management systems. Without efficient differencing algorithms, version tracking would be impractical for most applications.

Most uses stem from the fact that a delta is often one to two orders of magnitude smaller than the original, and significantly smaller than a direct compression of the original. For example, version control systems store multiple versions of programs, graphics, documents, and other data as deltas relative to a base version[10, 12]. Similarly, backup programs can save space by storing deltas. Checkpoints of large data spaces can be compressed dramatically by using deltas and can then be reloaded rapidly. Display updates can also be performed efficiently using a delta that exploits operations that move lines around[1]. Furthermore, changes of programs or data are most economically distributed as update scripts that generate the new data from the old. Transmitting the script, which is nothing but a delta, can save space, time, and network bandwidth. In addition, a delta provides an effective form of encoding; only the holder of the original can successfully generate the new version. This facility is becoming especially interesting in the Internet for distributing software updates.

Other uses of deltas are for highlighting the differences between two versions of a program or document and for merging or reconciling competing changes of a common original. Deltas are also needed for sequence comparison in molecular biology. The main focus of this paper, however, is the size of the deltas that various delta algorithms compute and the speed of compression and decompression.

The state of empirical comparisons of delta algorithms is poor. Miller and Myers[7] compare the runtime of their delta program, *fcomp*, with that of UNIX *diff* [2, 3]. Their first test involves two pairs of (highly untypical) files, and *fcomp* fails on one of them. Additional tests were run, but not enough particulars are given to repeat the tests independently. Obst[9] compares several difference algorithms on programs of about 3 Megabytes. No details are given that would permit the repetition of their experiment. In both instances, the claims are quite doubtful. The unreliability of the observations is underscored by outliers and irregularities.

The purpose of this paper is to both suggest a realistic benchmark for comparing the performance of delta algorithms and to present firm performance results for a set of such algorithms. The intent is to make the study reported here repeatable by anyone who wishes to check or extend the results. We also present a new delta algorithm called *vdelta* developed by David Korn and Phong Vo [13, 5].

2   Benchmark

The authors propose using the Longest Common Subsequence (LCS) as the reference against which to measure the effectiveness of a differencing algorithm applied to one dimensional data. In particular, they define the **difference** between two file as the average size of the two files minus the LCS. This yardstick is used to build a benchmark consisting of all files in two successive releases of Gnu *emacs*, releases 19.28 and 19.29, and of GNU *gcc*, releases 2.7.0 and 2.7.1. This benchmark contains 810 text files (C programs, Lisp programs, documentation) and 300 files with lisp byte code (binary files). The authors also compiled the 201 C program files present in both versions and included them in the study. The authors chose this benchmark because it is freely available and offers a large number of files of various types in successive revisions.

3   Algorithms

There are four differencing algorithms that are used for this study. The first—*longest common subsequence*—is used as a yardstick to measure the effectiveness of the other three because it is an exhaustive algorithm for finding the Longest Common Subsequences of any pair of files. UNIX *diff* finds an approximation of the Longest Common Subsequence by considering whole lines instead of characters as indivisible units. The last two—*bdiff*, and *vdelta* — piece together the second file out of blocks from the first file. Unlike *lcs*, these algorithms take the ordering of blocks into account. All three of these algorithms run enough faster than *lcs* to have practical applications. Both *bdiff* and *vdelta* offer additional compression on the resultant delta. For this reason, *diff* is also compared with *gzip* post processing.

3.1   *Longest Common Subsequence*

The *longest common subsequence* algorithm (*lcs*) is a textbook algorithm applied to strings[3, 8]. Its runtime is $O(nm)$ where n and m are the files sizes, so it is not practical for general use. However, it is a good point of reference, since it is guaranteed to find the Longest Common Subsequence of two linear character sequences. The **difference** between two files can be expressed as the mean size of the two files minus the size of the LCS.

3.2   **UNIX** *diff*

UNIX *diff* uses the *Longest Common Subsequence* algorithm computed on a line-by-line basis instead of a character-by-character basis[2]. It is much faster than *lcs* because it does not examine all possible combinations of characters. Only common lines can be found with *diff*. Since *diff* only produces output for text files, the contents of binary files must be folded into the ASCII printable range. A commonly used tool for this is *uuencode*.

3.3   *Bdiff*

Bdiff is a modification of W. F. Tichy's block-move algorithm[11]. It uses a two-stage approach. First it computes the difference between the two files. Then it uses a second step to compress the resulting difference description. These two parts run concurrently in that the first stage calls the second each time it generates output.

In the first phase, *bdiff* builds an index, called a suffix tree, for the first file. This tree is used to look up blocks, i.e. substrings, of the second file to find matches in the first file. A greedy strategy is used, i.e. every possible match is examined, to ensure that the longest possible match is found. The output from this phase is a sequence of copy blocks and character insertions that encode the second file in terms of the first. It can be shown that the algorithm produces the smallest number of blocks and runs in linear time. It also discovers crossing blocks, i.e., blocks whose order was permuted in the second file.

The second phase efficiently encodes the output of the first. A block is represented as a length and an offset into the first file. Characters and block lengths are encoded in the same space by adding 253 (256 minus the three unused lengths) to lengths before encoding. Blocks of lengths less than 4 are converted to character insertions. Characters and lengths are then encoded using a common splay tree[4]. The splay tree is used to generate a character encoding that ensures that frequently encoded characters are shorter than uncommon characters. Splay trees dynamically adapt to the statistics of the source without requiring an extra pass. A separate splay tree encodes the offsets.

Bdiff actually uses a sliding window of 64 KB on the first file, moving it in 16 KB increments. This means that the first phase actually builds four suffix trees that index 16 KB each of the first file. The window is shifted forward whenever the encoding of the second file crosses a 16 KB boundary, but in such a fashion that the top window position in the first file is always at least 16 KB ahead of the current encoding position in the second file. Whenever the window is shifted, the oldest of the four suffix trees is discarded and a new one built in its space. The decoder has to track the window shifts, but does not need to build the suffix trees. Position information is given as an offset from the beginning of the window.

3.4 *Vdelta*

Vdelta is a new technique that combines both data compression and data differencing. It is a refinement of W. F. Tichy's block-move algorithm[11], in that, instead of a suffix tree, *vdelta* uses a hash table approach inspired by the data parsing scheme in the 1978 Ziv-Lempel compression technique [14]. Like block-move, the Ziv-Lempel technique is also based on a greedy approach in which the input string is parsed by longest matches to previously seen data. Both Ziv-Lempel and block-move techniques have linear-time implementations [6]. However, implementations of both of these algorithms can be memory intensive and, without careful consideration, they can also be slow because the work required at each iteration is large. *Vdelta* generalizes Ziv-Lempel and block-move by allowing for string matching to be done both within the target data and between a source data and a target data. For efficiency, *vdelta* relaxes the greedy parsing rule so that matching prefixes are not always maximally long. This allows the construction of a simple string matching technique that runs efficiently and requires minimal main memory.

Building Difference For encoding, data differencing can be thought of as compression, where the compression algorithm is run over both sequences but output is only generated for the second sequence. The idea is to construct a hash table with enough indexes into the sequence for fast string matching. Each index is a position which is keyed by the four bytes starting at that position. In order to break a sequence into fragments and construct the necessary hash table, the sequence is processed from start to end; at each step the hash table is searched to find a match. Processing continues at each step as follows:

1. if there is no match,
   (a) insert and index for the current position into the hash table,
   (b) move the current position forward by 1, and
   (c) generate an insert when in output mode; or
2. if there is a match,
   (a) insert into the hash table indexes for the last 3 positions of the matched portion,
   (b) move the current position forward by the length of the match, and
   (c) generate a copy block when in output mode.

Each comparison is done by looking at the last three bytes of the current match plus one unmatched byte and checking to see if there is an index in the hash table that corresponds to a match. The new match candidate is checked backward to make sure that it is a real match before matching forward to extend the matched sequence. If there is no current match, i.e. just starting a new match, use the 4 bytes starting at the current position.

As an example, assume the sequence below with the beginning state as indicated (the ⇓ indicates the current position):

```
⇓
0  1  2  3  4  5  6  7  8  9  10 11 12 13 14 15 16 17 18 19
b  c  d  e  a  b  c  d  a  b  c  d  a  b  c  d  e  f  g  h
```

The algorithm starts at position 0. At this point the rest of the sequence is the entire sequence so there is no possible match to the left. Case 1 requires position 0 to be entered into the hash table (indicated with a * under it) then to advance the current position by 1.

```
   ⇓
0  1  2  3  4  5  6  7  8  9  10 11 12 13 14 15 16 17 18 19
b  c  d  e  a  b  c  d  a  b  c  d  a  b  c  d  e  f  g  h
*
```

This process continues until position 8 is reached. At that time, we have this configuration:

```
                  ⇓
0  1  2  3  4  5  6  7  8  9  10 11 12 13 14 15 16 17 18 19
b  c  d  e  a  b  c  d  a  b  c  d  a  b  c  d  e  f  g  h
*  *  *  *  *  *  *  *
```

Now the rest of the sequence is "abcdabcdedfg". The longest possible match to some part previously processed is "abcdabcd" which starts at location 4. Case 2 dictates entering the last 3 positions of the match (i.e., 13, 14, 15) into the hash table, then moving the current position forward by the length of the match. Thus the current position becomes 16 in this example.

```
                                             ⇓
0  1  2  3  4  5  6  7  8  9  10 11 12 13 14 15 16 17 18 19
b  c  d  e  a  b  c  d  a  b  c  d  a  b  c  d  e  f  g  h
*  *  *  *  *  *  *  *                 *  *  *
```

The final step is to match "efgh" and that fails so the last mark is on position 16. The current position moves to position 17 which now does not have enough data left so the algorithm stops.

```
                                                ⇓
0  1  2  3  4  5  6  7  8  9  10 11 12 13 14 15 16 17 18 19
b  c  d  e  a  b  c  d  a  b  c  d  a  b  c  d  e  f  g  h
*  *  *  *  *  *  *  *                 *  *  *  *
```

Note that the above matching algorithm will actually find the longest match if indexes are kept for every location in the string. The skip in step 2b prevents the algorithm from being able to always find the longest prefix; however, this rule saves considerable processing time and memory space. In fact, it is easy to see from the above hash table construction rules that the space requirement is directly proportional to the output. The more compressible a target data set is, the faster it is to compress it.

Difference Encoding In order to minimize the output generated, the block-move list generated above must be encoded. The output of *vdelta* consists of two types of instructions: **add** and **copy**. The **add** instruction has the length of the data followed by the data itself. The **copy** instruction has the size of the data followed by its address. Two caches are maintained as references to minimize the space required to store this address information.

Each instruction is coded starting with a control byte. Eight bits of the control byte are divided into two parts. The first 4 bits represent numbers from 0 to 15, each of which defines a type of instruction and a coding of some auxiliary information. Below is an enumeration of the first 10 values of the first 4 bits:

0: an **add** instruction,

1,2,3: a **copy** instruction with position in the **QUICK** cache,

4: a **copy** instruction with position coded as an absolute offset from the beginning of the file,

5: a **copy** instruction with position coded as an offset from current location, and

6,7,8,9: a **copy** instruction with position in the **RECENT** cache.

For the **add** instruction and the **copy** instructions above, the second 4 bits of the control byte, if not zero, codes the size of the data involved. If these bits are 0, the respective size is coded as a subsequent sequence of bytes.

The above mentioned caches—**QUICK** and **RECENT**—enable more compact coding of file positions. The **QUICK** cache and is an array of size 768 ($3 * 256$). Each index of this array contains the value p of the position of a recent **copy** instruction such that p modulo 768 is the array index. This cache is updated after each **copy** instruction is output (during coding) or processed (during decoding). A **copy** instruction of type 1, 2, or 3 will be immediately followed by a byte whose value is from 0 to 255 that must be added to 0, 256 or 512 respectively to compute the array index where the actual position is stored. The **RECENT** cache is an array with 4 indices storing the most recent 4 copying positions. Whenever a **copy** instruction is output (during coding) or processed (during decoding), its copying position replaces the oldest position in the cache. A **copy** instruction of type 6, 7, 8, or 9 corresponds to cache index 1, 2, 3, or 4 respectively. Its copying position is guaranteed to be larger than the position stored in the corresponding cache index and only the difference is coded.

It is a result of this encoding method that an **add** instruction is never followed by another **add** instruction. Frequently, an **add** instruction has data size less than or equal to 4 and the following **copy** instruction is also small. In such cases, it is advantageous to merge the two instructions into a single control byte. The values from 10 to 15 of the first 4 bits code such merged pairs of instructions. In such a case, the first 2 bits of the second 4 bits in the control byte code the size of the **add** instruction and the remaining 2 bits code the size of the **copy** instruction. Below is an enumeration of the values from 10 to 15 of the first 4 bits:

10: a merged **add/copy** instruction with copy position coded as itself,

11: a merged **add/copy** instruction with copy position coded as difference from the current position,

12,13,14,15: a merge **add/copy** instruction with copy position coded from a **RECENT** cache.

In order to elucidate the overall encoding scheme, consider the following files:

Version1: a b c d a b c d a b c d e f g h
Version2: a b c d x y x y x y x y b c d e f

The block-move output would be

1. **copy** 4 0		01000100 0
2. **add** 2 "xy"	which encodes to	00000010 "xy"
3. **copy** 6 20	(instruction in binary)	01000110 20
4. **copy** 5 9		01000101 9

Note that the third instruction copies from Version2. The address 20 for this instruction is $16 + 4$ where 16 is the length of Version1. Note also that the data to be copied is also being reconstructed. That is, *vdelta* knows about periodic sequences.

This output encoding is independent of the way the block-move lists are calculated, thus *bdiff* could be modified to use this encoding and *vdelta* could be modified to use splay coding.

4 Method

In order to test the various differencing algorithms, a large data set was needed. Thanks to the Free Software Foundation, quite a number of software projects are available in successive versions. The authors chose two versions of GNU *emacs*—19.28 and 19.29—and two versions of GNU *gcc*—2.7.0 and 2.7.1—as their test suite. These versions provide a broad spectrum of variation between one revision of any given file and the next.

Both versions of GNU *emacs* and GNU *gcc* were compiled so that successive revisions of object files were also available. A Longest Common Subsequence was computed for each pair. Then each algorithm was run on each pair of files. Files that existed in one version and not the other and files that did not differ at all were eliminated. All this was done on a DEC Alpha system.

The algorithms chosen were UNIX *diff -n* (as used by RCS), UNIX *diff* followed by compressing the results with *gzip*, *bdiff*, and *vdelta*. The files were broken up into three types: text files (mostly C and Elisp code), byte compiled Elisp code (ELC files), and object files. Since UNIX *diff* was not designed to work with non-printable characters, UNIX *uuencode* was used to remap problematic characters. UNIX *uuencode* was chosen, since it is used in some extension to RCS to provide for binary revisioning.

Each algorithm was run with each file pair both forward and reverse, e.g. revision 19.28 then 19.29 and revision 19.29 then 19.28. This was done so that the effect of differences where one file is much smaller than the other could be averaged out. Removing large sections from one file results in a small delta and adding large sections results in a large delta. In practice, this phenomena is "averaged out" in revisioning systems since one revision must be stored in its entirety.

Two types of data were collected: the size of the delta file and the time needed to encode and decode each pair. Since no dedicated decoder is available for UNIX *diff* -n files, RCS was used to time *diff* -n encoding and decoding. (The authors tried using *diff* -e and *ed*, but that proved to be ridiculously slow.) UNIX *wc* was used to measure file sizes and UNIX *time* was used to measure duration. Byte count and user plus system time are used to present the results below.

5   Results

There are two important measures for compression algorithms: the resultant compression ratio and the execution speed. The authors present the results of their study in graphic form below. These plots are presented using *gnuplot*. Results are given separately for text files, ELC files, and object files, since the behavior of some of the algorithms differ for these classes. ELC files were not combined with object files because they are mostly text.

5.1   Effectiveness

Since the *longest common subsequence* algorithm is known to produce optimal results (though at a great speed penalty), the *lcs* results are used as a point of comparison below. Specifically, the authors define the **difference** between two files as the average size of the two minus the LCS. An alternative would have been to just examine file sizes and compare them to the sum of the delta sizes. Although this number is also interesting, the LCS comparison used here sheds more light on the correlation between the actual changes between two revisions and the size of the delta. So, in each graph, a point is plotted for each file pair using each algorithm. Then a line is plotted for each algorithm that depicts the linear regression of all the data points using the standard least common squares algorithm.

In the first set of three graphs in figures 1, 2, and 3, the average size of the forward delta and reverse delta is plotted against the **difference**. The x axis is simply the average size of each pair minus the LCS size. The y axis is the average size of the forward *diff* and the reverse *diff* output. Here one can see how much better *bdiff* and *vdelta* correlate to the **difference** than *diff* and *diff* with *gzip*. Though *diff* with *gzip* performs as well as *bdiff* and *vdelta* for text files (figure 1), it performs much more poorly for ELC and object files. The outlying points correspond to files where the **difference** is much smaller than the file size. All

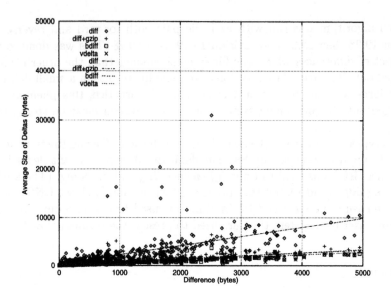

Correlations: diff 0.952; diff+gzip 0.976; bdiff 0.962; vdelta 0.976

Fig. 1. Plot of Delta Size for Text Files

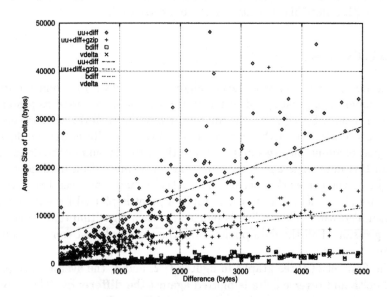

Correlations: uu+diff 0.805; uu+diff+gzip 0.804; bdiff 0.949; vdelta 0.959

Fig. 2. Plot of Delta Size for ELC Files

algorithms performed more poorly on the object file set (figure 3) than on the other sets.

The next set of three graphs in figures 4, 5, and 6 presents the same data as a log-log plot. The logarithmic scales permit the presentation of a much greater range of **differences** and delta sizes. As expected, the linear regression lines are not straight due to their nonzero y-intercepts. This is caused by the constant factor in execution time that is most likely related to program startup time. Here one can see the low end of the graph in more detail. The separation between the data points for the different algorithms can be seen more easily and the band for *diff* with *gzip* is much closer for those of *bdiff* and *vdelta* for text files than for the other categories.

The final set of three graphs in figures 7, 8, and 9 presents the average compression ratio against the ratio of **difference** to average file size. Here the x axis is given as one minus the LCS size divided by the average file size in each pair. This expresses how much the two files differ as a ratio. The y axis is the size of the delta produced by a given algorithm divided by the average file size for the pair. This expresses the size of the delta as a ratio to the file size. Here it becomes clear how badly *uuencode* disrupts the UNIX *diff* algorithm. Good correlation is obtained for *bdiff* and *vdelta*, whereas *diff* and *diff* with *gzip* appear to be independent of the **difference** ratio.

All these graphs show clear trends in the performance of *diff*, *diff* + *gzip*, *bdiff*, and *vdelta*.

5.2 Efficiency

Here the speed of both compression and decompression are given. Time is given as a sum of system and user time. This is plotted against the average file size. The first three plots in figures 10, 11, and 12 give encoding times in seconds and the remaining three plots in figures 13, 14, and 15 show decoding times in seconds. The scale is not the same for all plots, but the aspect ratio is held constant in each group. The reader should note the change in aspect ratio between the encode plots and the decode plots. Decoding is much faster for all algorithms. Though the relative performance for the others varies between encoding and decoding, *vdelta* is faster than all other algorithms for both.

6 Conclusion

Vdelta is the best algorithm overall. Its coding and decoding performance is high enough to be used for interactive applications. For example, it could be used to improve performance of raster display updates over a relatively slow networks links. Though *bdiff* generates output that is comparable in size to *vdelta*, *vdelta* is much faster. Both *vdelta* and *bdiff* result in delta sizes that correlate well with the **difference**. This is not true for *diff*. In the best case—text files—*diff* only reaches the effectiveness of *vdelta* and *bdiff* when it is combined with *gzip*. Using *uuencode* is not a good idea for binary files, since it breaks *diff*'s algorithm for

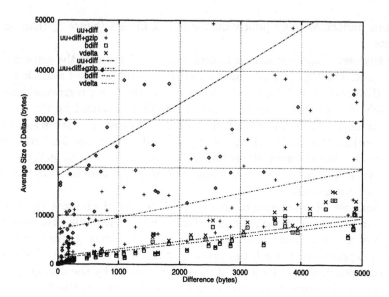

Correlations: uu+diff 0.847; uu+diff+gzip 0.857; bdiff 0.959; vdelta 0.937

Fig. 3. Plot of Delta Size for Object Files

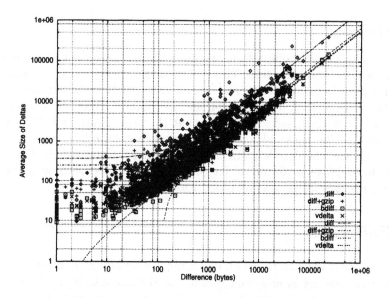

Correlations: diff 0.952; diff+gzip 0.976; bdiff 0.962; vdelta 0.976

Fig. 4. Log Plot of Delta Size for Text Files

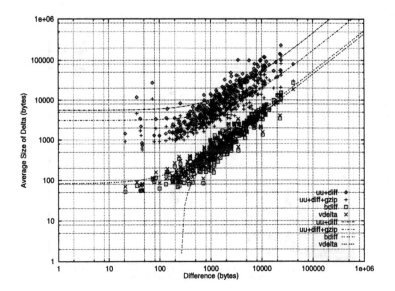

Correlations: uu+diff 0.805; uu+diff+gzip 0.804; bdiff 0.949; vdelta 0.959

Fig. 5. Log Plot of Delta Size for ELC Files

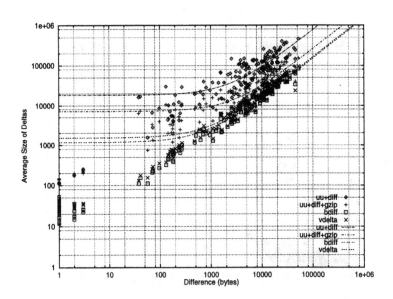

Correlations: uu+diff 0.847; uu+diff+gzip 0.857; bdiff 0.959; vdelta 0.937

Fig. 6. Log Plot of Delta Size for Object Files

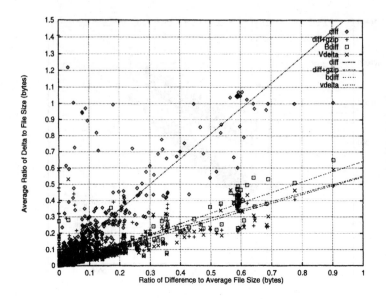

Correlations: diff 0.877; diff+gzip 0.545; bdiff 0.947; vdelta 0.870

Fig. 7. Plot of Compression Ratio for Text Files

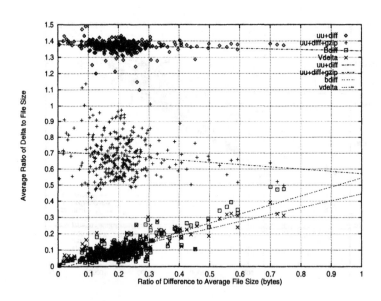

Correlations: uu+diff -0.111; uu+diff+gzip -0.118; bdiff 0.832; vdelta 0.778

Fig. 8. Plot of Compression Ratio for ELC Files

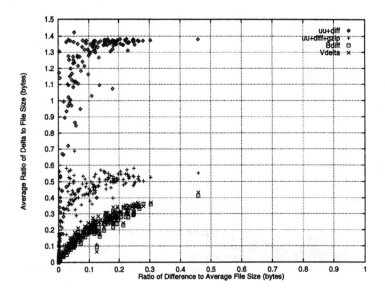

Correlations: uu+diff 0.742; uu+diff+gzip 0.736; bdiff 0.958; vdelta 0.945

Fig. 9. Plot of Compression Ratio for Object Files

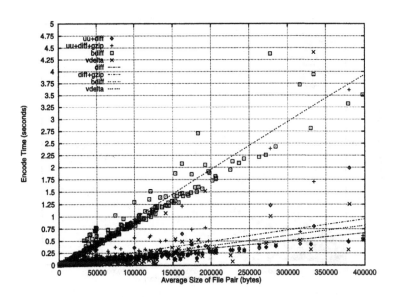

Correlations: diff 0.813; diff+gzip 0.672; bdiff 0.971; vdelta 0.599

Fig. 10. Plot of Encoding Time for Text Files

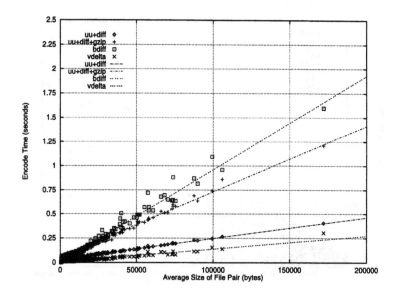

Correlations: uu+diff 0.993; uu+diff+gzip 0.996; bdiff 0.992; vdelta 0.965

Fig. 11. Plot of Encoding Time for ELC Files

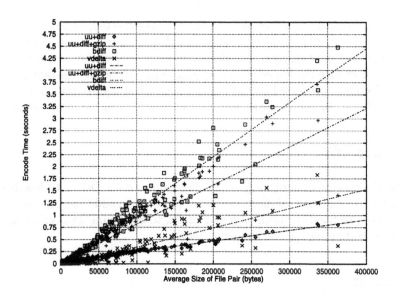

Correlations: uu+diff 0.994; uu+diff+gzip 0.875; bdiff 0.973; vdelta 0.855

Fig. 12. Plot of Encoding Time for Object Files

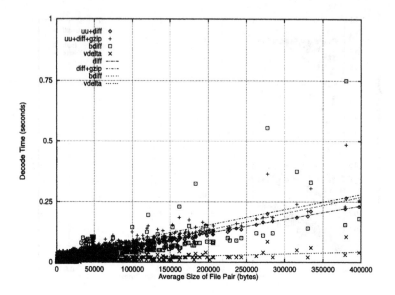

Correlations: diff 0.987; diff+gzip 0.927; bdiff 0.775; vdelta 0.612

Fig. 13. Plot of Decoding Time for Text Files

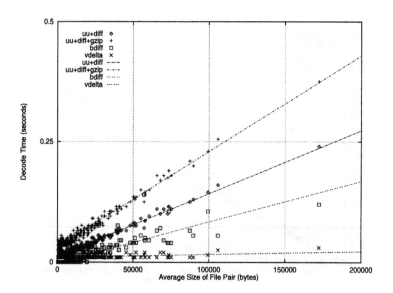

Correlations: uu+diff 0.985; uu+diff+gzip 0.987; bdiff 0.868; vdelta 0.395

Fig. 14. Plot of Decoding Time for ELC Files

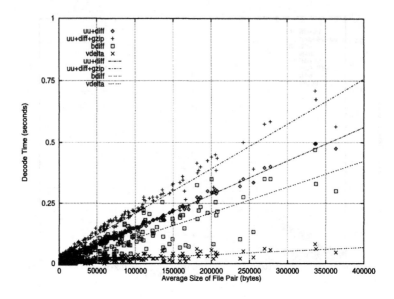

Correlations: uu+diff 0.997; uu+diff+gzip 0.976; bdiff 0.883; vdelta 0.787

Fig. 15. Plot of Decoding Time for Object Files

detecting unchanged sequences. This property was expected, because *uuencode* essentially removes all natural newlines and adds new ones at constant intervals. This means that only changes that do not modify the positions of unmodified characters or change the file length by an exact multiple of the constant interval can be effectively processed by *diff*. *Diff*'s only advantage is that it provides human readable differences; however, this can be added to the others as well.

7   Future Work

The result of this paper apply only to one dimensional data. Other studies should be done for two dimensional data such as for pictures. In addition, this test suite could be used to fine tune both *bdiff* and *vdelta*, to determine what effect block-move list encoding has on run time and delta size.

References

1. James A. Gosling. A redisplay algorithm. In *Proc. of the ACM SIGPLAN/SIGOA Symposium on Text Manipulation*, pages 123–129, 1981.
2. James W. Hunt and M.D. McIllroy. An algorithm for differential file comparison. Technical Report Computing Science Technical Report 41, Bell Laboratories, June 1976.

3. James W. Hunt and Thomas G. Szymanski. A fast algorithm for computing longest common subsequences. *Communications of the ACM*, 20(5):350–353, May 1977.

4. Douglas W. Jones. Application of splay trees to data compression. *Communications of the ACM*, 31(8):996–1007, August 1988.

5. David G. Korn and Kiem-Phong Vo. Vdelta: Efficient data differencing and compression. *In preparation*, 1995.

6. E. M. McCreight. A space economical suffix tree construction algorithm. *Journal of the ACM*, 32:262–272, 1976.

7. Webb Miller and Eugene W. Meyers. A file comparison program. *Software— Practice and Experience*, 15(11):1025–1039, November 1985.

8. Narao Nakatsu, Yahiko Kambayashi, and Shuzo Yajima. A longest common subsequence algorithm for similar text strings. *Acta Informatica*, 18:171–179, 1982.

9. Wolfgang Obst. Delta technique and string-to-string correction. In *Proc. of the First European Software Engineering Conference*, pages 69–73. AFCET, Springer Verlag, September 1987.

10. Marc J. Rochkind. The source code control system. *IEEE Transactions on Software Engineering*, SE-1(4):364–370, December 1975.

11. Walter F. Tichy. The string-to-string correction problem with block moves. *ACM Transactions on Computer Systems*, 2(4):309–321, November 1984.

12. Walter F. Tichy. RCS — a system for version control. *Software—Practice and Experience*, 15(7):637–654, July 1985.

13. Kiem-Phong Vo. A prefix matching algorithm suitable for data compression. *In preparation*, 1995.

14. J. Ziv and A. Lempel. Compression of individual sequences via variable-rate coding. *IEEE Trans. on Information Theory*, IT-24(5):5306, September 1978.

Inter-File Branching
A Practical Method for Representing Variants

Christopher Seiwald
P3 Software

Abstract Contemporary software configuration management (SCM) systems identify variants in the same namespace that identifies revisions. The variants -- the alternate implementations of a configuration item that must exist in parallel -- and revisions -- the iterative refinements that each variant takes on over time -- form a two dimensional version tree for a configuration item. So typically a configuration item will have two names: one that names the item and another that names the version.

This paper presents an alternate approach where the identification of a variant is moved into the name of the configuration item, leaving the version namespace only a linear set of revisions. Because this method has been realized in a working system where the configuration items are software source files, it is called *Inter-File Branching*. *Branching* is the act of creating variants, *files* are the configuration items, and *inter-file* reflects that fact that variants are separate files.

1 Introduction

This paper describes an new mechanism for handling file variants. First it describes the two major facets of the current method -- the way the variants are named and how they are created -- and cites their practical limitations. It then shows how a new approach called *Inter-File Branching* (IFB) does not suffer the same limitations, and describes the new mechanism in detail. It concludes with some empirical observations about using IFB.

2 Version-Tree Branching

2.1 The Version Names the Variant

A file is typically identified by two names: the name of the file itself and the name of the version of the file. The *version* itself decomposes into two pieces of information: the name of the variant and the name of the revision of the variant. The *variant* selects one of any alternate implementations that exist in parallel, while the *revision* selects one of the implementations of a variant that has evolved over time [4]. Usually, the first revision of a new variant is actually some revision of another variant; this is called the *branch point*. Joined at branch points, the variants and their revisions form a *version tree*, with each variant a branch in the tree and each revision a node on that branch.

In SCCS [5] and RCS [8] (and the many dozens of systems built upon these tools), the variants (in fact called "branches") are named with pairs of numbers and the revision is named by another pair of numbers. The "trunk branch" has an empty name. For example, 1.2.2.1.1.3 represents the 1.3 revision of variant 1.2.2.1, which itself is revision 2.1 of variant 1.2, which itself is revision 1.2 of the trunk. Obviously, remembering the significance of these numbers can become daunting for users, and so symbolic names are often applied to important versions.

Atria's ClearCase product [1] dispenses with revision numbers altogether and exposes a hierarchical version name to the user. For example, main/release2/bugfix/3 represents revision 3 of the bugfix branch, which is derived (at some point) from the release2 branch, which is derived from the main trunk. This naming is much more mnemonic than SCCS's numbering scheme, with the arguable liability that the branch point isn't explicitly named.

The approach of representing variants within the version namespace has several shortcomings:

Two Hierarchies. Each variant of a file is identified by the product of two hierarchical names -- the file's name and the variant name. While it is a subjective point, having files be identified by two hierarchies can leave users unable to visualize configurations. In theory, SCM systems are functional enough that users don't actually need such a convenience, but in practice engineers dealing with complex software products and their multiple releases often need to comprehend the "shape" of their product's file tree.

The picture can get especially murky if variants are created on-demand. Such a mechanism stores an update to a version not as a new revision of the same variant but as the first revision of a newly-created variant. The result of this is that, after some time, many files have many incidental variants, and important configurations may include differently named variants for different files.

Disparate semantics. Having one namespace for files and another for the variants of those files poses a dilemma for the user of existing SCM systems because those two namespaces are supported by different semantics. Specifically, the support for automated delta merging is normally tied into the version namespace: one can only merge deltas from one variant to another. (A delta is the change that leads from one revision to its successor.) On the other hand, only one variant of a file can be surfaced to the user at a time.

Thus if the user plans to merge deltas from one variant to another, they must be variants of a single file. On the other hand, if the user wants to access both variants at the same time then they must be different files. There are several real-world examples where this unsupported combination is desirable: in client/server systems, where client and server implementations of a protocol machine are similar but not identical; in multi-platform systems, where operating system specific files are similar but not identical; in systems migrating from one programming language to another, where perhaps C and C++ implementations must be kept in sync for the time being. In all these cases the files are variants of each other but by common practice they are in fact separate files.

Mainline-Centric. The representation of the version namespace assumes that one variant is the main branch from which all others descend. This mainline-centric view is often applicable to the early stages of a single software project, but rarely fits the structure of existing, mature products (especially those which began with poor SCM). These products are likely to have several "main lines" of the same source files, with active, disparate development on each.

The awkwardness of developing on multiple main variants can force users to set up separate repositories for files that would otherwise be variants of each other within the same repository. Doing so generally forgoes all the automated merging and tracking support afforded by the SCM system.

2.2. Creating Variants

Coupled with the common method for representing variants is the common method for creating them: for each file, the user selects an existing version and marks that as the starting point for a new variant. Typically, the existing version is marked with some sort of symbolic name, so that the user need not individually list each file's variant and revision. The new variant is similarly given a symbolic name, to make for easy future reference.

Users often talk about "a branch" to mean all files sharing a common variant name. But the variant creation does not support the semantics of a collective: it only creates variants of existing files, and not any files that may be created in the future. If the changes in one branch are to be merged into another, users then must take an extra step to create the new variants of any newly created files. More importantly, since the information used to create the variants was nothing more than a marked version for each file, there is no external means of telling if a new file *should* have a corresponding variant made as well.

To address this problem some SCM systems treat containers as configuration items and create variants of them as well. But this scheme can add considerable complexity and confusion: in addition to creating more namespaces that play into the identification of individual versions, it still fails to automate the creation of a variant when a new file is created.

3 Inter-File Branching (IFB)

IFB is an alternate approach that offers potential advantages over version-tree branching. The kernel concept is that creating a variant should be akin to the process fork in UNIX: a new file is created, related to the original in initial content and past history but with an unencumbered future.

This model is similar to what users without any SCM support typically must do when faced with the need to branch their software: they copy the files off and worry about any merging later. The difference between this primitive method and IFB is that the latter automates both the initial copying and the subsequent merging. In essence IFB is mostly a matter of extending the practical support for variants -- merging deltas and tracking merging history -- to span separate files.

With IFB different variants are differently named files. The file's name incorporates both what is normally considered the file name as well as the variant name, although the exact naming is left to the user. For example it is possible to have a file /release2.1/database/src/btree.c be a variant of /patch2.1.5/database/src/btree.c or /x/y/z be a variant of /a/b/c/d.

IFB builds upon a familiar practice: copying things to make variants of them. In doing so it gives users a natural way to express the relationship of a new variant to the old: by giving it a similar name. For example, sometimes a user will simply copy a file foo.c into foo.c.bak. A perhaps better example is when the user copies mainline/src/* into bob/src/*. Bob's files are variants of the mainline, and their names imply their relationship.

If this copying happens within the SCM repository rather than in a user's private workspace, the result is a repository namespace that is natural for the user to visualize. IFB gives users a single handle to identify the variant of a file, which makes the "shape" of configurations plain for the users to see. As in the example above, Bob knows that the configuration that describes his work is simply "what's in src/bob/* in the repository."

By treating variants as separate files, an SCM system supporting IFB can provide automated merging and tracking between any pair of files. The semantics for variants can even be applied *post hoc* to files that weren't originally related to each other. Thus it is possible to take two files (perhaps from before they were under SCM control) and begin treating them as variants of each other.

With IFB, variants have different names. In fact, the names don't even need to be similar. This makes it possible to create a variant of a whole configuration (i.e. variants of all of the files in a configuration), completely reorganizing the namespace in the process by naming the newly created variants in the desiring naming scheme. This can be useful in a variety of situations, most notably when software is branched into another project as a form of code sharing: the new project may very well need its copy of the software "reshaped" to fit its needs.

IFB relates variants through the namespace of the files. This makes it possible to relate whole configurations by expressing the relationship of the names of their component files. If this relationship expression leverages a natural organization of software, it can be quite compact. For example, to say that Bob's code is a variant of the mainline code is "bob/src/* is a variant of mainline/src/*". This expression relates not only the existing files but also any future files that may be created within the namespace.

Because the version namespace no longer holds the name of the variant, it can be reduced to a linear set of revision numbers (beginning at 1) for each file. This means that important configurations are often the tip (highest numbered, most recent) revisions of files within a certain part of the namespace. For example, Bob's latest work is the tip revisions of the files named bob/src/*.

3.1. Inter-File Branching Algorithm

The semantics which support this automation of merging stem from the following premise: that given a *source file* ("source"), any or all of its individual deltas can be meaningfully merged into the contents of a *target file* ("target"). This includes the initial delta that brings a file from empty content to its first revision. The distinguishing feature between the source and target files is their names. The user selects a source, some subset of its deltas, and the target. The following logic is then applied:

- If the deltas are not contiguous, they are broken into separate contiguous chunks and the remaining logic is applied individually to each chunk.

- If the target does not exist, it is created using the contents of the source at its highest selected revision. This is commonly referred to as "branching" -- starting a new variant with identical contents.

- If the target exists, the user must merge the current contents of the target with the contents of the source at its highest selected revision. The result of this merge will be the next sequential revision of the target. If a suitable base revision can be found then the merge might be automated with a common diff/merge algorithm. The basis for automated merges is the revision of the source one below the lowest selected revision. If the lowest selected revision is first revision of the source, then there is no basis, and the user will have to choose to replace the target's contents with that of the source, leave the target as-is, or manually produce a hybrid of the two.

- In any case, it is permanently recorded that the target now incorporates (at its new revision) the selected deltas of the source. At this point the source and target files can in fact be considered variants of each other.

3.2. Integration History

The record of deltas that have been merged from one file into another forms the integration history for that ordered pair of files. It serves two very important functions. First, if the integration history shows that any deltas have been merged from one file into another, it indicates that the target is a variant of the source. Second, the integration history can be used to compute what deltas have yet to be merged. Having this information relieves the user of having to select the source deltas for every merging.

Integration history can also be used as an audit trail and can make for comprehensive reporting. Through transitive closure, it is possible to compute for any revision of any file whatever deltas it incorporates from other files through first, second, third, etc. generation merges.

3.3. Branch Views.

If variant files are to be related by their names, something must express that relationship. This is the job of *branch views*. A branch view is a named, one-to-one mapping between the names of two sets of files: the source and the target of the intended branch. To apply the branch view, the name of every known file is mapped as a candidate source through the view. The resulting source/target pairs define the files to be branched or merged.

There are two important facets of this mechanism: first, even though each branch view allows only one-to-one mappings between sources and targets in the view, there can be multiple branch views with the same sources and/or targets. Thus the same source can be branched into many different targets or, perhaps less intuitively, the same target can be the variant of more than one source. Second, the mapping is applied only at the user's request, rather than as potential sources are created or updated. That is, only when the user requests to create or merge target files is the branch view applied.

Branch views merely document that a user had intended for a set of targets to reflect a set of sources. Actual merging is through the application of the branch view. On the user's request, the names of all existing files are projected through the view to produce a list of source/target pairs. For each pair the integration history is considered and the complementary integrations are proposed to the user. These proposed changes -- creating the first revision of new variants, creating new revisions of existing variants, or deleting variants whose sources had been deleted -- attempt to make the target set reflect the deltas in the source set. It is of course the user's choice as to whether these changes are to be incorporated wholesale, modified somewhat, or ignored altogether. It is rare that the user wishes to keep two configurations exactly identical.

3.4. Computing the Merge Basis

Previously we mentioned that integration history, which records individually what deltas of a source file have been merged to a target file, can be used to compute exactly what deltas have yet to be merged. A product of this computation is useful as the version to form the basis of a three-way file diff/merge. It is the revision of the source prior to the first to be merged.

The usual method for reconciling changes made to a file is to find a common ancestor and use that as a basis for the diff/merge process. This process involves computing the textual difference between the basis and each of the variant's revisions, and then merging those differences. This has been implemented in a wide variety of tools, from RCS's simple *rcsmerge* program to elaborate GUIs that colorfully illustrate the lines of text that have changed in each version.

Most systems use the original branch point as the common ancestor. Unfortunately, as the text of the two variants evolves further away from the ancestor, more and more of the changes in the variants appear to be in conflict or overlapping with each other. Thus each time the user merges the variants he must revisit any textual conflicts that had been resolved in previous merges. Another approach is to record the highest delta of the source that has been merged, as ClearCase does using *hyperlinks*. But this assumes that deltas will always be merged in order. Sometimes, for example, it is desirable to merge a single delta containing a bug fix immediately, while leaving the previous and subsequent deltas for later.

Tracking individual deltas merged makes it possible always to produce the optimum basis for merging, namely the revision of the source prior to the first to be merged. This minimizes the difference between the basis and the source head, and consequently minimizes the complexity of the merge.

3.5. "Pure" Integrations.

Because the integration history tracks individually deltas that are merged from one variant to another, a special advantage can be gained by recognizing *pure* integrations. A pure integration is one in which the new revision of the target incorporates *only* deltas from a single source. This is important in that a delta which is the result of a pure integration does not need to be merged back into the source.

Without integration history, the fact is lost that a target variant's new delta is only the merging of deltas from another variant. Any subsequent automated merge would find the new delta and attempt to merge it back into the source. If the delta was originally merged literally, the actual merge process should be a no-op and of little consequence to the user. But if the delta required conflict resolution or other editing when it was originally merged into the target, the user will have to revisit that resolution when merging the delta back.

With an integration history that records pure integrations, automated merges can avoid ever merging a delta back into its source. In practice, the user must provide some hint that the integration was kept pure: during conflict resolution the user has the opportunity to make other changes which may, in fact, need to be merged back. In the end, the user must actually confirm that the integration was kept pure, and the integration history can then record the fact. This record can then be used to suppress an automated attempt to merge the delta back into the source.

3.6. Namespace management.

If the hierarchical namespace of files is to serve double-duty as the name of variants, then room should be left in the file name for the name of the variant. This is largely a matter of individual use, but we find for simple cases that putting the variant name at the beginning of the file name renders the full file tree easy to grasp. For example, it is fairly easy for users to understand that the main line of development is under /main/src/... while the latest release has been branched into /release2.1/src/..., etc.

3.7. Client Views.

It is important that the name of the files in the SCM repository need not match the name of the file when in the hands (or filesystem) of the user. If the name must encode the variant, then it is desirable to be able to strip that information from the file name when file is delivered to the users. For this a *client view* can be used: each client workspace has a view (much like a branch view) that projects the names of the files in the repository onto the user's local filesystem. In this way, a single entity (the client view) specifies not only the files but also the variants that a user wishes to see. Such a view can bring two different variants onto the client merely by giving them distinct names on the client.

3.8. Variants as Virtual Copies

In practice, if branching a file means copying it in the repository then storage space can be a concern. A simple antidote is to perform a virtual copy, where the newly branched file makes use of the contents of the original file. This requires a level of indirection between the repository namespace and the actual underlying object store. When the branch is extended by adding a new revision, the branched file can acquire its own separate entity in the object store.

Supporting variants with virtual copies reduces the space requirement of a variant to be merely a record for the newly created variant that points to the original file. This is, more or less, no greater than the cost of a traditional variant.

This virtual copy can also be used when one variant is explicitly synchronized with another. If the user wishes to fold a branch back into a trunk and make the two identical, both can reference the same content at that point.

4. Discussion

4.1. Comparison with Existing Technology

IFB has been directly contrasted in this paper with the version tree model found in popular systems such as RCS and ClearCase. There are two other approaches to variant support that deserve mention.

4.1.1. Baseline Model

The baseline model [2] can be viewed as a much simplified attempt at IFB. Strictly speaking, a baseline is just a configuration that serves as the basis for future changes, but in common practice the configuration's contents is copied and the newly copied files become the actual baseline. In this respect, it resembles IFB's copying, because the new baseline itself has a name that distinguishes it from the original configuration.

Compared to IFB, the baseline model is limited in three ways: first, the relationship of the names is fixed -- usually the baselines are named, while the files within the baselines have names that are fixed across baselines. Second, a baseline is some predetermined set of files, usually a "project" or "product". It is not possible to create variants of just one or two files. Third, integration history, if present at all, is fairly limited with baselines. It doesn't, for example, track individual deltas merged from one variant to another.

4.1.2. Change Set Model/ICE Version Set Model

The change set model [7] and the version set model in ICE [10] are practically the antithesis of IFB. In both of these models, variants and revisions do not form a tree of named versions for each file. Instead, each file has a pool of deltas that can aritrarily be applied to produce a (possibly senseless) version. With the change set model, the combination of deltas to be applied is called a "change set", and a change set itself can be recorded as part of a named configuration. With ICE's version set model, the deltas have attributes (called "features") and are selected by finding those deltas with the right combination of attributes.

While both the change set model and ICE's version set model probably compare well with the version tree model, they are markedly different from IFB. IFB seeks to keep variants distinct in the repository namespace, so that user can view and handle them as independent files. Change sets and version sets, on the other hand, pile all variants of a file into a single entity and require users to select (or create) the desired version with every interaction. To put it on a continuum: with IFB important configurations can be identified with merely the names of the component files; with version tre there is a fair chance that important configurations are not on the trunk, and so the variants must be explicitly named; with changes sets and version sets, important configurations surely require explicit specification of the change set or feature list.

4.2. Empirical Evaluation

An earlier version of the IFB model was implemented at Ingres Corporation as part of an in-house SCM system called *Piccolo* [6]. It lacked the branch views and the detail in the integration history of the current model. Thus creating variants in the first place was cumbersome as the user had to enumerate specific files to be branched, and sometimes the system would (iteratively) insist that a delta be merged back after being merged into another file.

Nonetheless, IFB proved to be a solid foundation for carrying out parallel development and releases. Several hundred developers and other engineers spread across three continents used Piccolo's branching to support perhaps a dozen products totalling 12,000 files. At any one time, a dozen simultaneous releases were in progress.

For the most part, branches were made by perturbing the first component of the name of each file stored in the repository. The main line of descent was the development line and was called "main". From this were dozens of branches for individual developers or groups, each named after the developer or project. Also from the main line were branches at every major release, named after the release. These major releases became sub-main lines themselves, and from them patch branches were sprouted.

One of the unexpected benefits of IFB was that because branches were expressed as a relationship between the names of two arbitrary files, developers were free to create branches which had a different tree structure than the main line of code. This allowed them to build and maintain their product in an environment customized to their needs. For example, one group might be responsible for directories that were "far apart" in the name space of the main line. As a convenience, they could bring these directories together in their group's branch.

The current model for IFB, as described here, is implemented in a commercially available system called *P3*. P3 is a deliberate attempt to build upon the semantics of IFB while remedying the deficiencies found in the Piccolo implementation. P3 is new, but early experience shows the model to flexible, usable, and fairly complete. We expect that the record of integration history could prove to be a bounty of useful information in a large, mature software product, but we have no history for such a product yet.

5. Conclusion

The popularity of traditional variant handling belies a fundamentally unnatural model. Even though experienced users of current SCM systems understand the uses of a combined variant and revision namespace, the weakness in the foundations of this approach eventually lead to a collection of gaps in its total capability. IFB, on the other hand, begins with a natural model -- copying software files and renaming them -- and finishes it with a collection of techniques that make its model usable. Given the opportunity, IFB could rival the functionality of the traditional variant handling.

6. Bibliography

[1] Atria Corporation, *ClearCase Concepts Manual.* Natick Massachusetts, 1994

[2] Bersoff, Henderson, Siegel, *Software Configuration Management*. Prentice-Hall, 1980.

[3] Susan Dart, *The Past, Present, and Future of Configuration Management*. Technical Report CMU/SEI-92-TR-8, Software Engineering Institute, Carnegie Mellon University, 1992.

[4] Stephen MacKay, The State of the Art in Concurrent, Distributed Configuration Management. *Proceedings of the 5th International Workshop on Software Configuration Management*, Seattle, WA, 1995.

[5] Rochkind, The Source Code Control System. *IEEE Transactions on Software Engineering*, Volume SE-1, December 1975.

[6] Roger Rohrbach and Christopher Seiwald, Galileo: A Software Maintenance Environment. *Proceedings of the International Workshop on Software Version and Configuration Control*, Grassau, 1988.

[7] Software Maintenance and Development Systems (SMDS). *Aide-de-Camp Users Manual*, Concord Mass, 1993.

[8] Walter Tichy, RCS -- a system for version control. *Software -- Practice and Experience*, July 1985.

[9] Walter Tichy, Tools for Software Configuration Management. *Proceedings of the International Workshop on Software Version and Configuration Control*, Grassau, 1988.

[10] Andreas Zeller, *Smooth Operations with Square Operators -- The Version Set Model in ICE*. Informatik-Bericht No. 95-08, Technical University of Braunschweig, Germany, 1995.

An Architecture for a Construction System

David Tibrook

qef Advance Software Inc.
dt@qef.com

Abstract. Most organizations do not have a comprehensive or effective approach to the management of the software construction process. This paper describes **QEF** (Quod Erat Faciendum, that which was to be made), a system for large scale software construction developed by the author over the last twelve years and in use at a number of major organizations. The rationale, strengths and weaknesses of the architecture are discussed.

1   Introduction

Many organizations have a great deal of difficulty actually producing their software products from source. Furthermore, most organizations do not have a comprehensive approach for the porting of their product to new platforms, the safe development of their product without interfering with production or other developers, the management and fixing of old releases, or the simultaneous use of multiple releases on the same platform.

Measuring the cost of the lack of these capabilities is virtually impossible. But it is the author's belief and experience that the reliable, timely and efficient approach to the management of the software construction process in a way that promotes an effective development process can yield substantial benefits both in terms of decreased costs and increased quality.

This paper describes the architecture of the **qef** system. **qef** is a family of tools used to manage processes typically used to do software construction. In the beginning, circa 1983, **qef** was developed to provide a mechanism whereby the construction of software products could be described in a host-independent way. Over the years it has been enhanced to encourage and support a better software process and a comprehensive approach to software development and maintenance and release engineering.

In hindsight, the major objectives of the **qef** implementation were to achieve the following:

Simplified Expression of the Construction — the expression of the construction process as provided by the user should be as simple as possible. Simple statements of what is to be done should be all that is required.

Effective Full and Incremental Constructions — the system must ensure correct, accurate and efficient construction of the products. Furthermore, the system must ensure that an incremental build (i.e., using previously built temporary files) ensures consistency between the resulting product and which that would be built by a full construction.

Effective Parameterization/Configuration Mechanism — comprehensive mechanisms must be provided to specify, test and use parameters and configuration controls throughout the construction and software process.

Effective Process Control and Monitoring — mechanisms to launch and monitor the construction process must be provided.

Promote an Effective Software Process — the system must support and encourage the use of better software development strategies throughout the software life cycle.

Whereas the objectives of the **qef** implementation and research were to achieve the above, one must examine at length the major objective or purpose of a construction system. A construction system manages the processes that transform source into a product. The organizations that can produce their products from source, and only source, reliably, efficiently and on demand are in a very small minority. The construction system must provide the mechanisms whereby the ability to produce the product from the source is almost taken for granted but can be tested easily, cheaply and frequently.

An important implicit assumption of this objective is that if the construction system is applied a second time to the same sources, it will produce the same product. Unfortunately even fewer organizations can reproduce the identical product if the source is relocated or some other aspect of the run-time environment has changed (e.g., a different user with a different environment). The construction system should help ensure that the ability to reproduce the product depends as little as possible on things that are not administered source. Furthermore, the construction system must provide an incremental build facility, that is given that some or all of the product and its intermediate build-files exist, the system skips processes that are not required to make the product identical to the version of the product that would be produced by rerunning the entire production from source alone. In other words, if a target exists and the process that produces it and its inputs have not changed, then the target does not need to be recreated — the target is assumed to be already "up-to-date".

In meeting these stated objectives a number of characteristics and features have evolved as being of paramount importance.

Portable — The user provided construction system input must be the same for all systems.

Flexible — The construction system must support the use of the most appropriate tool. The system should have a simple and consistent way to specify the tool to be run and its input.

Complete and Comprehensive — The construction system must facilitate and encourage the provision of the complete set of construction options. The construction system must also provide mechanisms whereby all aspects of the system are managed using the same mechanism in a consistent manner.

Dynamic and Responsive — Managing software construction is about responding to change. A construction system must respond appropriately to changes in the file system, the files themselves and the build parameters.

The appearance or disappearance of a file should be appropriately reflected in the construction commands. Changes in the files that would be found by various search paths (e.g., the cc -I flag) should result in the appropriate recalibration of the dependencies.

Consistent — The construction system should present a consistent and simple interface across all platforms, projects, and users. Constructing a software product should not require any special knowledge.

Clear and Concise — The actual processing involved in a construction can be described very simply, but comprehensive and complete **make** files can run to hundreds of lines. The system should derive everything else required automatically, while still providing simple mechanisms to override defaults in the general and specific cases.

Simple — This is indeed one of the most difficult characteristics to achieve — software construction is exceedingly complex — but must be if the system is to be accepted and used successfully.

Highly and easily configurable — When dealing with software that is to be built on many different platforms by many different users, the number of configuration parameters that can be required is staggering. Most projects will require scores of parameters to specify construction controls, names of tools, tool flags, search paths, special directories and files, and other build and semantic options and controls. The construction system must provide a comprehensive, universal, debuggable, and extendible mechanisms to specify, test, manipulate, and use parameters. Furthermore, it is imperative that these parameters be available to any tool — not just the construction system. Note: the C preprocessor is not such a mechanism!

Facilitates and encourages complete source and object separation — It is absolutely essential that a construction system support and encourage the total separation of the master source, source under development, and object files. There should be one and only one true read-only source file system which is shared by all users. Files to be modified should be copied to and changed in a user's own work space, thereby ensuring that their changes are not visible to others until ready and authorized. It should be trivial to create and link the separate directories. Furthermore, it is essential that the source path mechanism be usable by any application (e.g., the version system).

Provides suitable controls — A construction system must provide a simple consistent mechanism to manage large trees of directories and to support the constructions of part or all of those trees. Furthermore, it the construction system should provide mechanisms to monitor its progress and to halt it.

2 QEF's Architecture

As a construction system must be oriented towards the management of the construction of large complex systems on multiple platforms simultaneously, a major feature of the system is dealing with the complexity of the construction process. **qef** uses a structured, layered approach to deal with this complexity.

In many ways, this architecture parallels the use of structured programming and high-level programming languages to deal with and create large programs. Abstraction and information-hiding is used to control the amount of information that one must deal with at any level.

In some ways, **qef** is similar to **make**[Feldman 78]. There is an text-file that contains the construction control script; the user invokes **qef** with arguments specifying files or constructs to be created; ultimately, commands are invoked, often by a **make**-like process, to create the required objects or perform the required tasks. As such, **qef** can be viewed as a **make** replacement. However, the most important features of **qef** are for configuring and controlling processes and preparing the input for the back-end.

Thus **qef** is primarily a driver of other processes. Rather than attempting to solve all the problems using a monolithic program, **qef** provides facilities and structures to select, configure and control other processes. As will be seen, this approach provides great flexibility in configuring the construction process, while ensuring that there is a single universal interface.

qef's processing is roughly divided into three stages: construction of the build parameters/configuration database, script preparation, and back-end processing.

2.1   The Parameter/Configuration Database Construction

The first stage invokes a program called **lclvrs** which prepares a database of the build parameters and configuration information for use by other programs. The information is represented in a heirarchical database at the top of the current tree and distributed through the source tree. Configuration files at a particular level of the tree apply to all sublevels of the tree. This parallels the lexical scoping used in programming languages — configuration information is only visible where it is required.

lclvrs finds and processes the relevant files for the current directory and outputs a binary file that can be directly loaded by other programs to retrieve the various parameters, options and controls provided via the **lclvrs** files. Parameters are used to specify search paths, process controls, build options, the names of special files and directories, tool names and flags, and so on. In this and other documents the convention used to specify the use of a **lclvrs** variable's value is either **@Variable** or **@Array**[*value*], '@' being the **lclvrs** precursor variable escape.

2.2   Script Preparation

The major purpose of the script preparation stage is to transform an as simple as possible specification of the processing to be done, into the back-end command to be run and the input to that command. This transformation can range from the naming of a back-end process and its input file via **lclvrs** parameters, to the more common three stage process of the creation of a list of source files, script generation using the source list as arguments or input, and the macro processing of the generated script. Practically any command may serve as a script generator, but two programs, **qsg** and **qefdirs**, are used most of the time. **qsg, qefdirs** and the macro processor are described briefly later.

2.3 Back End Interpretation

The third stage is the back-end which usually does the real work. In most instances this will be a shell or **make**-like program. Some back-ends that are specifically designed for **qef** use are discussed in later sections. The actual back-end to be run is specified by **lclvrs** variable or a preprocessor symbol.

2.4 The Commonest Implementations

While this architecture allows a wide range of processing models, in practice, two models are used in the majority of directories that contain conventional processing.

In directories of directories the user provides a list of the directories that contain constructions, the type of processing the directories support, and their dependencies on other directories. The list may also partition sets of directories into individually selectable sets. The script preparation stage invokes the program **qefdirs** which transforms this information into a **make**-like script which provides labels (i.e., targets) to perform aggregate operations (e.g., All, Install, Post, Test), or processing for named directories or sets of directories. The recipes for an operation are usually just to invoke **qef** in the named directory with the appropriate argument.

The commonest model (used in approximately 75% of 1200 directories examined in various Toronto sites) is used for directories that contain source files to be processed. Once the configuration database has been assembled, a snapshot of the file system is generated. This generation uses configuration information to determine the search paths to be used and the suffixes of relevant files. The source database is typically input to the script generation stage.

That this database is created at the beginning of processing is significant. It has benefits both in terms of debugging the construction as the initial conditions are preserved and it is also efficient. Tools that combine view-pathing and rule-inference result in many unnecessary accesses to the file-system meta-data.

The script preparation is done using **qsg**, an algorithmic programming language. The configuration and source databases and a **qsg** script is processed to generate the necessary recipes to do the construction. **qsg**'s output is processed then by the macro processor the output of which is input to the back-end **qmk**, a **make**-like program described later.

Although the above may appear complicated, most users are unaware of the actual processing. A **qeffile** that invokes the above is often as simple as:

```
Begin qsg -M

commands @argv
```

This example is not that far-fetched. — the average size of the 1,200 sample **qeffiles** was seven lines.

3 qef, et al.

This section describes some of the more important features of the major **qef** tools.

3.1 lclvrs

lclvrs is run as part of **qef**'s initialization to find and interpret the **lclvrs** files for the current directory, and build a temporary database of variable/value pairs that other tools will access directly. **lclvrs** files are used to specify process controls, build options, the names of special files and directories, search paths, tool names and flags, special library mappings and search mechanisms, and other such values. **lclvrs** provides a variety of options to select the form of the output, list the selected files, report where specified variables are set, or to output special values.

In most situations, **lclvrs** will find and interpret:

root.vrs at the top of the current tree — provided by developer (using the program **rootvrs**) to indicate the root of a tree and specify links to other trees;

config.vrs at the top of the current tree — copied from annotated prototype and modified by developer as required — used to contain all configuration settings and user options;

tree.vrs at the top of the master tree — used to specify project parameters and controls;

hostsys.vrs a host provided file containing host specific controls such as library mappings and search paths; and

qeffile in the corresponding source directory — the directory specific settings and local construction controls. The **qeffile** also usually contains the input to the script generator or the back-end.

In addition to the above, a user can create files called **leaf.vrs** and **branch.vrs** in the current tree to specify temporary **lclvrs** settings without changing source files. **lclvrs** settings can also be specified via the **qef -L** flag. This feature is often used to specify the type of binaries to be produced as in:

```
qef -LDEBUGGING echo # {\rm produce debuggable echo program}
qef -LPROFILING echo # {\rm produce profiling echo program}
```

The **hostsys.vrs** file will set the C flags and library search mechanisms as required to create the requested type of binary.

The **lclvrs** language provides simple keywords to set, manipulate and test variables, paths and associative array elements, to do flow control ("**if**" and "**switch**" — no loops), and output fatal or non-fatal diagnostics. **lclvrs** also offers a set of functions that can be used in keyword argument lists to test and manipulate strings and/or variables, search or test for files, and to retrieve user or environment information.

One of the most important **lclvrs** features is that it is a separate program whose sole purpose is to process the configuration files and prepare data for other processes use. Any tool that requires **lclvrs** settings either executes **lclvrs** or reads a previously prepared **lclvrs** output. Configuration information need not be passed via command line arguments or environment variables thereby ensuring consistent application of the tool no matter through whatever invocation mechanism was used.

3.2   Script Generation

qef's ability to invoke an arbitrary shell command coupled with the preprocessor to prepare the input to an arbitrary back-end is an extremely powerful and important feature that has been a crucial component of the **qef** system since its birth[Tilbrook 86]. In **qef**'s early years there were a large number of special purpose script generators but all but one (**qefdirs**) have been replaced or superceded by **qsg** which is used about 80% of the time.

qsg is a fairly simple programming language, specifically designed to create input for other processors from simple shell-like commands. Because **qsg** is used to generate data to be read by arbitrary languages it has a number of lexical characteristics such as minimal quoting — consider as a contrary example the difficulty of running **awk** from **tcl**. For performance reasons it is compiled to a very efficient intermediate representation either at run-time or to prepare object files for possible inclusion in a library of **qsg** scripts. The library mechanism facilitates provision of a rich set of standard procedures. These standard library functions can, for most constructions, reduce the entire build specifications as provided by the user to single simple host independent one line commands.

The set of **qsg** library scripts deliver the type of functionality that **make** inference rules are intended to supply. The actual construction details are hidden in the library allowing the end-user to trivially create portable construction specifications.

qsg commands consist of a keyword or the name of a procedure, file or **qsg** library member, and an argument list. The keywords provide flow and I/O control, variable manipulation, procedure and flag definition, and debugging controls. Argument lists are simply strings that may incorporate the values of variables and/or functions. The value of a variable is used by '@' followed by the variable's name as in:

```
# {\rm invoke commands script for the arguments (i.e., variable argv)}
commands @argv
```

Functions are provided to read files or pipes, evaluate **lclvrs** expressions, find or check files, etc. Function calls look like "@(*function flags args ...*)" as in:

```
# {\rm read line from previously opened file or pipeline}
set var @(readline fid)
```

Various manipulations of a variable or function value can be performed using tilde postfix operators. For example, "@argv 1" is replaced by the number of elements in the variable **argv**. Tilde operators are provided to select matched elements, selected parts of individual elements (e.g., the directory name, tail, suffix), or to perform substring replacements. However, the normal user uses a very small subset of **qsg**'s facilities when creating a **qeffile**. Most **qeffiles** will consist of a few invocations of the **qsg** library members as in:

```
# {\rm install *.dat source files in directory _DestDir_/lib}
install -d _DestDir_/lib @argv~x/dat/

# {\rm compile and link example.c and parser.y}
program example.c parser.y

# {\rm create and install dtree library with a version module}
library -v -n dtree @argv~x/c.y.l/
```

In the above "install", "program", and "library" are **qsg** scripts that have been compiled into the **qsg** pseudo-code and installed in an archive. A typical **qsg** library script will produce output in a form suitable for the chosen back-end. The **qsg** scripts are built to deal with host-dependent conventions, although in many cases they output **qefpp** macros to deal with host dependent names and mappings.

An example of **qsg** output would be of limited value. "**program file.c**" will generate 30 to 60 lines, depending on the host. The output would contain recipes and dependencies to produce the program, the installed program, the object modules, the assembler versions, the **purify**, **quantify**, and **pixie** versions (if supported), to **lint file.c**, and to remove any intermediate and/or installed files.

One of the significant advantages of this approach, when compared with **make**'s inference/suffix rules or **imake**'s macros, is that **qsg** creates scripts that provide complete and comprehensive facilities from succinct portable specifications. Many **qeffiles** consist of one or two **qsg** commands, yet the equivalent **make** scripts are huge. In one of the author's source directories (containing 70 c, lex, yacc, and shell programs) a three line **qsg** script produces the equivalent of a 3,500 line **make** script.

3.3   The Preprocessor — qefpp()

qefpp()'s primary role is much the same as the C preprocessor — to define macros and replace embedded instances of those macros by their values and to provide primitive flow control. However, **qefpp()** offers a number of important features far beyond cpp's capabilities as illustrated by part of **qsg**'s output for "**program eg.c**":

```
eg: _Touch_(cc) _Libs_(_FndSrc_(eg.c)) eg.o
_T_cc _F_cc _F_cc_o _F_cc_o[eg] eg.o _CcLibs_() -o eg
```

The above uses the following **qefpp** built-in macros:

Touch(cc) replaced by list of files called **cc** in the **@TouchPath** directories. Thus the target file "eg" is dependent on any existing "Touch cc" file. To force the recompilation of all C sources, one touches a file called "cc" in a **@TouchPath** directories. The script generators output these Touch dependencies for every significant tool thereby providing a simple and consistent way to force the reexecution of processes.

FndSrc(eg.c) **qefpp** searches the **@SrcPath** directories for the first instance of a file called "eg.c" and replaces the macro by its path.

Libs(eg.c) Replaced by the libraries for file **eg.c** A variety of configuration parameters are used to create this list. The "_CcLibs_()" is almost the same except that the list of libraries might be modified to be suitable for a **cc** command.

_T_cc, _F_cc, _F_cc_o[eg] Symbols beginning with "_T_" and "_F_" are for tool names and flags respectively. Such symbols are treated specially in that they are automatically imported from the **lclvrs** database as predefined symbols and also have special default values (the symbol name minus the "_T_" prefix for _T_ symbols, the empty string for _F_). Also note that associated array elements are support to allow the specification of tool flags for specific files.

In the initial implementation of **qef** (circa 1983) the preprocessor played a much more important role. Its importance has been greatly reduced as the script generators and **lclvrs** now provide better mechanisms for managing variables and special constructions. However, it still serves to perform simple macro processing and variable substitution which greatly reduces the complexity of the script generation process.

4 The Back-Ends

Almost any non-interactive program may be used as a **qef** back-end. As such **qef** has been used for a wide range of applications, not just software construction (e.g., driving **empire**). Using standard tools (e.g., **make**, **sh**, **tar**, **rdist**) is not uncommon. In some instances programs have been created to be used as **qef** back-end for a single application. However, three programs (**qsh**, **mimk**, and **qmk**), were created to be general purpose **qef** back-ends and one of them is used in most directories.

4.1 QSH

qsh is just a much reduced shell command interpreter, with features to control command echo and exit on failure. It also monitors the **qef** halt file so as to stop processing when required. **qsh** is used when the required constructions are unconditional or can be selected by the script generator (i.e., **make** would just get in the way).

4.2 MIMK and QMK

For the first 4 years, **qef** used **make** as its primary back-end, but that caused a number of problems. **make** is not standard (implementations vary greatly); does not provide the required consistency mechanisms; does not provide some of the required semantics such as monitoring the **qef** halt file; and cannot run recipes in parallel.

mimk was developed in the mid-80s to be the **qef**'s engine of consistency. **mimk** is based on **make** with extensions to provide recipe and dependency attributes, improved consistency checking and parallel recipe executions. **mimk** was designed to be a back-end for **qef**. As such it does not need some of **make**'s facilities. It does not have suffix rules — the script generators provide complete recipes. It does not have variables — **qefpp** does it all.

However, **mimk** has its own limitations and is being replaced by **qmk**. **qmk** is **make/mimk**-like in purpose. However, its syntax has been extended to provide for extended control and attribute semantics and easier generation by **qsg**. The major reason for its creation is to provide an improved consistency checker and lazy dynamic dependency list generation.

5   The QEF Software Process

One of the major objectives listed in the first section was the promotion of an effective software process. **qef** does not require any particular process methodology — users may use **qef** in much the same way they would use **make**. However, a number of tools and features have been implemented to support the total separation of the source and object trees and source view pathing. These mechanisms allow multiple independ constructions to share a common source tree. Furthermore each build can specify the optional insertion of a user's own source override tree to contain those files modified by the user.

A typical **qef** using site will set into place procedures whereby someone (e.g., a librarian) will be responsible for maintaining a version of the product that is consistent with a master source tree. This responsibility is usually fulfilled by running **qef** at the top of an object tree for each required platform and checking the results on a daily basis. These product trees will be searched for any product files that the developers need during construction that are not being built by the developers themselves. Meanwhile developers make their source modifications to files copied to or created in their own source trees, thereby protecting the master source users and other developers from their changes. Developers will then build a version of the product incorporating their modifications in their own directories. The simple configuration mechanism, the run-time script generation and the comprehensive consistency mechanism ensures that the constructed products are virtually identical to that that would be built from the current master sources if it incorporated the modified files.

Some mechanisms are required to facilitate interfacing to the versioning system being used (e.g., to check files in and out from a remote directory) and some procedures or policies are necessary to ensure that librarian has the required control over the publication process, but both are fairly easily created for most versioning systems.

One of the benefits of the qef system is that the construction scripts themselves, due to their simplicity and portability and run-time processing, rarely need modification by the developers to incorporate new constructions. If modifications are required, they will normally be platform independent thereby eliminating any need for extensive work by the system librarian to adapt to those platforms that the developer did not test.

Adaptation of such a scheme is not necessary to take advantage of qef's benefits, but those organizations that have used such an approach do claim substantial rewards, albeit subjectively.

6 QEF Drawbacks

There may be a small performance penalty using qef. The overhead of running lclvrs, sls, qsg, and qefpp() is not negligible but not excessive — less than a second per directory on a 486, sgi, sparc, or rs6000. But many of the scripts and tools use techniques to avoid gratuitous time stamp propagation, thus in many situations qef avoids work that other systems would perform. Furthermore, the parallel process facility and other features actually reduce the build cycle time. One site that audits build cycle times reported a 66% reduction in the time taken to build their product.

Gaining acceptance from developers is sometimes difficult due to their resistance to change and their suspicion of radically different or novel approaches. Furthermore, a lot of the problems qef solves are problems that do not concern programmers or ones that they don't believe they have. There was a similar resistance to make initially. However, when challenged on programmer acceptance of qef, the author asked a user how he would feel about going back to using make. His reply was that it would be similar to going back to DOS.

One of the necessary characteristics for a construction system that was listed in the first section was that the system needed to be simple. make is fairly simple in its syntax and semantics, but the make files themselves and the actual use of make to control large scale projects can be exceedingly complex. qef uses a collection of small languages which may make it seem complicated. Indeed, qef's processing is complex, but its complexity is largely hidden from its users. The greatest difficulty in promoting qef is presenting it to an audience that currently uses make. Programmers are notoriously reactionary and resistant to change. They expect to understand qef sufficiently to deal with complex problems in the first ten minutes and forget how long it took them to achieve a similar understanding of make. qef is a complex system, although the individual components are simple and the qeffiles are invariably tiny. The complexity lies in their combination to achieve the other requirements.

7 Conclusion

The major differences between **qef** and other construction systems is the separation of the parameters system (i.e., **lclvrs**), the flexible run-time script generation and preparation and the ability to specify the use of arbitrary back-end interpreters. While these unconventional approaches and the unfamiliar representations do present marketing problems, the resulting system does meet the objectives discussed in the first section. Testimonials from satisfied and enthusiastic users could be presented as a more objective defence of this claim, but will not be in the interest of ensuring that this paper does not appear to be a marketing document.

However, a demonstration copy of **qef** will be available via anonymous FTP in the second or third quarter of 1996. Complete documentation and unlimited use will be available as a supported product in the same time period.

References

[Feldman 78] S. I. Feldman: *Make — A Program for Maintaining Computer Programs.* Unix Programmer's Manual, Volume 2A, Seventh Edition, January 1979; Bell Laboratories, N.J.

[Stenning 89] Vic Stenning: *Project Hygiene.* Usenix Software Management Workshop, New Orleans, 1989.

[Tilbrook 86] D. M. Tilbrook and P. R. H. Place: *Tools for the Maintenance and Installation of a Large Software Distribution.* EUUG Florence Conference Proceedings, April 1986, USENIX Atlanta Conference Proceedings, June 1986.

[Tilbrook 90] David Tilbrook and John McMullen: *Washing Behind Your Ears — or — The Principles of Software Hygiene.* Keynote address, EurOpen Fall Conference, Nice, 1990.

Configuring Versioned Software Products

Reidar Conradi[1] and Bernhard Westfechtel[2]*

[1] Department of Computer Systems and Telematics
Norwegian Institute of Technology (NTH), N-7034 Trondheim
conradi@idt.unit.no
[2] Lehrstuhl für Informatik III, RWTH Aachen
Ahornstr. 55, D-52074 Aachen
bernhard@i3.informatik.rwth-aachen.de

Abstract. Despite recent advances in software configuration management (SCM), constructing consistent configurations of large and complex versioned software products still remains a challenge. We provide an overview of existing approaches which address this problem. These approaches are compared by means of a taxonomy which is based on an analogy to deductive databases: construction of a configuration corresponds to evaluation of a query against a versioned database with stored version selection rules.

1   Introduction

Consistently configuring a large product existing in many versions is a difficult task. Many *constraints* on combining revisions and variants must be taken into account. Frequently, these constraints are neither documented properly nor specified formally. Then, it is up to the user of a SCM system to select consistent combinations of versions. Furthermore, dependencies between changes must also be taken into account, e.g. bug fixes may require other bug fixes to be included. If the user commits an error, this may turn out only after testing the selected source configuration, or even by failures at the customer site.

This paper provides an overview of existing approaches to configuring versioned products. From the perspective of *deductive databases* [20], configuring a versioned product corresponds to evaluating a query against a versioned database with stored version selection rules. In section 2, a taxonomy is developed which is based on this analogy.

SCM systems are based on a wide spectrum of different *version models*. A version model defines the objects to be versioned, version identification and organization, as well as operations for retrieving existing versions and constructing new versions. This paper focuses on support for configuring versioned products from an intensional description. In our survey, we distinguish between two classes of version models which are treated in sections 3 and 4, respectively:

---

* This work was carried out during a research stay at NTH. Support from NTH is gratefully acknowledged.

- *Version-oriented models* describe configurations (i.e. product versions) in terms of explicit versions of components. Component versions are arranged in version graphs describing their evolution histories. A configuration is described by version rules which select appropriate versions with the help of attributes and history information. Constraints refer to consistent combinations of versions of different components (in general, only a small fraction of all potential combinations are actually compatible). Differences between versions are described by deltas which, however, are not referenced in the version rules.

- *Change-oriented models* describe configurations in terms of changes relative to some base configuration. There are no version graphs, just version rules describing potential combinations of changes. Changes differ from deltas in several ways: changes are named, they comprise logically related modifications to multiple components, and they can be applied in a flexible way (while a delta is tied to a specific pair of versions). In contrast to version-oriented models, change-oriented models do not maintain (and are not restricted to use) explicit component versions. Rather, new component versions are implicitly constructed by merging changes, resulting in higher flexibility than in version-oriented models. However, this combinability also has a drawback: inconsistent configurations may be produced easily. Therefore, constraints are required to express conditions on consistent change combinations.

At the ends of sections 3 and 4, a table is presented which summarizes the main points of the comparison. A final conclusion is given in section 5.

2   Conceptual Framework

This section defines the terminology used throughout the rest of this paper and lays the foundations for comparing specific approaches in the next sections. Let us start with some general definitions (along the lines of [27] and [2]):

- A *(software) object* (item) is any kind of identifiable entity put under SCM control. An object may be either *atomic*, i.e. it is not decomposed any further (internals are irrelevant to SCM), or *composite*. A composite object is related to its components by *composition relationships*. Furthermore, there may be *dependency relationships* between dependent and master objects.

- A *version* is an implicit or explicit instance of a versioned object which groups "similar" objects sharing some properties. We distinguish between *revisions* (historical versioning) and *variants* (parallel versions).

- A *configuration* is a consistent and complete version of a composite object, i.e. a set of component versions and their relationships. A configuration is called *bound* if it exclusively contains versions as its components. Conversely, an *unbound* configuration exclusively consists of versioned objects. A *partly bound* configuration lies in between.

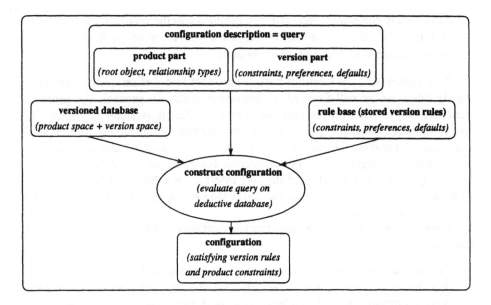

Fig. 1. Construction of a configuration from a deductive database perspective

Construction of a configuration may be regarded as a search problem on a *deductive database* (Fig. 1): A configuration description is a query which is evaluated against a versioned database augmented with a rule base for version selection. The configuration to be constructed is the result of evaluating the query.

The *versioned database* contains the versioned products to be configured. It consists of two parts:

- The *product space* is composed of the stored objects (items) and their relationships. Typical software objects (often documents) are requirements specifications, source files, relocatable files, user documentation, test data, review forms, measurement data, project plans, etc. The product space is organized by relationships between objects, e.g. composition relationships (part-of, e.g. a file is part of a directory) and dependency relationships (e.g. include dependencies in C programs or traceability dependencies between lifecycle documents).
- The *version space* is composed of version structures, e.g. version rules and/or histories that are characterized by version attributes with specified domains. Such attributes may be globally or locally defined.
  In version-oriented models, *version graphs* are used to describe the revisions (historical versioning) and variants (parallel versions) of software objects, annotated by given attribute values. The version space is an N-dimensional space, where one dimension corresponds to time and there is one dimension for each variant attribute.
  In change-oriented models, versions are described by *changes* which can be

dynamically combined ("merged") to produce specific versions. Each change, described by an attribute value, defines a dimension of an N-dimensional space characterizing all potential versions.

Before discussing the relations between product and version space more thoroughly later, let us pull forward an important point: In general, the product structure may depend on the versions selected; different versions may have different outgoing relationships (*versioned relationships*). Conversely, the version space may depend on the product space, i.e. the version attributes may depend on the part of the product to be configured. For example, there may be an attribute characterizing the style of the user interface, e.g. Motif or OpenWindows. This attribute does not apply to the database part of the product, which may e.g. be Oracle or Ingres.

A *configuration description* specifies the configuration to be constructed and consists of two parts:

- The *product part* describes the product as a composite object. This can be done by specifying one *root object* (or a set of such) and a set of *relationship types* (composition or dependency relationships). A product is constructed by a transitive closure from the root object following the specified relationship types.
- The *version part* contains the version selection rules, which constrain and guide the search (see below).

Further selection rules are contained in a *rule base* of stored rules. The rule base exists independently from the query. We may distinguish between the following kinds of *version rules* (this classification applies both to the rule base and the configuration description):

- A *constraint* is a mandatory rule which must be satisfied. Any violation of a constraint indicates an inconsistency, e.g. the SUN and the VAX variant must not be selected simultaneously.
- A *preference* is an optional rule which is only applied when it may be satisfied. It corresponds to a property which is preferred but not enforced, e.g. released module versions are preferred.
- A *default* is also an optional rule, but it is weaker than a preference. A default rule is only applied when otherwise no unique selection could be performed, e.g. the latest version of the main branch in a version graph may be selected by default.

A tool which constructs a configuration by evaluating a configuration description with respect to a versioned database and a rule base is called a *configurator*. Note that we intentionally avoid the notion of builder here, since we are only concerned with source configurations (no classical builds using tool-based rederivations are considered).

We use *AND/OR graphs* [25] both for describing the structure of a versioned product and for explaining how version selections are performed during the configuration process. An AND node represents a product part. When an AND node

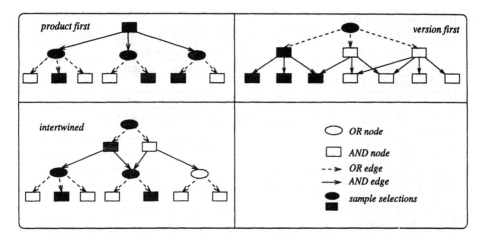

Fig. 2. Different kinds of AND/OR graphs and selection orders

is selected, all outgoing edges (relationships) need to be followed for constructing a configuration. An OR node represents a version group from which one member must be selected.

The following kinds of *selection orders* may be distinguished (Fig. 2):

Product first. First, the entire product structure is selected (AND selection). In this case, we have a composite object consisting of a known set of components. Each component may expand into multiple versions (OR selection).

Version first. This is the inverse approach: The product version is selected first (OR selection). Subsequently, an AND selection is performed to obtain all components belonging to the selected version. In general, the set of components depends on the version selected.

Intertwined. Product selections are intermixed with version selections (multi-level selections). Often, the AND/OR graphs are structured such that AND and OR selections alternate (bipartite AND/OR graph).

During the configuration process, non-deterministic selections (e.g. based on defaults) may need to be performed. These selections can be performed either automatically (*automatic configurator*) or with user assistance (*interactive configurator*). In either case, a non-deterministic choice may be wrong, and the configurator must therefore be able to *backtrack* from wrong selections.

Furthermore, configurators may be classified according to when references to versioned objects are bound to specific versions. *Static binding* means that a mapping is constructed beforehand. In case of *dynamic binding*, the configuration description is evaluated only when an object is actually accessed.

We still have to define *consistency*: A configuration is consistent when it satisfies the constraints (mandatory conditions) both in the configuration description and the rule base. In this paper, we concentrate on *version-level consistency*, i.e.

versioned database	
selection order	product first, version first, intertwined
product space	files, modular programs, ...
version space	revisions, variants, changes, ...
configuration description	
formalism	SQL-like queries, boolean expressions, ...
rule classes	constraints, preferences, defaults
rule base	
formalism	(see above)
rule classes	(see above)
configurator	
binding modes	static, dyamic
degree of automation	automatic, interactive
backtracking	yes, no

Table 1. Taxonomy for comparing configurators

on constraints describing legal version combinations. Typical examples are "select the same operating system variant throughout the whole configuration" or "include change c together with all changes on which c depends". We do not address *product-related consistency*, which must also be satisfied by a consistent configuration. In particular, the configurators described in this paper do not guarantee syntactic or semantic consistency of the result of a configuration process. Product-related consistency has been treated in module interconnection languages and systems which are based on such languages, e.g. SVCE [10], NuMil [18], and Inscape [19].

The framework developed above applies to both version-oriented and change-oriented models. However, there are some specific points which are discussed below:

- In version-oriented models, version rules refer to versioned components. In change-oriented models, (versions of) components are not mentioned in the version rules.
- In change-oriented models, the *version* (of the whole product) is always selected *first*. In version-oriented models, any selection order can be applied.
- In version-oriented models, *explicit versions* of components are used to construct configurations. For a product consisting of m modules existing in v versions, there exist v^m potential configurations, i.e. the number of potential configurations grows polynomially in v. The actual number may be very large, e.g. 5^{1000} for 1000 modules each of which exists in 5 versions.
- In change-oriented models, construction of a configuration does not rely on explicit component versions. Rather, *versions* of components are constructed *implicitly* by merging changes at a fine-grained level, e.g. text lines rather than files. In case of unconstrained combination of changes (each change

---

Product **foo** supports different operating systems (e.g. **DOS**, **Unix**, **VMS**), window systems (e.g. **X11**, **SunView**, **Windows**), and database systems (e.g. **Oracle**, **Informix**, **dbase**).

There are some straightforward constraints among these variants, e. g. **dbase** is not available under **VMS**, or **X11** does not run under **DOS**.

Furthermore, various changes are performed during maintenance of **foo**, such as e.g. bug fixes which are denoted by **Fix1**, **Fix2**, etc. Changes may be mutually exclusive; they may also depend on each other.

Finally, versions of (components of) **foo** have states indicating their degree of consistency (e.g. **coded**, **tested**, **released**).

Fig. 3. Running example

---

may either be applied or skipped), there are 2^v potential configurations for v changes, i.e. the number of potential configurations even grows exponentially in v. For example, for 1000 changes there are 2^{1000} potential combinations.

Table 1 shows a taxonomy which we will use for the comparisons in sections 3 and 4. The taxonomy is structured according to Fig. 1. Fig. 3 shows a small running example which will be used in sections 3 and 4, as well.

3 Version-Oriented Models

In the following, we survey version-oriented configurators. Each of them is based on some sort of *AND/OR graph* which is used to represent the versioned product to be configured. The AND/OR graph is traversed starting from some root node, with version selections performed at OR nodes.

3.1 RCS

RCS [26] is a successor of SCCS [21] and manages versions of text files. RCS selects the *product first* and thus cannot express versioned relationships. A version is a member of a *version group* which is contained in some directory. The members of a version group are arranged in a *version graph*, which consists of several branches (variants) each of which is composed of a sequence of revisions. An example is given in Fig. 4, where our sample product **foo** is represented by a directory containing version groups for the source files and the make file[3].

Configuration descriptions take the simple form of options supplied to a **checkout** command. Options describe *preferences* in terms of values of built-in version attributes. For example, the following command retrieves the latest versions with state **Released** which were created before the specified date:

---

[3] For the sake of convenience, a version group is represented by an oval surrounding its members.

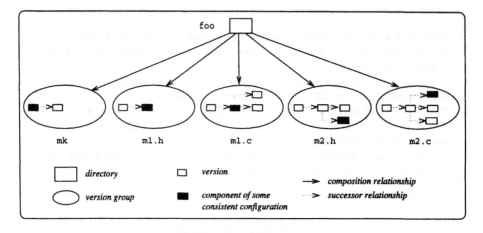

Fig. 4. RCS

```
co -d''1995/05/05'' -sReleased *,v
```

RCS does not support a rule base for version selection. Consistent version selections are difficult to perform. A consistent configuration may consist of versions which are located at different places of the respective version graphs (see the grey boxes in Fig. 4). A configuration may be regarded as a *thread* through the version graphs. Such a thread may be represented by tagging all versions with the same symbolic name.

For each version group, the `checkout` command selects the latest version satisfying all options. If no matching version exists or no options are specified, the latest version on the main branch is selected by default.

3.2 ClearCase

ClearCase [12], a successor to DSEE [13], adopts like many other SCM systems the SCCS/RCS approach to versioning of individual files. In addition, directories may be versioned, e.g. directory `foo` in Fig. 5). All kinds of versioned objects (files/directories) are uniformly denoted as *elements*. In contrast to RCS, ClearCase selects the *version first*. A single-version *view* is established on the versioned file system by a configuration description. The view is a filter which dynamically binds generic references to specific versions. The filter is used for both read and write accesses. It excludes components which are not used in the specified configuration (`m3.h` in Fig. 5).

A configuration description consists of a *sequence* of *rules*. There is no distinction between constraints, preferences, and defaults. The product part of a rule describes its scope, which may be a specific element, all elements in a certain subtree, or simply all visible elements. The version part is a boolean expression which refers to version numbers, branches, or values of version attributes. For example, in the configuration description

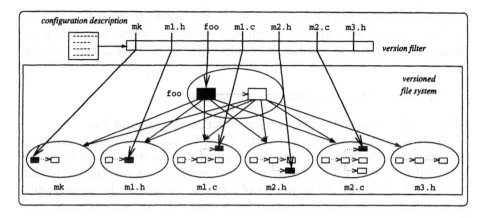

Fig. 5. ClearCase

```
element /foo/... /X11
element /foo/... /Oracle -time 10-Oct
element /foo/... /Unix   -time 10-Oct
element /foo/... /main   -time 10-Oct
```

/foo/... denotes the product part (subtree), X11, Oracle, ... specify branches, and a cut-off date is given by the time option[4].

ClearCase does not support stored version rules in addition to the configuration description. In particular, there is no way to state constraints, e.g. "X11 and DOS are not compatible".

An operating system process, e.g. for compiling and linking a program, is executed under some configuration description which is supplied at process start. The configuration description is evaluated only when an element is accessed. Rules are evaluated sequentially, the ordering of rules indicates their priority. Evaluation stops when a unique match is found or all versions returned by a query reside on the same branch. In this case, the latest version on that branch is selected. An error is reported when no matching rule has been found.

3.3 CONFIG

CONFIG is a language-independent approach for configuring *modular programs* [28]. Versions of modular programs are represented by a bipartite AND/OR graph as given in Fig. 2. Accordingly, CONFIG performs *intertwined selections*.

CONFIG distinguishes between *revisions* and *variants*. A modular program evolves into a set of revisions which are denoted by natural numbers below. The structure of the evolution history is irrelevant to CONFIG. Each program revision may exist in multiple variants. Variants are characterized by attributes.

---

[4] This description can be used to perform changes specific to X11 in a stable work context.

A *configuration description* is a pair *(re,va)*, where *re* denotes a revision and *va* a tuple of attribute values. For all attributes characterizing a program variant, a value must be specified; incomplete specifications are not allowed. For example,

```
(1, (os = DOS, ws = Windows, db = dbase))
```

selects a PC variant of the first revision of our sample program foo.

The rule base consists of two parts. First, for each version of a module a *version description set*, denoted as *VD*, is maintained which consists of pairs such as described above. *VD* indicates to which configurations the module version belongs. The version description sets of different versions of the same module must be mutually disjoint. For example, a version of the main module may have the following version description set:

```
{(1, (os = DOS, ws = Windows, db = dbase)),
 (1, (os = Unix, ws = X11, db = Oracle)),
 (2, (os = DOS, ws = Windows, db = dbase)),
 (2, (os = Unix, ws = X11, db = Oracle))}
```

According to lines 1 and 2 (3 and 4), this version is used in both the DOS and the Unix variant of program revision 1 (2).

Second, each version puts constraints on the versions of modules on which it depends. These constraints are attached to dependencies. A constraint is defined by a *mapping* from the version description *vd* of the current module to a version description *vd'* of a used module. In the simplest case, this mapping is the identity, e.g.

```
USE m VERS = (SAME, SAME)
```

propagates the current version description to the used module m.

The configuration process starts with a complete configuration description *vd* (=*(re,va)*, see above) at the root module. *vd* uniquely selects a version, and new version descriptions are computed for selecting versions of used modules. Since the version description sets of different module versions are mutually disjoint, the configurator operates in a deterministic way (no non-deterministic choices and hence no backtracking). If a module is used by multiple modules, the first selection wins, and inconsistencies between different selections are not detected.

3.4 Adele

Like CONFIG, the Adele configuration manager [4, 5, 6] performs sophisticated, *intertwined* product and version *selections* when configuring a modular program. In Adele, modular programs are organized into *families*. The structure of a family and relationships between families are depicted in Fig. 6[5]. Each family may

---

[5] For the sake of convenience, we make use of hybrid AND/OR nodes to represent interfaces and variants.

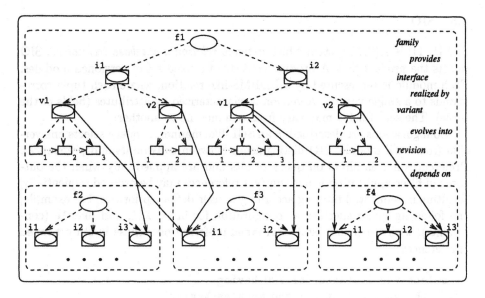

Fig. 6. Adele

have multiple interfaces, realized by alternative variants evolving into sequences of revisions. Note that realization variants may be both module bodies and previously constructed subconfigurations. Dependencies emanate from interfaces and variants, and they end at interfaces.

Adele supports both configuration descriptions and stored version rules, the latter of which are attached to families. Configuration descriptions and stored version rules are specified using the same language. *Version rules* are similar to those used in ClearCase. The product part of a rule defines its scope, which may be a specific family or a set of families below some root family. The version part consists of a boolean expression over version attributes, e.g.

```
([os = Unix] and [ws = SunViews]
  and [db = Informix] and [state = tested])
```

Unlike ClearCase, Adele explicitly distinguishes three different classes of rules, namely *constraints*, *preferences*, and *defaults*. Using these rules, short intensional descriptions can be given for large and complex configurations.

Given a configuration description for an interface, the *configurator* traverses the AND/OR graph of families, selecting one revision for each family. The configurator maintains a set of version rules V initialized with the configuration description. V is extended gradually by adding the stored rules attached to selected versions. To avoid wrong choices, version selection for some family f is performed only after all constraints are known. This is the case when versions of all families above f have been selected. However, once a selection has been made (possibly with the help of preferences and defaults), it cannot be retracted (no backtracking).

3.5   SIO

SIO [1, 11] is a SCM system which extends *relational database technology*. SIO selects the *product first*. A product consists of a fixed set of versioned modules. Each module is represented by a RDBMS-like relation, where each tuple corresponds to a single version. A version is characterized by attributes (fields of the tuple). The set of fields may vary from one module to another.

Configurations are described in an SQL-like manner. A query selects one version from each module. SIO distinguishes between *constraints* and *preferences*. Preferences act as filters on query results and are applied only when the outcome of filter application is not empty. Preferences may be ordered sequentially, resulting in sequential filtering according to user-defined priorities. For example, the following query specifies a configuration for Unix, X11, and Oracle (constraints), with versions in state released preferred over those in state tested (preferences):

```
select the instances of FOO having
   the versions of all the modules having
      os = Unix and ws = X11 and db = Oracle
from which prefer those having
   the versions of all the modules having state = released
from which prefer those having
   the versions of all the modules having state = tested
```

The rule base contains constraints which are specified by *compatibility rules*. A compatibility rule is an assertion in a restricted first order predicate calculus. The conditions under which two versions from different modules are compatible are stated in terms of version attributes. Constraints which quantify over (versions of) all modules are not supported. Due to the restricted form of constraints, SIO can efficiently check for contradictions between them.

A configuration description is evaluated against a database of module relations, taking compatibility rules into account. The *query evaluator* is a deductive component which goes beyond conventional database technology. In addition to checking the compatibility rules when constructing a new configuration, SIO analyses whether existing configurations would satisfy a new compatibility rule. Modification of the rule base is disallowed if it makes any existing configuration inconsistent.

3.6   NORA

ICE [31, 30], the SCM system of the software development environment NORA, is based on *feature logic*. A feature denotes a property of some object, e.g. the feature os denotes the underlying operating system. In its simplest form, a *feature term* q consists of a list of pairs of features and values, e.g.

```
q = [os : Unix, ws : X11, db : Oracle]
```

Feature terms are used both for configuration descriptions and stored rules. q serves as an example of a configuration description (query). All feature terms describe *constraints*; preferences and defaults are not supported. Versions of some object are represented by feature terms containing a special object feature whose value is an object identifier. For example, the following terms denote two versions of some user interface module and database module, respectively[6]:

```
ui1 = [object : UI, ws : X11, os : Unix]
ui2 = [object : UI, ws : Windows, os : DOS]
db1 = [object : DB, db : dbase, os : DOS]
db2 = [object : DB, db : Oracle, os : {VMS, Unix}]
```

The feature term of a configuration is constructed by an intersection operator (*unification*) which handles the object feature in a special way (union of the values instead of intersection). An intersection fails if corresponding features cannot be unified (mutually inconsistent constraints). For example, ui1 may be combined with db2, but not with db1:

```
c1 = ui1 ⊓ db2 =
    [object : {UI, DB}, ws : X11, os : Unix, db : Oracle]
c2 = ui1 ⊓ db1 = ⊥
```

NORA supports *incremental construction* of a configuration with constraint-based guidance. Features can be specified step by step by selection from menus (rather than simultaneously as in the query q above); inconsistent choices are disabled by NORA. In our example, selecting Unix as operating system uniquely identifies the configuration c1, eliminating the need for further choices.

As used above, NORA may be classified as a version-oriented approach. However, it is interesting to note that feature logic can be applied to SCM in a more general way. In [30], Zeller proposes a unified version model for SCM which covers both version-oriented and change-oriented versioning. In particular, changes are modeled as features which can be either included or omitted (see also COV in the next section).

3.7 Summary

Table 2 summarizes the approaches described in this section. Different selection orders are used (version first, product first, intertwined). The product space is composed of files, components (with no assumption about object contents), or modular programs, either flat or hierarchical. The formalisms for describing version rules differ widely, ranging from command options to fully developed query languages. Only Adele and NORA represent configuration descriptions and stored rules in a uniform way. Except ClearCase, all approaches perform static binding. Only NORA and Adele support interactive construction of a configuration. Finally, not all approaches supporting constraints can backtrack from wrong choices (CONFIG even excludes non-determinism at all).

---

[6] In db2, the feature os is set-valued, which is indicated by braces.

	RCS	ClearCase	CONFIG	Adele	SIO	NORA
vers. db.						
selection order	product first	version first	intertwined	intertwined	product first	product first
product space	flat files	file hierarchy	flat modular programs	hierarchical modular programs	component hierarchy	nested components
version space	version graphs	version graphs	revisions variants	variants revisions	version sets	version sets
conf. descr.						
formalism	checkout options	first-order expressions	attribute tuple	first-order expressions	extended SQL	feature terms
rule classes	preferences	priority-ordered rules	constraints	constraints preferences defaults	constraints preferences	constraints
rule base						
formalism	—	—	attribute functions	first-order expressions	first-order expressions	feature terms
rule classes	—	—	constraints	constraints preferences defaults	constraints	constraints
configurator						
binding modes	static	dynamic	static	static	static	static
degree of automation	automatic	automatic	automatic	automatic interactive	automatic	interactive
backtracking	—	—	no	no	yes	yes

Table 2. Comparison of version-oriented approaches

4   Change-Oriented Models

In the following, we survey change-oriented configurators. While version-oriented configurators are based on AND/OR graphs, change-oriented configurators rather origin from *conditional compilation*. Conditional compilation addresses the multiple maintenance problem by storing multiple versions in a single file and using preprocessor statements to control the visibilies of fragments (sequences of text lines). Editing source files with many embedded preprocessor statements may become very confusing. Therefore, all change-oriented approaches described below automate management of visibilities and hide the corresponding control expressions from the users who are offered a single-version view on the versioned database.

4.1 PIE

An early approach to change-oriented versioning has been developed at XE-ROX PARC [7]. PIE manages configurations of Smalltalk programs which are internally represented by graph-like data structures. Each change is placed in a *layer*. Layers are aggregated into *contexts* which act as search paths through the layers[7].

When constructing a context, there are two degrees of freedom: First, each layer may either be included or omitted; second, the layers included can be arranged in any sequential order. This combinatorial complexity can be overcome by defining contexts in terms of other contexts (*aggregates*) which contain consistent and reusable combinations of layers. Furthermore, PIE provides *relationships* to document constraints for the combination of layers. For example, A **depends on** B implies that each context containing A should include B, as well. Conversely, B **repairs** A indicates that a bug in layer A has been fixed in layer B. Therefore, B should be included whenever A is selected. However, PIE does not enforce any constraints. Rather, the documented relationships are merely used to warn the user of possible inconsistencies.

4.2 Aide-de-Camp

Aide-de-Camp [3, 23] describes versions of products in terms of *change sets* relative to a base version. A change set describes a physical change which may affect multiple files. The finest grain of change is a text line. In contrast to layers, change sets are totally ordered according to their creation times. If change set $c1$ was created before $c2$, $c1$ will be applied before $c2$ when both change sets are included in some product version. Each change set may be viewed as a switch which can either be turned on or off.

Aide-de-Camp detects *physical conflicts* when a change set is applied to some product version. A conflict occurs when a modification included in the change set refers to text lines which are not part of that product version. Furthermore, Aide-de-Camp provides a 3-way *merge tool* which combines alternative versions with respect to a common base and detects contradictory modifications to the same text lines. Unlike PIE, Aide-de-Camp does not support relationships which can be used to detect inconsistent combinations of change sets.

4.3 MVPE

MVPE [22] is a text editor which supports simultaneous editing of multiple versions of a text file. A text file consists of a collection of fragments (sequences of words). To each fragment, a *visibility* is attached which determines the versions to which the fragment belongs. A versioned file may vary along multiple dimensions. The version space is modeled as a table whose columns correspond to these dimensions and whose rows represent specific versions (Fig.7).

---

[7] DaSC [15] is based on a similar approach.

versions			edit set		
os	ws	db	os	ws	db
DOS	Windows	dbase	Unix	*	*
Unix	X11	Oracle			
Unix	SunViews	Informix		view	
Unix	X11	Informix			
...	...	...	os	ws	db
			Unix	X11	Informix

Fig. 7. MVPE

MVPE distinguishes between an edit set and a view. An *edit set* is a write filter controlling which versions will be affected by a change. The edit set is specified in a query-by-example style with the help of regular expressions (e.g. the edit set in Fig. 7 denotes all Unix versions). A *view* is a read filter and selects from the edit set a single version which is displayed to the user[8].

MVPE does not support stored version rules. In particular, there is no way to state constraints on combinations of different dimensions.

4.4 COV

Change-oriented versioning [14, 17] emphasizes management of *logical changes*. The version space is structured by global *options*. Each option defines a dimension of the version space. Options may denote variants, e.g. Unix, DOS, and VMS define different variants of the underlying operating system. Options may also be used to represent changes, e.g. Fix1 and Fix2 represent certain bug fixes. An option may be bound to either true or false, or it may be left unbound. A set of option bindings corresponds to a region of an N-dimensional version space.

A versioned database consists of a collection of *versioned fragments*. An example is given in Fig. 8 (see the box "database before update" on the left-hand side). The sample database consists of three fragments, denoted by f1, f2, and f3. While there is only a single version of f3, f1 and f2 both exist in two versions, denoted by f11, f12, and f21, f22, respectively. To each fragment version, a *visibility* is attached. The visibility of a fragment version is a boolean expression describing the product versions to which the fragment version belongs. For example, the visibility of f11 is Unix. This means that f11 is contained in all Unix versions, regardless of the window system selected.

Like MVPE, COV has been designed for multi-version editing and distinguishes between a read filter, called *choice*, and a write filter, named *ambition*. Changes are performed in transactions, which have both an ambition and a choice. Both ambition and choice are sets of option bindings. The choice extends the ambition, i.e. all option bindings of the ambition are included in the

---

[8] Note that ClearCase, which also sets up a view on a versioned database, does not distinguish between read and write filter.

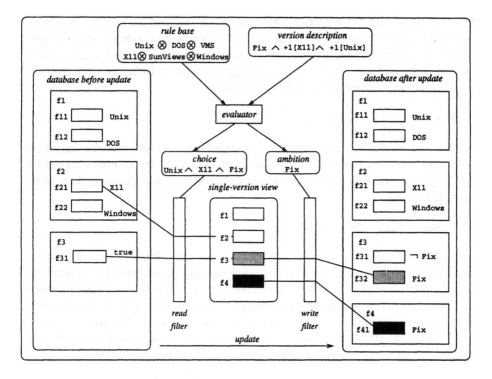

Fig. 8. Change-oriented Versioning

choice. The choice corresponds to a single point in the version space. This point is contained in the region corresponding to the ambition.

For example, in Fig. 8 the choice is

Unix ∧ X11 ∧ Fix

In particular, this means that the change is performed in a version which runs under Unix and makes use of the X11 window system. The ambition is set to Fix. This indicates that a bug fix is applied, being valid regardless of the operating system and the window system. The scope of changes is reflected in the visibilities which are assigned to updated or inserted fragments. In Fig. 8, f3 is updated and f4 is inserted. Fragment versions f32 and f41 both have the visibility Fix.

On top of these base mechanisms, more high-level concepts are provided [9]. *Validities* are used to express states of versions, e.g. **tested**, **released**, etc. Validities are global, they refer to the whole product rather than to individual components. A validity is defined by a boolean expression. It may be referenced in a version description (see below) to ensure that the selected product version has a certain state, e.g. we may want to work on a **tested** version.

A *version description* consists of *constraints* and *preferences*. A constraint is a mandatory condition on option bindings. A preference consists of option bindings which are not enforced. Preferences are weighted by rational numbers. A positive number means that binding of an option to a certain value is preferred; analogously, a negative number indicates that the option binding should be avoided. In Fig. 8, the version description requires inclusion of Fix (constraint) and prefers inclusion of X11 and Unix:

Fix ∧ +1[X11] ∧ +1[Unix]

To keep version descriptions short, *aggregates* are introduced. An aggregate is a named version rule which refers to a set of mandatory or preferred option bindings. For example, the following aggregate denotes a sequence of fixes to be applied together:

Fixes = Fix1 ∧ Fix2 ∧ Fix3

The *rule base* consists of version rules of the same form as used in version descriptions. Aggregates stored in the rule base may be referenced in version descriptions. Note that aggregates can be used to modularize the rule base; modules can be activated as required by mentioning their names in version descriptions. Furthermore, *defaults* are added implicitly when a version description is evaluated. In Fig. 8, all version rules are defaults which express *mutual exclusion* of options. These constraints are defined by means of the operator ⊗:

Unix ⊗ DOS ⊗ VMS

X11 ⊗ SunViews ⊗ Windows

The *evaluator* takes the version description and the rule base and calculates a choice (or an ambition). In general, there is no unique "best" solution satisfying a version description. A heuristic algorithm searches for a solution, guided by preferences. In case of an ambition, the algorithm tries to minimize the number of option bindings; in case of a choice, it tries to maximize the number of options set to true. In our example, the ambition evaluates to Fix, i.e. preferences do not narrow the ambition. However, they do affect the choice (options X11 and Unix).

Recent work on high-level extensions of change-oriented versioning is described in a companion paper [16]. That paper introduces additional types of constraints not covered above, e.g. option dependencies, and it also describes tools for managing the option space and supporting consistent version selection.

4.5 Summary

Table 3 summarizes the change-oriented models which we have presented in this section. The many blank entries clearly indicate that more research in version rules is required. Only COV addresses this issue to some extent.

	PIE	Aide-de-Camp	MVPE	COV
vers. db.				
selection order	version first	version first	version first	version first
product space	Smalltalk programs	ER database (file entities)	text files	EER database (file entities)
version space	layers	change sets	dimensions	options
conf. descr.				
formalism	(extensional only)	(extensional only)	query by example	boolean expressions
rule classes	—	—	no distinction	constraints preferences
rule base				
formalism	relationships between layers	—	—	boolean expressions
rule classes	constraints	—	—	constraints preferences defaults validities

Table 3. Comparison of change-oriented approaches

5 Conclusion

Table 4 contrasts the main features of version-oriented and change-oriented approaches to configuring versioned products. Let us summarize their *strengths* and *weaknesses*:

- Change-oriented models have a nice link to change requests and long transactions. The user directly refers to a change spanning multiple components and is not bothered with the tedious task of bookkeeping which component versions make up a logical change. The flexibility is extremely high, since new component versions can be constructed as required by merging changes. However, constraints on change combinations have to be managed carefully; raw merging often yields an inconsistent result.
- In version-oriented models, the product structure is referenced in the version rules (white box approach). Therefore, version-oriented models may express product-related version concepts — e.g. alternative realization variants of an interface, see Adele — which go beyond the black box approach of change-oriented models. On the other hand, version-oriented models lack grouping of logical changes affecting multiple components. Furthermore, flexibility is limited since only already existing component versions can be used for the construction of a configuration (no implicit merges).

We suggest the following topics to be addressed by future work:

	version-oriented models	change-oriented models
version space	version graphs (revisions and variants) version attributes	product-level changes attributes controlling change application
configuration	$\sum$ component versions	base version $+ \sum$ changes
product structure	white box approach (query references the structure)	black box approach (structure transparent to the query)
version rules	expressions over version attributes	expressions over change attributes
constraints	conditions on version attributes (e.g. consistent variant selection)	conditions on change combinations (e.g. c_1 implies c_2)
versioning	explicit (members of the version graph)	implicit (any change combination)
combinability	v^m (m modules in v versions)	2^v (v changes)

Table 4. Comparison of version-oriented and change-oriented models

- Change-oriented and version-oriented models have complementary strengths. Initial attempts to combine these approaches have been undertaken, but more work has to be done to come up with a *unified model*.
- In this paper, construction of a configuration is viewed as evaluation of a query against a *deductive database*. However, deductive databases are not yet used widely, neither in general nor in SCM. The potentials of applying deductive databases need to be investigated further.
- We have focused primarily on technical issues, in particular concerning the formalisms used for writing version rules. *Experiences* gained from actual use of configurators have to be discussed, as well.
- Many configurators operate on a low *semantic level*, e.g. raw text-oriented merges in change-oriented approaches or composition of versioned files in version-oriented approaches. Raising this semantic level may improve detection of inconsistencies and conflicts.
- More support is required for *managing* the complexity of the *version space*. In both version- and change-oriented models, the version space may become untractable when a large software product evolves over a long period. Constraints excluding inconsistent combinations of versions or changes are essential for managing complexity. Furthermore, appropriate *visualization* techniques may prove very helpful, see e.g. [8].
- Finally, we have tacitly assumed that the rule base is located on top of the versioned database, without being versioned itself. However, the rule base is

subject to change as the underlying product evolves. *Versioning* of the *rule base* raises some difficult modeling issues, concerning e.g. relations between evolution of the rule base and the product, or meta rules for configuring the rule base.

Acknowledgements

We would like to thank the anonymous reviewers as well as Bjørn Gulla and Bjørn Munch for helpful and constructive comments on this paper.

References

1. Y. Bernard, M. Lacroix, P. Lavency, and M. Vanhoedenaghe. Configuration management in an open environment. In G. Goos and J. Hartmanis, editors, *Proceedings of the 1st European Software Engineering Conference*, LNCS 289, pages 35–43. Springer-Verlag, Sept. 1987.
2. R. Conradi. Configuration management. Course material, NTH, June 1995.
3. R. D. Cronk. Tributaries and deltas. *BYTE*, pages 177–186, January 1992.
4. J. Estublier. A configuration manager: The Adele data base of programs. In *Proceedings of the Workshop on Software Engineering Environments for Programming-in-the-Large*, pages 140–147, Harwichport, Massachusetts, June 1985.
5. J. Estublier. Configuration management: The notion and the tools. In Winkler [29], pages 38–61.
6. J. Estublier and R. Casallas. The Adele configuration manager. In Tichy [24], pages 99–134.
7. I. P. Goldstein and D. G. Bobrow. A layered approach to software design. Technical Report CSL-80-5, XEROX PARC, 1980.
8. B. Gulla. *User Support Facilities for Software Configuration Management*. PhD thesis, NTH Trondheim, 1996.
9. B. Gulla, E.-A. Karlsson, and D. Yeh. Change-oriented version descriptions in EPOS. *Software Engineering Journal*, 6(6):378–386, Nov. 1991.
10. G. E. Kaiser and A. N. Habermann. An environment for system version control. In *Digest of Papers of Spring CompCon '83*, pages 415–420. IEEE Computer Society Press, Feb. 1983.
11. P. Lavency and M. Vanhoedenaghe. Knowledge based configuration management. In B. Shriver, editor, *Proceedings of the 21st Annual Hawaii International Conference on System Sciences*, pages 83–92, 1988.
12. D. Leblang. The CM challenge: Configuration management that works. In Tichy [24], pages 1–38.
13. D. B. Leblang and G. D. McLean, Jr. Configuration management for large-scale software development efforts. In *Proceedings of the Workshop on Software Engineering Environments for Programming-in-the-Large*, pages 122–127, Harwichport, Massachusetts, June 1985.
14. A. Lie, R. Conradi, T. Didriksen, E. Karlsson, S. O. Hallsteinsen, and P. Holager. Change oriented versioning. In C. Ghezzi and J. A. McDermid, editors, *Proceedings of the 2nd European Software Engineering Conference*, LNCS 387, pages 191–202. Springer-Verlag, Sept. 1989.

109

15. S. A. MacKay. The state-of-the-art in concurrent, distributed configuration management. In J. Estublier, editor, *Proceedings of the 5th International Workshop on Software Configuration Management*, LNCS 1005, pages 180–194. Springer Verlag, 1995.
16. B. Munch. HiCOV: Managing the version space. In *Proceedings of the 6th International Workshop on Software Configuration Management*, 1996.
17. B. P. Munch, J.-O. Larsen, B. Gulla, R. Conradi, and E.-A. Karlsson. Uniform versioning: The change-oriented model. In *Proceedings of the 4th International Workshop on Software Configuration Management (Preprint)*, pages 188–196, Baltimore, MD, May 1993.
18. K. Narayanaswamy and W. Scacchi. Maintaining configurations of evolving software systems. *IEEE Transactions on Software Engineering*, SE-13(3):324–334, Mar. 1987.
19. D. E. Perry. Version control in the Inscape environment. In *Proceedings of the 9th International Conference on Software Engineering*, pages 142–149, Monterey, CA, Mar. 1987.
20. K. Ramamohanarao and J. Harland. An introduction to deductive database languages and systems. *The VLDB Journal*, 3(2):107–122, April 1994.
21. M. J. Rochkind. The source code control system. *IEEE Transactions on Software Engineering*, SE-1(4):364–370, Dec. 1975.
22. N. Sarnak, R. Bernstein, and V. Kruskal. Creation and maintenance of multiple versions. In Winkler [29], pages 264–275.
23. Software Maintenance and Development Systems. *Aide-de-Camp Product Overview*, 1990.
24. W. Tichy, editor. *Configuration Management*. John Wiley and Sons, New York, 1994.
25. W. F. Tichy. A data model for programming support environments. In *Proceedings of the IFIP WG 8.1 Working Conference on Automated Tools for Information System Design and Development*, pages 31–48, Jan. 1982.
26. W. F. Tichy. RCS – A system for version control. *Software–Practice and Experience*, 15(7):637–654, July 1985.
27. W. F. Tichy. Tools for software configuration management. In Winkler [29], pages 1–20.
28. J. F. H. Winkler. Version control in families of large programs. In *Proceedings of the 9th International Conference on Software Engineering*, pages 150–161, Monterey, CA, Mar. 1987.
29. J. F. H. Winkler, editor. *Proceedings of the International Workshop on Software Version and Configuration Control*, Stuttgart, Germany, 1988. German Chapter of the ACM, B.G. Teubner.
30. A. Zeller. A unified version model for configuration management. In *Proceedings of the ACM SIGSOFT '95 Symposium on the Foundations of Software Engineering*, pages 151–160, 1995.
31. A. Zeller and G. Snelting. Handling version sets through feature logic. In *Proceedings 5th European Software Engineering Conference*, LNCS 989, pages 191–204. Springer Verlag, 1995.

HiCoV: **Managing the Version Space**

Bjørn P. Munch

Telenor Research & Development, N-7005 Trondheim, Norway

Abstract. This paper presents HiCoV, high-level extensions to our Change Oriented Versioning model (CoV), which will reduce the inherent complexity of selecting versions based on this model. Thus, we hope to eliminate the largest obstacle to making CoV practically usable.

1 The Complexities of Version Selection

A central part of software configuration management (SCM) is the *selection* of a configuration. By configuration, we mean a complete and consistent set of software objects. Since most SCM systems can manage also different *versions* of the software objects (henceforth called *components*), the selection process actually consist of two parts:

- Selecting the correct software objects which will make up the configuration. This is related to the *product space*.
- Selecting appropriate versions of each component. This is related to the *version space*.

For a large configuration where each component (or at least many of them) exists in many versions, this selection is not trivial. There are usually a number of more or less well-defined restrictions to which component versions can be selected together as part of a consistent configuration.

Those restrictions may be represented in several ways:

- Explicit relationships between software objects, stating that a version of one component requires a certain version (or one within a range of versions) of another component. Simple systems based on e.g. RCS [12] may use this method.
- Hierarchical version representations: configuration and sub-configurations are versioned, and each version of a (sub)configuration is defined to include specific versions of its constituent parts. An example of this is CVS [2].
- Attribute based selection, where attribute values on the versions decide which get chosen. Attribute values on already selected versions, and rules associated with them, may also be used to restrict further choices. An example of this is Adele [1].

---

* This work was done at Department of Computer Systems and Telematics, Norwegian Institute of Technology.

– Intensional selection, where some logical expression defined over the whole database defines the version of the configuration, and which version to pick of each component can be deduced from this. An example of this is Aide-de-Camp [11].

Whichever way the configuration restrictions (CRs) are represented, the SCM system must give appropriate support to the developers. This includes:

– Manually specifying CRs.
– Automatically maintaining CRs, based on work units.
– Using CRs for guiding the user to a valid selection.
– Disallowing user selections which are in conflict with the CRs.
– Supporting queries over the CRs.

An overview of the state-of-the-art in selecting configurations of a versioned software product can be found in [3].

The rest of this paper is organized as follows: Section 2 briefly describes our versioning model CoV and explains the particular problems this model introduces. Section 3 then describes a set of version rules which are intended to alleviate some of the problems. We take this further into a description of planned support tools in Section 4. Section 5 describes some initial experience with CoV. We give a conclusion and indicates further work in Section 6.

2 Our Background: CoV

2.1 Definitions

Change Oriented Versioning (CoV) falls into the "intensional selection" category of representing restrictions. Versions are defined via global, logical variables called **options**. Each option corresponds to some property of the product. The user may create a new option whenever he adds a new property to the product or part of it.

Options will be identified by their name. Examples could be:

GUI : Set to TRUE for versions of programs which supply a graphical user interface. Can also be used for the documentation.
SunOS : Set to TRUE for program versions specially adapted for being run under the SunOS operating system.
OptSpeed : Set to TRUE for versions specifically optimized for speed.

In order to select a version of a configuration, the user will specify a version choice, in CoV simply called **choice**. This is a list of bindings of options to either TRUE or FALSE. The choice will define which version of every object is included in the configuration, and also which objects are part of it.

When a set of changes is applied to the versioned product, the user must set an **ambition** defining the scope of the changes. An ambition is also a set of option bindings (usually binding fewer options than the choice). This ambition limits which versions are being affected by the changes. Once the set of changes (which may touch a single component, or span the whole product) have been committed to storage, they will be included in any future version selection based on a choice which includes all the option bindings of the ambition.

For example, if the ambition GUI ∧ OptSpeed is used on a set of changes, those will later be included whenever the user specifies a choice binding both these options to TRUE, irrespective of which other bindings the choice includes.

In the above example, the user will introduce changes which are specific to this *combination* of two options, and which will only take effect when both are set to TRUE. Thus, one can make the combined version quite different from what is produced by the automatic merge. This will be completely transparent to the user.

For a more thorough description of CoV, see e.g. [7, 9].

2.2 Problems

While CoV completely solves the problem of deciding which component versions go together, the selection problem is far from being solved; it has simply been transformed into another dimension. Instead of having a selection problem in the *product* space, we now have a problem in the *version* space. We have to manage rules about what *options* go together, rather than what *objects*.

In other words, the selection process should not be based solely on option, but also on "meta" rules about how to combine the options, and an algorithm guiding the selection.

The *external* complexity has traditionally been the major criticism against CoV and similar systems, like those based on change sets. We also believe it is the greatest obstacle in the way of making CoV practically usable. The problems facing the CoV user can be classified into a number of sub-problems:

- What options are available, and what do they mean?
- Which options are relevant for this part of my product, and which ones can I ignore?
- What are the restriction on which options go together? Having selected an option:
  - Which other options are then not selectable?
  - Does that option depend on some other option also being selected?
- Which versions have passed through various stages of testing, QA etc., and can thus be used for a certain purpose?
- Which versions have been "frozen" and should not be modified in the future, e.g. because they have been delivered to customers?

2.3 Moving the Selection Problem

In comparison with traditional, "version-oriented" approaches, we can see from the above that we have moved the selection problem into the *version space*. Our problem is not to select the product given a version description, but to select the version description in the first place; the product then "falls out" automatically. The purpose of HiCoV is to ease the first phase of the configuration selection process for the user.

In the rest of the paper, we will look at various techniques to reduce the selection problem in this version space

3 Adding Version Rules

The rules described in this section are similar to the high level version descriptions that were introduced in [6]. Examples will be jointly presented in Section 3.7.

In addition to all the version rules, all options which are not bound through any other mechanism in a version choice, are interpreted as though bound to FALSE. This ensures that a choice is complete and identifies a unique version.

3.1 Option Constraints

Not all option combinations make sense. Some options may be mutually exclusive, some may depend on others, and these constraints restrict how options can be combined. Typical examples of the former include options for different hardware or different language in user interface text. An example of the latter can be options for deciding layout of a graphical user interface, which make no sense unless GUI is selected in the first place.

We will require option constraints to be *fixed*, i.e. once a constraint has been added it cannot be revoked. This is necessary to maintain order in the version space, and also because the fixed nature makes it possible to exploit option constraints for internal optimization in the CoV kernel.

Mutual Exclusion. Mutual exclusion means that at most one of a set of options may be bound to TRUE. We cannot model this by relationships directly between the involved options. That will be inconvenient when we have many options, and also makes it impossible to model an option which is member of more than one mutually exclusive set.

Instead, we introduce a concept of **option set**. An option set represents a set of (at least two) mutually exclusive options; no more than one of the options in a set may be bound to TRUE in any ambition or choice. An option may be the member of any number of sets. The members of an option set are not fixed; the set may expand over time by more options being incorporated.

An option set would presumably be created (manually) together with the first member option(s). The semantic meanings of the options would guide the decision; it is not something that HiCoV can deduce.

Option Dependency. Dependency of one option on another means that the option cannot be bound explicitly to either TRUE or FALSE in an ambition or choice unless another option is bound to TRUE. This is naturally a relationship between the two options, and from this one can construct a dependency graph.

We should point out that an option dependency is not simply a matter of stating "this feature requires that feature", but rather *"this feature does not even make sense to talk about, unless we have that other feature first"*.

Since this dependency is not a standard logical implication, we need some other syntax to describe it. One possibility is shown below, indicating that fix3_unix depends on UNIX:

$$Dep: \quad fix3\_unix \hookrightarrow UNIX \tag{1}$$

We will also allow an option to be dependent on an option set (as defined above). Such a dependency means the option requires one of those in the option set to be bound to TRUE. More informally, "this feature also requires *one* of these other features to be selected". A possible use is e.g. to force the user to select among interface languages.

Sub-Options. Another typical dependency can be:

$$Dep: \quad SunOS \hookrightarrow UNIX \tag{2}$$

This example is actually a case of what we call *sub-options*, since SunOS can be thought of as one of several possible specializations of UNIX. All sub-options of UNIX will naturally form an option set, since we can only choose one of them.

If an option set is created with the same name as an already existing option, the set (and hence indirectly all its members) is automatically made dependent on the option. The members of this option set will be called "sub-options". Note that the dependency does not go the other way: you don't have to select any of the sub-options after having selected UNIX.

3.2 Product Specific Options

Just as some option combinations do not make sense, not all option/product combinations are useful either. For example, it would not matter what the option GUI is bound to when you are making changes to a database kernel. On the other hand, some options may apply to the kernel only, such as alternative B-tree algorithms.

By making some options local to a specific (sub-)product, we can achieve two things:

- The user will not have to consider all options for other (sub-)products than the one he is working with.
- We do not have to worry about whether the combination of two local options for non-overlapping sub-products are compatible. Since their changes cannot touch the same components, they will not be in conflict.

The product local option is only allowed to be bound if the configuration includes parts of the product to which the option belongs. Thus, the decision about using the option is *not* a pure CoV decision but has to be done by a tool which also knows the product structure.

Note that the option is still globally applicable, thus not breaking with the basic philosophy of CoV. The product locality only restricts the scope within which is is visible, and thus selectable, by the user. This also implies that a local option may be given a larger scope later, if the user finds out is has a more global perspective than originally assumed.

3.3 Aggregates

It is a quite common situation that a developer or team performs a number of sequential bug-fixes or correction to a product. This will often happen e.g. after the first version of a new or enhanced product has entered testing.

In these situations, there will often be little need for picking only some of those corrections in a choice. One would normally select none (to get the original, non-corrected version) or all (to get a version with as few errors left as possible). Instead of having to name each of the bugfix options, we can make things simpler by introducing the concept of **aggregate options**.

An aggregate option is simply a single entity representing a number of options; it is not a real option in itself. The user can select it as he selects a normal option. When the aggregate is chosen, the system will expand it and actually set all the part options to TRUE. It is thus a short-cut for a list of options, and does not preclude the possibility to select only some of them individually.

3.4 Validities

A validity is, simply stated, a disjunction ("OR") of not necessarily complete version choices (see 2.1 for the definition of version choice):

$$Val = VC_1 \lor VC_2 \lor \ldots \lor VC_i \tag{3}$$

These choices, or *validity terms* are built up like choices and ambitions: each is a conjunction ("AND") of option bindings, as was described in Section 2.1.

A validity indicates that the included versions have some common property. It is generally up to the user or application to interpret the semantics of these properties, and to decide when to add new terms to them. HiCoV provides support for maintaining the validities.

A typical use is to assign some form of status value to different versions depending on how "good" they are conceived to be. Examples could include "compiled", "module tested", "integration tested", "accepted" etc. There will be one validity for each such value.

Note that we are here talking about **global** properties of the versions, that will be used to guide choice selection. If status values on (versions of) particular objects are desired, attributes or other data values individual to each object can of course be used in addition.

The validities do not take part in the versioning itself, so all the existing rules and algorithms for handling choices and ambitions remain the same. Validities will not cause any overhead in normal use. What they *will* affect, is the user's selection of ambitions and version choices.

Stability. The *stability* is built up just like other validities, but it is used in another way. As the name suggests, all versions covered by the stability are *stable*, or immutable. We want to prevent any update to them. A simple way to achieve that goal, is to prevent the user from ever working with an ambition that overlaps with the stability. Another important distinction is that this restriction will *always* take place "behind the scenes" with no need for user interaction.

In general terms, we can say that the normal validities are meant to limit which versions we can *read*, while the purpose of the stability is, within the same formalism, to limit what version we can *write* to.

The checking of ambition/choice against stability/validity is done by the **evaluator**, which logically is an integral part of the CoV service. It cannot be a stand-alone tool, since we must ensure that the stability is *always* enforced.

3.5 Overview of Option Relationships

Figure 1 shows an example of some options and the logical relationships between them. Note that only the dependency relationships are actually represented this way; the mutex and sub-option relationships are internally represented in other ways[2].

This (global) option graph is in some ways similar to the (local) version graphs of Tichy [Tic88]. The dependency relation corresponds to **revision_of**, while the mutex corresponds to **variant_of**.

Of course, our option "graph" is not a version graph, as there are many more possible versions than options. And the existence of independent and freely combinable options have no equivalent in Tichy's version graph model, nor do the aggregates.

The figure is shown here to illustrate a point; it does not necessarily reflect how a similar graph might be shown buy a visualization tool. See [5] for a description of such a tool.

3.6 Preferences

Preferences were described in [6] as a means for the user to indicate desirability of having certain options bindings included in the choice, without insisting. These would be used by the heuristics to select among different alternatives, or for overriding the defaults.

---

[2] For a discussion of some of the representation issues, see [8].

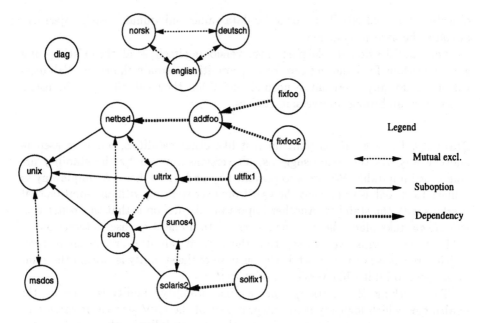

Fig. 1. Example of relationships between options.

We have chosen not to support preferences at this time. We feel that the described set of rules are already quite challenging to implement and support, and preferences possibly the most complicated of all. We are also rather unsure about how these would be used in practice; some experience with the rest of the HiCoV rules may give us a better understanding.

3.7 Examples of Use

The rules described in this section serve two purposes, namely to restrict what choices are legal *and* to automate some of the selection process. In order to better illustrate the usefulness of these rules, we will construct a simple example and show how the user is helped by them in setting his ambition/choice.

Option Constraints. In the following description[3], **mutex <setname>:** means the following options are mutually exclusive, **dep:** means the first option depends on the second, **subopt <name>:** and **aggr <name>:** means the following options are sub-options, resp. aggregate members.

```
mutex opsys: unix msdos os2
subopt unix: aix ultrix sunos
subopt sunos: sunos4 solaris
mutex language: english deutsch norsk
```

---

[3] This is not any actual syntax; it's just been made for this example

```
dep: menus gui
dep: scrollbar gui
dep: help language
dep: helpmenu help menus
dep: msdos intel
aggr scrollfix: bug12 bug14 bug19
dep: #scrollfix scrollbar
```

Given the above version rules, here are some examples of how user specified version choice will be expanded[4] (! is a negated option, # names an aggregate):

Explicit	After Expansion
help msdos	help english[5] !deutsch !norsk intel !unix !os2
helpmenu solaris	helpmenu help norsk menus gui sunos unix
	!english !deutsch !sunos4
bug19 os2	bug19 scrollbar gui os2 !unix !msdos
#scrollfix deutsch aix	bug12 bug14 bug19 scrollbar gui deutsch !english
	!norsk unix !ultrix !sunos !msdos !os2
unix !gui	unix !msdos !os2 !menus !helpmenu !scrollbar
	!bug12 !bug14 !bug19
aix english norsk	ILLEGAL
ultrix bug14 !gui	ILLEGAL
!intel help	!intel !msdos help deutsch

Note that the explicit choice on the left is also the one that will be presented as the "offical" choice when the user asks to see it. Just as he will not have to enter all the extra binding, he should not have to be bothered with them later as part of his work specification. The effective full choice can of course also be asked for explicitly.

Validities. Let us assume that we have the following validities:

```
stability: (os2 english !gui !help) v
           (sunos4 norsk !gui !help) v
           (sunos4 norsk gui help !helpmenu)
tested:    (os2 english !gui) v
           (os2 english gui !menus !scrollbar !help) v
           (os2 deutsch !gui !help) v
           (unix norsk !gui !help) v
           (sunos norsk !gui) v
           (sunos4 norsk gui !scrollbar)
```

Ambitions have to be restricted so that they do *not* overlap the stability. Some examples of ambitions and additional option binding that the system may add[6]:

---

[4] More precisely, how they would have had to be specified without version rules.

[5] The user is forced to choose a language; may be another one.

[6] Note that this is non-deterministic; there may be more than one possibility

```
os2 !gui                      # !english
os2 english                   # help
os2 english !gui !help intel # ILLEGAL
os2 deutsch                   # OK (!english is implicit)
ultrix menus                  # OK
sunos4 norsk gui              # !help
```

Choices have to be restricted so they overlap completely with the validity the user want to comply with. If he has requested **tested**:

```
os2 gui !help      # deutsch
os2 !gui help      # english
os2 gui help       # ILLEGAL
solaris norsk help # !gui (sunos is implicit)
sunos norsk gui    # sunos4 !scrollbar
aix help           # ILLEGAL
msdos              # ILLEGAL
```

4   The HiCoV Tools

COVST and VRMAN, the two tools described here, will become an integrated part of our environment. They will be implemented on top of our graphical environment CHAT, which in turn is based on ECM which was mentioned in Section 5.1. We will first make a textual-interface prototype of both in order to get experience with the basic functionality. This work is now in progress.

4.1   VRMAN: Version Rule Manager

The main task of VRMAN is to give the user an interface for creating and manipulating the version rules. Since most of the operations supported by VRMAN are rather trivial, we will not go into detail about them in this paper, but only mention a few non-trivial ones.

Creating a new Option. The central part of this operation is for the user to provide a name (we will not give any help in choosing names), which will be checked for uniqueness, and a descriptive text.

Calls to this part of the VRMAN tool may come from COVST. In that case, it will already be established into what relationships the new option belongs. In other cases, the user will be prompted for the relevant relationships.

In order to help the user find options and option sets, rather than having to remember the names, an **option space browser** will be provided. This should work similarly to the COVST menu system, except that there is no concept of selecting or un-selecting items.

Manipulating Validities. To *create* a new validity is trivial: just supply a name and a description. By default, validities start out empty (meaning FALSE).

When adding a term to a validity (except for the stability, which we will manage separately), it will usually be, in fact it should in principle *always* be, the current choice of a transaction in which we have checked that the version in question indeed has the property defined by the validity. Thus, VRMAN supplies an operation which just adds the current choice to a named validity and makes no more fuss about it.

Adding a term to the stability is another matter. Here we may start off with the current, or last, ambition and let the user modify this if possible. He will also be prompted with a list of options he might want to add negated to the term in order not to block off the possibilities of further development too much.

4.2   COVST: the version Selection Tool

The main purpose of COVST is to help the user select ambition and choice for his work. This will be done through a menu-based interface, which lets the user see what options are currently available for selection. COVST will also relieve him from the error-prone task of typing in the option names manually, as it has to be done now.

We use the term **selection** to refer to the ambition or choice which is in the process of being specified by the COVST user. We assume that the user already knows (this will be the task of other parts of the EPOS environment) which product he is going to work on, i.e. the software object representing the root of his product hierarchy.

Selection Menus. Selection of options is based on a hierarchical selection menu which at any time lists all **items** ready for selection. These items can be independent options, options on which others depend, options sets or aggregates.

The different kinds of items are marked with different fonts, colors or additional symbols; see Figure 2 for an example. Note that an option set may be an option with sub-options; this fact will of course also be noted.

If an independent option is selected, it is simply removed. If another item is selected, a **sub-menu** appears in which the user may select one or (except in the case of option sets) more other items. This operation may recurse, if the sub-menu contains non-simple options.

If the rest of the items on the sub-menu are put back on the parent menu, they will be indented to to indicate the fact that they are not "top level" items, or they may be "hidden" inside the parent item, which must be marked as "opened". An option having sub-options is also marked as "opened" if it has itself been selected, but none of the sub-options have been.

Any item may be **unselected** at any time, in which case it is deleted from the menu and any selection already done "inside" it (see below) are deleted as well. The exception to this is the ambition, which is frozen when we are selecting the choice.

The user can at any time request information such as the textual description, for any item on the selection menu.

COVST does not care about validities, only option constraints, and so its operation is the same for selecting ambition as for selecting choice. The natural way to proceed, is to first select the ambition, then freeze that selection and proceed to bind more options for the choice. The latter may be repeated if the user wants to change his current choice. A similar operation will be done when setting the ambition for a sub-transaction (sub-WS); the settings of the parent are fixed.

Menu Example. Figure 2 shows how the menu might look like at a few stages during the selection process, based on the options and rules form the example in Section 3.7. On the left is the menu at start-up, with only the "top-level" options available. In the middle is a fully expanded sub-menu structure, with no selections yet made. On the right, the options **sunos** and **menus** have been selected, **help** and **intel** unselected, and the **language** sub-menu closed.

Checking against Validities and Stability. Before starting the actual selection process, the user will be allowed to specify which (if any) validities to evaluate the choice against. Before "submitting" the version selection, COVST calls the evaluator to check whether the selection is legal related to the stability or validity, and if it is, what additional option bindings, if any, have to be added.

If the selection is restricted by additional option bindings, the user will then be prompted with the result and asked if it's OK. If it is, the transaction (workspace) will be started. If not, we may be able to provide alternatives.

The ambition and choice which will be registered as the one we used, and which may in turn be the basis for a future selection, are the ones explicitly requested by the user, *before* validities and stability were taken into account.

Re-using Previous Version Selections. COVST should remember the last selection the user made, since he is quite likely to want the same or something quite close to it for the next job. At start-up, he will be allowed to pick this directly, or to enter the selection tool with the last selection pre-made so he can make a few changes to it.

The user may also define his "base ambition" and "base choice" containing the most used options. By default, COVST will then startup with this selections pre-made.

In this base selection the user may refer to an aggregate option as such, so that the base choice will include all the part options of the aggregate at any given time, not just the ones that existed when the base choice was defined.

Product Dependent Options. At start-up, COVST will ask the user to specify the product root of his coming workspace (or may get that information from

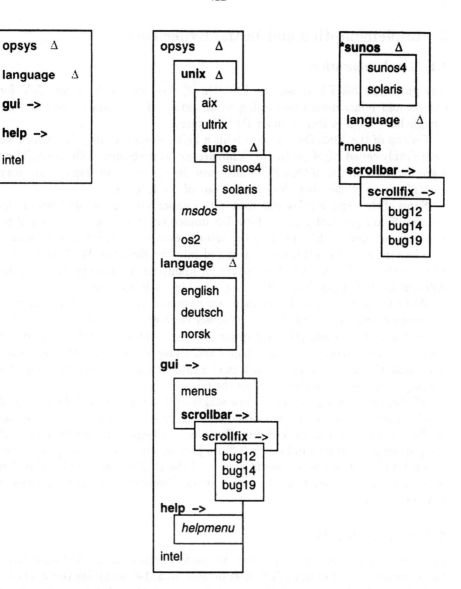

Fig. 2. Examples of a COVST menu during selection.

the work environment). Based on this, COVST can eliminate all options local to any product or sub-product outside this workspace root.

Note that when starting a workspace with product root R, an option O depending on product P can be:

- Used in the *ambition* only if if R is P or a sub-product of P.
- Used in the *choice* also if P is a sub-product of R.

5 Implementation and Initial Experience

5.1 Implementation

Our prototype SE Database, the EPOSDB [8] implements the basic CoV for objects and relationships (according to an extended ER data model) and for "longfields", i.e. files stored under DBMS control.

On top of the EPOSDB, we have built a higher-level user interface which we have simply called ECM (= EPOS Configuration Management). We are building a graphical UI on top of this. ECM also manages the user's workspace directory and takes care of checking files into and out of the EPOSDB.

Some of the version rules described in this paper have previously been implemented [6] independently of the EPOSDB implementation. Much of this will be reused in our new tools, especially the validity evaluation which is non-trivial.

The version rules will have to be stored into the EPOSDB. We have written additions to the Prolog (ECM) interface for manipulating and operating all the different kinds of rules. The HICoV tools will be built upon these.

After ECM became stable enough, we have started to use it for managing some own development, which was previously done with RCS. That includes this paper, where some parts (the description of version rules and tools) exist in two main versions: a short one for this paper and a longer one for an internal design document. Common changes to both can be applied with a ambition not binding the **paper** option which distinguishes the two.

We begun by using ECM for some stages of development and debugging of itself. Apart from some initial chicken-and-egg problems of this particular use of the system, it it has worked fine. However, we began running into some of the problems mentioned in Section 2.2. As part of our development process, we wrote down a list of how we *would* have used the HICoV functionality if it had been available, and even from this rather small example we can see that it would have helped us.

5.2 CoV in Real Use

ECM consists of about 20 components. We performed six changes and introduced the same number of options. The first option "`usable`" identifies the upgrades needed to make the system stable enough that we could use it for installing itself and running the first change job. Four of the other options depend on this, while the sixth is independent.

Those four options all identify bug fixes, so it was natural to want to select all in the choice when doing later updates. Each one is also specific to one of the two sub-products of ECM.

Finally, ECM seems fairly stable after we did these fixes, so we would like to define the version choice including all as a validity. Thus, we can later check out according to this validity to retrieve a version to use, without getting not-yet-tested further developments.

If all the above had been modeled using HICoV, the developer would have avoided these problems (which were real problems that actually occurred):

- Remembering and correctly typing in the option names; these had to be looked up elsewhere.
- Forgetting to add **usable** to the ambition when doing the changes that depended on it. With HiCoV, this would automatically be added to the choice and may in fact be optimized away from the ambition.
- While doing a bug fix to one of the sub-product, identified by a supposedly product-local option, a small error was discovered and fixed in the other sub-product. This was possible because the whole ECM had been specified as the product. The extra fix had to be redone later with an appropriate ambition. HiCoV would have prevented this from happening by not allowing this combination of option and product root.
- Forgetting to add all previous bugfix options to the choice. The result was that a buggy version was checked out, and testing of the new bugfix could not be done properly. Again, HiCoV would have helped us by use of the aggregate mechanism.

As the number of options increase, and we start introducing variability and the need for stability, we expect it to become increasingly difficult to enter the full ambitions and choices manually and correctly.

6 Conclusion and Further Work

6.1 The benefits of HiCoV

Though our experience so far is rather limited, we have already seen ourselves that we run into problems that HiCoV could have solved for us. We would of course have to specify the version rules (in our case, option dependencies and aggregates). This could be just a few extra parameters to the "create option" command. It would have been much less work than having to redo some changes because we had checked out a buggy version and thus could not test the system; this happened to us on one occasion.

From the examples in section 3.7 we see that HiCoV will be able to reduce considerably the number of options the user have to explicitly specify.

We can conclude that HiCoV will give a number of benefits to the CoV user:

- Navigation through the set of available options.
- Much fewer options (ideally only those the user are really interested in) have to be specified.
- Illegal or nonsensical combinations are prevented.
- Aggregates help the user getting "all those changes" without having to list them all.
- Stability will prevent accidental changes to versions which were supposedly fixed.

In addition, knowledge about option constraints may be utilized for internal optimization of CoV, further reducing the *internal* complexity[7].

---

[7] Discussion of this is outside the scope of this paper.

The only disadvantage we can see, is the added work for the user in establishing the version rules in the first place. In most cases, the corresponding rules will be known by the user who creates a new option, so it should not be much added burden. This is especially true if we allow an option to be created from within a sub-menu in COVST; then the appropriate rules are given by the context.

6.2 Future Work

Our future work in this field consists of these main parts:

- An initial test system, where the rules are not stored in the database, and not managed by any HiCoV tools. The rules will be manually edited as Prolog statements in an external file, and evaluated outside the database. This can be done quite quickly, and may give us some further insight before we start the "real" implementation.
- Implementing the HiCoV as specified is of course our main task. This consists of two main parts: the support functions in the EposDb which actually enforce the rules, and the user interface tools described here.
- Continued use of CoV for our own development, including a planned major upgrade of the EposDb.
- Evaluating previous history of the EposDb source code, documentation etc. to see how CoV and HiCoV could have been used.
- We hope also to be able to acquire some change history of real products from industry. This may be even better input that our own code, which is mostly just sequential revisions of one canonical variant.

We feel confident that the HiCoV extensions will make CoV much easier to use, both for ourselves and in the future hopefully also for other users. We look forward to getting more hand-on experience with CoV with help of these tools.

References

1. Noureddine Belkhatir, Jacky Estublier, and Walcelio Melo. Software Process Model and Work Space Control in the Adele System. In *[10]*, pages 2–11, 1993.
2. Brian Berliner. CVS II: Parallelizing software development. In *Proceedings of USENIX Winter 1990, Washington, D.C.*, 1990.
3. Reidar Conradi and Bernhard Westfechtel. Configuring versioned software products. March 1996. To be published.
4. Stuart I. Feldman, editor. *Proceedings of the Fourth International Workshop on Software Configuration Management (SCM-4)*, Baltimore, Maryland, May 21–22, 1993.
5. Bjørn Gulla. The constraint diagram: an approach to visualizing the version space. In *[4]*, pages 112–122, 1993.
6. Bjørn Gulla, Even-André Karlsson, and Dashing Yeh. Change-Oriented Version Descriptions in EPOS. *Software Engineering Journal*, 6(6):378–386, November 1991.

7. Anund Lie. Versioning in Software Engineering Databases. Technical Report 1/90, EPOS TR 95, ISBN 82-7119-155-1, DCST, NTH, Trondheim, Norway, January 1990. 166 p. (PhD thesis NTH 1990:2).

8. Bjørn P. Munch. *Versioning in a Software Engineering Database — the Change Oriented Way.* PhD thesis, DCST, NTH, Trondheim, Norway, August 1993. 265 p. (PhD thesis NTH 1993:78).

9. Bjørn P. Munch, Jens-Otto Larsen, Bjørn Gulla, Reidar Conradi, and Even-André Karlsson. Uniform Versioning: The Change-Oriented Model. In *[4]*, pages 188–196, 1993.

10. Leon Osterweil, editor. *Proc. 2nd Int'l Conference on Software Process (ICSP'2), Berlin. 170 p.* IEEE-CS Press, March 1993.

11. Software Maintenance & Development Systems, Incorporated, Concord Massachusetts. *Aide-de-Camp, Product Overview*, 7.2 edition, 1990.

12. Walter F. Tichy. RCS — A System for Version Control. *Software — Practice and Experience*, 15(7):637–654, 1985.

Work Space Management in Software Engineering Environments

Jacky Estublier

L.S.R.. BP 53 38041 Grenoble Cedex 9
FRANCE. jacky@imag.fr

Abstract. A Software Engineering Environment (SEE) must satisfy a number of difficult requirements. Among others there is a need for (1) maintaining numerous complex artifacts, thus involving databases with high modelling power, (2) supporting the day-to-day work of engineers thus necessitating the support of so called Work Spaces, and (3) supporting cooperation among team members. Each one of these aspects is still a research topic in its own right.

A number of research communities: Software Configuration Management, Distributed AI, Operating Systems, Databases, and Process Technology feel concerned by only a sub set of these aspects, while what we need is a consistent approach which covers all facets simultaneously.

A WS manager must support the synchronization of objects when shared by concurrent WSs: this is a collaboration policy problem and it links Process Support field with the one of Software Engineering. In this paper we concentrate on how collaboration is handled in the Adele Work Space manager.

The claim here is that the WS concept provides a bridge between different areas. It unifies in a consistent way aspects which were previously disparate, taking the best from the different domains involved, instead of trying to build a complete solution by simply extending a single technology within a single domain.

1 Introduction

Software Engineering Environments (SEEs) have to satisfy numerous conflicting requirements. Among others we have identified the following.

1.1 Supporting the artifacts: a Database

In a modern SEE, numerous resources and software artifacts are managed. The modelling and management of these artifacts and their versions need a powerful object manager for which almost any concept, any kind of abstract and/or complex object, any version model, any software definition, team structure, as well as history dimension can (at least in theory) be defined. This a Database (DB) problem. What kind of database is needed for SEE is still a research topic, but clearly it is needed powerful high modelling services based on high level functionalities. This paper does not address this topic directly.

1.2 Supporting the Engineering Work: Work Spaces

SEE is specific in that most artifacts are electronic objects (i.e. represented in one way or another by a file), and in that numerous tools are available to deal with these files. The work is performed essentially by humans, applying tools to artifacts, creating artifacts, etc. Supporting SE work means the environment must be able to:

- **Identify** the data to be worked with (all the artifacts required and only these).
- **Provide** the data where it is needed (server, station, LAN, WAN),
- **Represent** the data in the form required by tools and humans (file, others).

A Work Space manager is intended to solve these problems by providing engineers with the data and tools they need, in the form they need it, in their preferred form and desired location (computer). Most current SEEs rephrase it as follows: provide a well defined part of the software product, somewhere in a file system, while protecting the other files from unintended or malicious use.

1.3 Supporting the Project: Cooperative Work and Process support.

Until recently, parallel work was prohibited because of its complex management aspects, the high risk of introducing inconsistencies and to work duplication. Parallel work means work on shared artifacts that is not sequential, also called concurrent engineering.

As software projects get bigger and bigger, development teams become larger and larger, and the pressure to reduce the time to market higher and higher. Therefore it was obvious parallel work could not be banned any longer; it has become unavoidable. The increasing capabilities for controlling the processes by which software products are produced and maintained means that parallel work comes to be recommended.

Thus a very strong requirement for a modern SEE is its ability to support parallel work:

- Engineers must be able to work in **isolation** (point 1 and 2 below),
- WSs must **share** artifacts (point 3),
- WSs must **collaborate** i.e. synchronize the changes on shared artifacts (point 4):

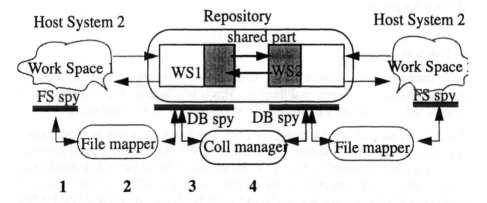

The 4 main aspects we identified are: (1) the file control, (2) the mapping between files and a repository, (3) the organisation of the repository, and (4) the collaboration between WSs.

Currently, depending on the area of concern, only one aspect of WS management is taken into account. SEE [Mil89] and SCM [Leb94] tools focus essentially on a File System representation Tic85 (point 1), but offer weak data-modelling capabilities (point 2), and no or hard-wired collaboration policies (point 4).

In Computer Supported Cooperative Work (CSCW) [Ell92], the focus is on information sharing (point 4). Multiple representation is not addressed, and data modelling is often low level. Usually there are no explicit collaboration policies, a single one is imposed, or the sharing protocol is left to applications.

In databases, the focus is on modelling power (point 3); consistency is enforced prohibiting activities (transactions) to modify objects concurrently. Until recently a unique representation (the DB one) was allowed, whilst some prototype sought to provide a FS representation [GJR94, ACM93, MW94]. But no WS is provided. We think the attempts for breaking the transaction limitations, providing exotic transaction mechanisms [DBAV94, Kai90] are doomed to failure since the DB is not aware of collaboration policies [BK91].

In Process Support, cooperative work is a hot topic (point 4) [Fer92, BGR+94, JPSW94, CHL94, God93]. The need for dynamic data exchange, sophisticated and negotiated protocols has been identified, but there is no satisfactory solution yet and the representation problem is not been addressed.

This research seeks to unify these different aspects, whilst proposing highly efficient, usable and evolutive solutions. Our proposal is based on an SEE database, providing high modelling power with sub-DBs for the support of reference space (point 3); a file mapper for translating a RS to the convenient location and format (currently limited to the Unix FS) (Point 1 and 2), and a collaboration manager for the definition and automation of advanced collaboration policies (point 4).

2 The Approach

2.1 Isolation

While complete sharing is often "easily" implemented, complete isolation, in long-term persistent WSs, raises numerous difficulties. This is why isolation is provided, in most systems, only as a full copy of files in a file system (point 1 is provided only).

Work Spaces are isolated if a change in a WS is only visible in that WS. We implemented this feature using dynamic versioning [EC95]. Each time a shared object is changed in a WS, in a significant way[1], a new version of that object is *dynamically* and *transparently* created[2] and replaces the previous one in that WS. In particular, objects created in a WS are only created locally, and, if not synchronized, will be deleted at WS completion. Conversely, an object deleted in a WS is only removed from the WS, and not really deleted.

Transparency implies all dynamic versions of the same object must have same identity.

The different dynamic versions are resynchronized (i.e. merged), at a later time, depending on the collaboration policies. The merge semantics also depend on the collaboration policy[1] and object type.

The *shared* policy is one extreme, wherein any change is significant, and resynchronization is carried out immediately[2]. Complete isolation is the other extreme, where any change is significant, and resynchronization is done at WS completion only (if completion is allowed at all!).

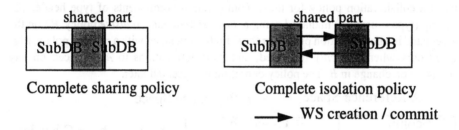

Complete sharing policy   Complete isolation policy

⟶ WS creation / commit

2.2 Collaboration policies

We will exemplify WS collaboration policies using a simple but nevertheless realistic situation. WSs A and B are sharing a configuration C (comprising numerous header and body files), and may contain other objects, not discussed here. Let us denote $A(C)$, the configuration C as in WS A, and $C->comp$ components X of configuration C ($C->comp$ is the set of objects reached following relationship *comp*, starting from C). Finally $X.a$ refers to attribute a of object X.

Each object is in fact a (logical) pair of objects, one in WS A, and the other in WS B [3]. A collaboration policy must be defined for such each pair. The collaboration policy defines how and when a change in one element of the pair is propagated to the other. A

---

1. "significant" is defined by the type of collaboration policy. By default only change in the file content is significant; but any attribute, relationship, or composition change can also be significant.
2. The exact content of the dynamic copy depends on the type of collaboration policy.
1. The default merge is the interactive and graphical Adele merger, classically based on the common ancestor comparison, but specific mergers can be defined and used instead. In particular attribute and relationship merges must be explicitly defined.
2. For obvious reasons of efficiency, default *sharing* policy is implemented as a physical sharing, not as the creation of a dynamic version immediately resynchronized and deleted.

collaboration policy is defined for each group (or sub group) of object using the same collaboration policy.

A collaboration policy is defined by

Policy_name = { set_of_objects } ;{ policy (when) }

where *set_of_objects* is an Adele query returning a set of objects [EC95]; *policy* is a collaboration policy identifier, and *when*, optionally expresses on which condition the collaboration policy is to be triggered.

For example[1]:

P1 = C->comp(type = header); local_shared(WS.state = valid), exclusive;
P2 = C->comp(type = body); resynch (explicit), notify (comp_change = true);

P1 is a collaboration policy for the C configuration components of type header (C->comp (type = header)) managed using a *local_shared* and *exclusive* policy. P2 on the other hand is a collaboration policy for the C bodies managed with a *resynch* policy, triggered only when *explicitly* requested, and with notifications to A produced on any composition change in B. The policy definition is presented later.

A Reference Space   B Reference Space

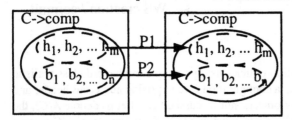

$h_1, h_2, ... h_m$ = C headers

$b_1, b_2, ... b_n$ = C bodies.

A collaboration policy is NOT symmetric. For example A can be a *development* WS, and B an *official* WS. WS A may want to incorporate all changes realized in WS B as soon as possible, but not conversely. A symmetric policy is simply a pair of policies of the same type, one in each direction.

2.3 Composite Object Management

Previous policy definition can only synchronize pairs of atomic objects. It is also fundamental to synchronize the composition changes of so-called composite or complex objects. Suppose that, in WS B, a header h_i is split into two files h_{i1} and h_{i2}, and then h_1 is removed. How this change is to be synchronized into WS A?.

---

3. The default *private* policy is copy_on_write; i.e as long as the object is unchanged, both WSs are really sharing the same object; but they can still be consided as 2 objects with same value; from users point of view it is equivalent, since the isolation mechanism maintains the same identity for all dynamic versions.

1. The syntax presented is the abstract syntax as used in the graphical interface currently under design. The textual syntax will presented in more detail later.

A WS being isolated, an object created in a WS is, by default, temporary and local to that WS, i.e. it is not visible from anywhere else and it will be deleted upon WS completion. Any change, including composition change, triggers the collaboration policy, which can then add/delete the new object in the slave WS.

In our example, the *local_shared* policy is defined such that existing objects are physically shared, while inserted/created/deleted objects are local changes, until requested. In our example these composition changes will be propagated into WS A when the *state* of WS B will be *valid*. The *shared* policy makes any change, including creation/deletion immediately visible in both WSs.

The P2 policy only notifies (*notify* policy, by email and warning) when event comp_notify is true, i.e when C composition changes; the corresponding composition propagation will be carried out only when explicitly requested (command "resynch C - update -delete").

Explicit synchronization is performed by the *resynch* command, but its precise behaviour depends on the collaboration policy definition.

2.4 Creating and Committing Work Spaces.

The complete DB is the original WS, called Root_WS, which is the ancestor of any other WS.

In order to be as reusable as possible, a WS type does not make any assumption with respect to the context in which its instances will be used. Instead, each WS "knows" how to create, synchronize and make its own sub WSs collaborate.

A WS is created by the command "mkws WSname -t WStype -ct {content} -u U...."; in our example, the A WS can be created executing

    mkws A -t TA -ct C,.... -u U

with *TA* the type of WS A, and U, the user that will work in the A WS, and C the name of the configuration. Suppose this command is executed from WS called D. Command *mkws* creates the Database WS for the new WS A, initialises its content with D(C), i.e. a logical copy of those versions visible from the WS D (by default), the explicitly referred to WS otherwise.

If *TA* is a File System WS, the same command also builds up the corresponding FS WS, under identity U, on the usual U computer location on the network. To do this, the WS manager executing the *mkws* command, sends a BMS message to the WS manager running for user U, giving the new A DataBase WS as parameter. The U WS manager can thus create the A FS WS for user U even on a computer and in an FS invisible and inaccessible to the person who created the WS.

For the sake of our example, suppose WS D, of type *TD*, is in charge of creating and controlling an arbitrary number of WSs of type *TA* and *TB*. The way in which *TA* and

TB WSs collaborate must be defined in *TD*, but also how *TA* and *D*, and *TB* and *D* collaborate, i.e. their collaboration policy. This is illustrated by the following figure.

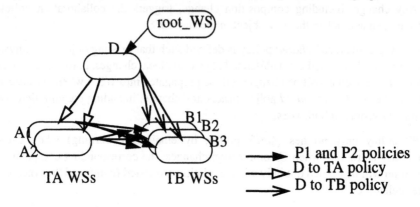

A WS definition contains 2 parts: one is executed when an instance is created (after "ON created_ws"), the other when creating another WS (after "ON creating_ws"). WS type *TD*, for example can be defined as follows:

```
TYPEOBJECT TD IS Work_Space ;
1 FSWS := true ;                        -- Indicates a FS WS is needed.
2 PRE ON creating_ws (newWS) DO
3     IF newWS.type = TA THEN
4               synchronize (SELF, newWS , C, local, "cmd = promote") ;
5               synchronize (SELF, newWS , C, private) ;
6               synchronize (newWS, SELF->sonWS(type = TB), C->comp (type = header),
                    local_shared, "newWS.status = valid") ;
7               synchronize(newWS, SELF->sonWS(type = TB), C->comp (type = header),
                    exclusive) ;
8               synchronize(newWS, SELF->sonWS(type = TB), C->comp (type = body),
                    notify, "comp_change = true") ;
9               synchronize(newWS, SELF->sonWS(type = TB), C->comp (type = body),
                    resynch) ;
      IF newWS.type = TB THEN ....        -- Defining how TB WSs are synchronized.

   PRE ON created_ws ( .... ) DO -- Initialising D content
   .......
END TD ;

TYPEOBJECT  TA IS Work_Space ;
   FSWS := true ;                        -- Indicates a FS WS is needed.
   PRE ON creating_ws (newWS) DO
   -- How to coordine sub WSs (if any) .
10 PRE ON created_ws (C, MR) DO
11   create_object (C) ;
12   create_object .... ;
END TA ;
```

Line 1 indicates that *TD* WSs need a File System representation; line 2 is a trigger which is fired when a WS, *newWS*, is created by a *TD* WS, called *SELF* in the following block. Lines 3 to 8 are executed if the new WS is of type *TA*.

The function "synchronize (origin_WS, slave_WS, Object, policy, condition)" instanti-ates the *policy* collaboration when *Object* is shared between *slave_WS* and *origin_WS*. The policy is triggered when the *condition* becomes true, explicitly if omitted.

Lines 4 and 5 instantiate a *local* and *private* collaboration policy for C between the creating and created WS; condition *cmd = promote* means the composition changes are propagated only when command *promote* is executed by a user i.e. it is an explicit synchronization. Lines 4 and 5 define the collaboration policy. *Local* means that changes performed on C in the created WS are to be propagated into the creating WS at completion and/or when the command *promote* is executed; *private* means the new WS is isolated from its creator.

Lines 6 and 7 instantiate the collaboration policies called P1 and lines 8 and 9 the collab-oration called P2 in 4.2. SELF->sonWS(type = TB) refers to all WSs of type TB, son of the current WS, thus P1 and P2 are instantiated between the new WS and all existing WSs of type B, son of the current WS.

Lines 10 is a trigger fired when an instance of a TA WS is created; the parameters are the objects to be instantiated. Lines 11 and 12 create the content of the WS from the parameters provided.

2.5 Summary.

At creation time, a WS only needs the references to the objects it requires, thus maxi-mizing the independence with respect with its context of utilization.

The synchronize command can instantiate, at any time, a collaboration policy between any existing WSs, not only between father and son WSs, as found in most propositions like [God93], [CAL+94], [CHL94], and not only at creation time. When automated synchronization is defined, it is based on dynamic predicate evaluation. It can involve object state, attributes, relationships and composition, time constraints, complex object dependencies and so on. It is not limited to read/write operations as found in all DB approaches to collaboration, nor to predefined read/write sequences pairs as in relative serializability [DBAV94].

Collaboration policies can thus be changed at any moment, but the protocols are nego-tiated at the process coordination level. We believe that this WS manager is powerful and flexible enough to support almost any collaboration policies.

We provide a small library of basic and classic collaboration policies, which the user is able to extend and customize[1].

---

1. Currently 11 such relationships are defined. For example *shared* and *local_shared* (see 2.3), *exclusive* which ensures a single WS can changes the object, *private* which is the most usual one, implementing isolation with a copy on write semantics, *RO* for read only, different *notify* for different kind of notifi-cation and so on.

3 Implementation

This WS manager was first prototyped in June 1994, the second version came out in September, and the third in January 1995. It has been extensively reworked since to address protection and efficiency issues. The initial WS manager is fully implemented using Adele triggers. Once line 8 has been executed, we have the following situation in the DB.

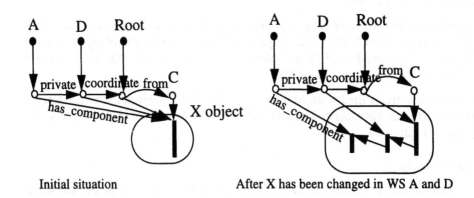

Initial situation   After X has been changed in WS A and D

This schema shows only the situation for an object (X), which is a component of configuration C. The synchronize function creates a virtual object C in WS A, and instantiates a *has_component* relationship between A(C) and all components satisfying the condition (*type = body*). The *has_component* relationship propagates toward A(C) all actions executed on X.

```
TYPERELATION private IS origin;
DOMAIN WS_content -> WS_content ;
1  EVENT obj_modified = (!cmd = propagate AND !modified = true) ;
2  PRE ORIGIN obj_modified DO
              { creates a dynamic version of the modified object ;
              moves relationship has_component from previous version to the new one}
```

Line 1 defines the event *obj_modified* as occurring each time the command *propagate* is executed and the database is modified (*!modified* is a built-in attribute, true when the current (sub)transaction have modified the DB). Line 2 is a trigger fired when the object (X) has been modified in the current WS. The semantics of the *private* relationship indicates that a dynamic version (of X) for the current WS needs to be created. *Private* is one of the 11 policies provided in standard in our collaboration policy library.

The complete WS manager was around 3000 trigger lines. All the usual collaboration strategies are easy to implement (and are already contained in the current one we provide). A new collaboration policy is most often defined in less than 10 lines and a new WS type in 5 to 20 lines.

These initial versions suffers some limitations. Dynamic versioning being only partially implemented in the Adele kernel, dynamic versions are not fully transparent[1]. n-DFS has not yet been integrated. The representations in WS are limited to Unix FS representations, as there are no requirements for any other one.

We are currently supporting large WSs in real industrial applications. In the Dassault customer, for example, WSs contain up to 20 000 files, the WS hierarchy is in average 9 levels deep, 5 WS types are defined, with non trivial collaboration policies; 400 engineers will be supported concurrently by mid 95.

4 Conclusion

The objective of such a work is to address, in a unique and consistent framework, a number of topics currently addressed partially in different domains. We need to provide high level concepts and mechanism, but hiding the complexity of the involved technology.

Consequently, in this work, we seek to provide highly efficient, usable and evolutive solutions. Our proposal is based on an SEE database, providing high modelling power, sub-DBs for the support of reference space; a file mapper for translating a DataBase WS to the convenient location and format, and a collaboration manager for the definition and automation of advanced collaboration policies.

From a practical point of view, the goal of this WS manager is twofold:

To become ultimately a commercial tool used by large software projects,

To support sophisticated and novel process formalism and cooperation policies

As a consequence, great attention has been devoted to efficiency, usability, completeness and robustness. The experience, however, showed that a 100% trigger solution have efficiency deficiencies, event if still usable. Based on the experience we have accumulated, we are currently working in defining which basic concepts and mechanisms must be included in the Software Engineering Database kernel.

For the conceptual aspects: power, flexibility, adaptability and extensibility the solution involves formally defined collaboration policies. Collaboration policies are implemented as semantic relationships, dynamically activated by triggers. It is sufficient to create such a relationship between two (complex) objects to automate a collaboration policy between these objects. Thus collaboration between WSs can be highly evolutive and protocols can be negotiated and modified at any moment, still with an explicit and formal collaboration model. Our system provides a small library of basic and common policies.

---

1. For instance the new version starts at revision 1. The history of the original object is no longer accessible.

We are currently designing and testing sophisticated cooperation/coordination policies, as found in [BSK94] for example. More generally the support of process formalisms is under investigation.

It is our belief that our goals: (1) providing a practical tool (i.e. efficient and robust) and (2) a state of the art collaboration manager (i.e. versatile, evolutive, extensible and powerful) have been reached.

References

[ACM93] S. Abiteboul, S. Cluet, and T. Milo. Querying and updating the file. In *19th VLDB*, pages 73–84, Dublin, Ireland, Agust 1993.

[AF94] B. Nuseibeh A. Finkelstein, J. Kramer, editor. *Software Process Modelling and Technology*. John Willey and Son inc, Research Study Press, Tauton Somerset, England, 1994.

[BGR⁺94] R.F. Bruynooghe, R.M. Greenwood, I. Robertsson, J. Sa, and B.C. Warboy. *PADM: Towards a Total Process Modelling System*. In A. Finkelstein AF94, 1994.

[BK91] N. S. Barghouti and G. E. Kaiser. Concurrency control in advanced database application. *ACM Computing Surveys*, 23(3):269–317, 1991.

[BSK94] I.Z. Ben-Shaul and G. E. Kaiser. A paradigm for decentralized process modeling and its realization in the oz environment. In *Proc. of the 16th Int'l Conf. on Software Engineering*, Sorrento, Italy, May 1994.

[CAL⁺94] R. Conradi, M. Agasseth, J. Larsen, M. Nguyen, P. Munch, P.H. Westbyand L. Jacchieri, and C. Liu. EPOS: Object-oriented cooperative process modelling. In A. Finkelstein AF94, chapter Software Process Modelling and Technology, pages 33–64.

[CHL94] R. Conradi, M. Hagasseth, and C. Lui. Support for collaborating transactions in epos. In *CAISE 94*, pages 2–13, Uthecht, Germany, June 1994.

[DBAV94] D.Agrawal, J.L. Bruno, El Abbadi, and V.Krishnaswamy. Relative serializability: An approach for relaxing the atomicity of transaction. In *Proceedings of the ACM SIGACT/SIGMOD Symposium on Preinciples of DatabaseSystem*, pages 139–149, May 1994.

[DHB93] H. Dai, J.G. Hughes, and D.A. Bell. A distributed real-time knowledge based system and its implementation using o.o. techniques. In *Int. Conf on Intellignet and Cooperative Information Systems. ICISIS93*, Rotterdam, Nehterland, May 1993.

[EC95] J. Estublier and R. Casallas. Three dimentional versionning. In J. Estublier, editor, *Proc. of 5th Int'l Workshop on Software Configuration Management*, LNCS 1005, Seatle, Washington, USA, May 1995. Springer Verlag.

[Ell92] C. Ellis. A model and algorithm for concurrent access within groupware. Technical Report CU-CS-593-92, University of Boulder at Colorado,, Dep. of Comp. Science, 1992 1992.

[Fer92] C. Fernstrom. Computer aided process support: State-of-the-art and state-of-the-market. Technical report, Cap Gemini Innovation, 1992.

[GJR94] N.H. Gehani, H.V. Jagadish, and W.D. Roome. Odefs: A file system interface to an object oriented database. In *20th VLDB*, pages 249–260, Santiago, Chile, May 1994.

[God93] C. Godart. Coo: A transaction model to support cooperation software developers COOrdinaton. In I. Sommerville and M. Paul, editors, *4th European Soft. Eng. Conference*, volume 717 of *LNCS*. Spring-Verlag, September 1993.

[JPSW94] G. Junkerman, B. Peuchel, W. Schaefer, and S. Wolf. *MERLIN: Supporting Cooperation in Software Developemnt Through a Knowledge-Based Environment*. In A. Finkelstein AF94, 1994.

[Kai90] G. Kaiser. A flexible transaction model for software engineering. In *6th Int. Conf. on Data Engineering*, pages 560–567, 1990.

[Leb94] D. Leblang. *The CM Challenge: Configuration Management thats work*, chapter 1, pages 1–37. Trends in Software. J. Wiley and Sons, Baffins Lane, Chichester West Sussex, PO19 1UD, England, 1994.

[Mil89] T. Miller. Configuration management with the NSE. In F. Long, editor, *Proc. of Int'l Workshop on Software Engineering Environments*, volume 467 of *LNCS*, pages 99–106. Springer-Verlag, Berlin, 1990, Chinon, France, September 18–20 1989.

[MW94] U. Manber and S. Wu. Glimpse, a tool to search through entire file system. In *Proc USENIX winter Conf.*, January 1994.

[Tic85] W.F. Tichy. Rcs — a system for version control. *Software—Practice and Experience*, 15:637–654, 1985.

System Compositions and Shared Dependencies

Dewayne E. Perry

Bell Laboratories, 600 Mountain Avenue, Murray Hill, NJ 07974 USA

Abstract. Much of the work in configuration management has addressed the problems of version history and derivation. Little has been done to address the problems of reasoning about the consistency of composed components or the effects of substituting one version for another. In my paper, "Version Control in the Inscape Environment" [13], I defined a number of concepts to be used in reasoning about substituting one component for another. In this paper, I discuss the problem of shared dependencies (that is, substituting one of more interdependent components in a context), propose an approach for specifying such dependencies, and show how this approach can be used to reason about the substitution in the context of interdependent components in a configuration.

1 Introduction

In building software systems from components, there are two important concerns that we must address: keeping track of how components in a system are derived, and determining that the components comprising a system are consistent with each other.

Much of the past and current work in version and configuration management has been focused on determining and keeping track of how components are derived. We have systems, such as SCCS [16], RCS [18], and NSE [1], to help us manage version and configuration histories. Typically, these tools use trees or graphs to represent the derivation of source versions. We have tools, such as various forms of Make [6] and such opportunistic processors as Marvel [9], to automatically derive objects we need to build executable versions of our systems. Typically, these tools use (unit or syntactic) dependency [12] descriptions as the basis for their automation. In general, we have a fairly deep understanding of how to manage the derivation relationships both for manually derived and for automatically derived components [3].

The problem of component consistency, however, has received much less attention by researchers in configuration management. Instead of using tools specific to programming-in-the-large, we manage consistency checking with basic component-building and systems-building tools, such as compilers and link-loaders, and with laborious and (necessarily) incomplete testing.

There are two basic problems that motivate our interest in the consistency of atomic and composed components: that of putting them together so that the resulting system is consistent, and that of substituting one component for another in an existing composition in such a way that consistency is preserved.

The well-formedness of system compositions from components that meet basic constraints (about the provided and required facilities in the syntactic interface of the component) is the foundation for building syntactically and semantically consistent systems. See Habermann and Perry [7] for a complete discussion of the various aspects of syntactically well-formed systems.

Once we have basic syntactic consistency, we must then worry about semantic consistency. It is for this reason that such approaches as found in the Inscape Environment [14] and Narayanaswamy and Scacchi [11] are important. The primary concern of Inscape has been exploring the constructive use of interface specifications in sequential programs. Thus, Inscape provides us a way of constructing the *semantic interconnections* [12] among components that provides the basis for reasoning about the initial consistency of system compositions and the preservation of consistency when substituting one component for another.

In my paper on version control in Inscape [13], I addressed the problem of reasoning about independent substitutions in system composition.s In this paper, I address the problem of interdependent substitutions — that is, the substitution of components that participate in shared dependencies. I first explain shared dependencies in section 2, the current state of the art in section 3, and then discuss the necessary groundwork in section 4. I discuss my approach to reasoning about shared dependencies in section 5. I first introduce the form of shared-dependency specifications and the method for constructing them in section 5.1. I next present the rules for determining the well-formedness of those specifications in section 5.2, and the rules for determining their satisfaction by compositions in section 5.3. I summarize the results of the paper in section 6.

2   Shared Dependencies

Shared dependencies among components arise naturally in the way we build systems and are not necessarily the result of having built them badly. Because of our desire to separate concerns, encapsulate and abstract, we break up our complex systems into distinct components that cannot, of necessity, be completely independent.

It is also increasingly common that our software systems have multiple dimensions of organizations, particularly large and complex systems. For example, we have the notion of features in telephone switching systems that are often orthogonal to the design structure [20] — that is, the implementation of a feature is to be found distributed among design components that also share in the implementation of other features. This kind of organizational complexity is further compounded by such considerations as specialization, optioning and portability. We note in passing that the occurrence of multiple dimensions of organization is a general problem, not one endemic to switching systems.

A common form of shared dependency occurs where several components share data structures. These dependencies are implicit in the assumptions about the state of the shared structures that each component makes when using those shared structures. The shared use of devices is another example of this form of shared dependency.

We find that a similar but more complicated form of sharing occurs when several components share in the implementation of a complex algorithm. This form is similar to the previous one because the distributed processing is usually glued together by means of a shared data structure, or set of data structures. Not only is the assumed state important to the processing by each component, but there is an invariant, or set of invariants, that must be maintained for the shared structure or structures.

Producers and consumers interacting and communicating by sharing a queue is a simple example of the first form of shared dependencies. A slightly more complicated example is that where one component opens a file, another components reads and processes some of the contents, another makes use of that information, and yet another closes the file. In each case, the components have assumptions about the state of the shared structures.

Two problems arise from these shared dependencies. First, one must treat the components together in context and not in isolation. In evolving any one of these components, one must often change other components participating in the shared dependency as well. Second, this problem of context is compounded by the fact that it is not unusual for a component to participate in several shared dependencies. This is particularly true in large complex systems where there are multiple dimensions of organization. In both cases, substitution in a system composition is not a simple consideration. Because shared dependencies involving a single component often extend in several different directions simultaneously, integration of individual component changes is complex and error prone.

3 Current State of the Art and Research

The current state of the art in handling shared dependencies is represented by two different kinds of approaches: attribute-based configuration management systems and language-based programming-in-the-large facilities.

Two such CM systems are Adelle [5] and Workshop [4]. Both provide facilities at what I call the *unit interconnection* level — that is, dependencies are expressed between rather large-grained units (files, procedures, etc.). In Adelle, objects have attributes that may be used to indicate shared traits. For example, attributes may be used to indicate that certain versions are for a particular machine or for particular options. In Workshop, attributes are attached by the system to all objects edited in a particular workshop session. These attributes then indicate related sets of changes and can be used in a relatively coarse-grained way to indicate shared dependencies.

Two programming languages that offer some help with shared dependencies are ML and Ada. Both enable one to pass objects to modules and thus explicitly specify when objects are being shared between several modules. They provide what I call *syntactic interconnections* — that is, dependencies between syntactic entities in the languages. In ML, one can specify the sharing of data structures by means of functors. In Ada, one can specify the sharing of data structures as parameters to generic instantiations of modules.

The attribute-based approach has the advantage of indicating which components share a particular dependency. It does not however indicate what the dependent data structures are nor what the actual semantic dependencies are between those components. The language-based approach has the advantage of making explicit what the dependent data structures are. Unfortunately, that is all that it does indicate. It only indirectly indicates what components are involved, but does not offer much assistance when multiple data structures are involved. Neither does it provide any information about the actual semantic dependencies among the components.

SVCE [8] provides programming-in-the-large (again, *syntactic interconnections* facilities for both encapsulation and system composition. Both the encapsulation facilities and the system composition facilities enable one to group collections of related components together. Thus, one can indicate what is being shared and bound the scope of that sharing by either of these means. However, these facilities only work where any of the components only participate in a single shared dependency. SVCE also suffers from the disadvantage of not expressing the semantic dependencies between components.

To our knowledge, these approaches represent not only the current state of the art, but the current state of research as well. Mahler in his article about Shape [10] mentions the problems of multiple variances and the problems of semantic consistency in the presence of building compositions where components share in such multiple variances, but does not address them in that paper.

Batory and Geraci [2] come to grips with some of these problems in the context of their domain-specific system generators, adjusting the choice of some of the components dependent on other component choices to generate a consistent domain-specific system. Their mechanisms for doing this consistent generation are analogous to my approach in Inscape, but using only primitive predicates. Their rules of composition are similar to those of Inscape [15].

4 Preliminary Groundwork

The approach I present in the next section is based on the approach that I have previously taken in the Inscape Environment: specifying module interfaces in Instress [14], reasoning about the composition of components in the construction and evolution of systems [17], and reasoning about the relationships among component interfaces [13].

4.1 Interface Specifications

Instress module specifications contain three components: predicate definitions, data specifications, and operation specifications. Predicates may be defined as primitive (that is, uninterpreted), or in terms of other defined predicates and/or boolean predicates. Data specifications consist of a declaration with additional properties to further constrain the values of the type or object. Operation specifications consists of a function or procedure declaration, a set of preconditions (a conjunct of predicates), and a set of results. Each result consist of a set of postconditions and a set of obligations (both are conjuncts of predicates) — see the example of an operation specification in Instress.

Postconditions define what is known to be true as a result of the operation's execution. Obligations define what must become true at some time in the future of the computation — that is, the computation is obliged to fulfill the obligation or it is a semantically incorrect computation. Obligations are generally used to indicate either the relationship of bracketing operations (such as open and close, allocate and deallocate) or the expression of an invariant among components. It is this last purpose that is of particular importance in the sequel.

The definition of consistency is straightforward:

> A predicate or set of predicates P is *consistent* if and only if it is not the case that P ⊢ false [1].

The consistency of a specification as a whole, then depends on the consistency of the various parts.

> An Interface Specification S = (P, D, O) is consistent if and only if
> - the definition of each predicate P_i in P is consistent,
> - the set of properties defined for each data object D_i in D is consistent, and
> - each set of preconditions, postconditions and obligations for each operation O_i in O is consistent.

4.2 Interface Relationships

These formal descriptions of interfaces are the basis for reasoning about the relationships among various components and versions of components. Because of the semantic interconnections established during construction of the software, we can reason about the substitution of one version for another both dependent on the context of that construction and independent of it.

On the basis of Inscape's interface formalism, I defined the concepts of identity, equivalence, strict compatibility, upward compatibility, and various forms of implementation-dependent compatibility [13]. I separated the notion of compatibility into two distinct concepts: dependency preserving compatibility (strict) and functionality preserving compatibility (upward).

Of the two forms of context-independent upward compatibility, the more useful in reasoning about single substitution was strict compatibility. That utility is due precisely to its focus on dependency preservation.

> Operation O2 is a *strictly* compatible version of O1 if and only if

---

[1] In the reamining discussion, the logical notions are those of a standard first order predicate logic.

OpenFile(<in> filename fn, <out> fileptr fp)
　　returns unsigned int status
Synopsis:
　　If a file exists with the file name in fn, then the file is opened for I/O and a
　　pointer to the file is returned for all further I/O operations.
Preconditions:
　　[V] LegalFileName(fn)
　　[V] FileExists(FileNamedBy(fn))
{Successful result}
　　Determined by:
　　　status' == 0
　　Synopsis:
　　　The file named in fn is open for i/o and fp references that file.
　　Postconditions:
　　　LegalFileName(fn)
　　　FileExists(FileNamedBy(fn))
　　　FileOpen(*fp')
　　　ValidFilePtr(fp')
　　　FileNamedBy(fn) == *fp'
　　Obligations:
　　　FileClosed(*fp')
{Exception Result: IllegalFileName}
　　Determined By:
　　　status' == 1
　　Synopsis:
　　　The file name is not a legal one.
　　Precondition failure:
　　　LegalFileName(fn)
　　Postconditions:
　　　not: LegalFileName(fn)
　　Obligations:
　　　<none>
　　Recovery Method:
　　　Correct the file name.
{Exception Result: NonExistantFile}
　　Determined By:
　　　status' == 3
　　Synopsis:
　　　The file named by fn does not exists.
　　Precondition failure:
　　　FileExists(FileNamedBy(fn))
　　Postconditions:
　　　LegalFileName(fn)
　　　not: FileExists(FileNamedBy(fn))
　　Obligations:
　　　<none>
　　Recovery Method:
　　　Choose a name for a file that exists.

- PRE(O1) ⊢ PRE(O2) and
- POST(O2) ⊢ POST(O1) and
- OBL(O2) ⊢ OBL(O1) and OBL(O1) ⊢ OBL(O2).

That is, O2 requires no more than O1, produces no less and obligates equally. We shall see below that the more useful concept in reasoning about shared dependencies is upward compatibility, precisely for its emphasis on functionality (or if you will, behavioral) preservation.

The definition used in the rest of the paper for upward compatibility is that an upwardly compatible version preserves the original functionality or behavior while extending it.

Operation O2 is an *upwardly compatible* version of O1 if and only if
- PRE(O2) ⊢ PRE(O1) and
- POST(O2) ⊢ POST(O1) and
- OBL(O2) ⊢ OBL(O1).

Formally, the base component interface is derivable from the upwardly compatible component interface — that is, the preconditions, postconditions and obligations of the base component are derivable from the preconditions, postconditions and obligations of the upwardly compatible component.

4.3 Composition

Instress's formal interface specifications are also the basis for reasoning about the constructive composition of these components into implementations. In my paper "The Logic of Propagation in the Inscape Environment" [15], I defined the rules of composition for sequence, selection and iteration. On the basis of rules about function invocation and assignment, the rules for sequence, selection and iteration enable one to compose program fragments (and derive their interfaces by the rules of the propagation logic) which can be further composed with other fragments until an implementation sequence has been composed for the desired operation.

It is this notion of a composed sequence that will be of importance in the discussion of reasoning about shared dependencies. An important aspect of a composed sequence is whether it is *complete* or not — that is, whether all the preconditions and obligations have been handled properly according to the basic rule in Inscape: all preconditions and obligations in a composed fragment must be either satisfied within that fragment or propagated to the interface of that fragment.

Germane to the definition of the completeness of a program fragment are the notions of *precondition ceilings* and *obligation floors* [15]. In the propagation of preconditions and obligations when constructing program fragments, the preconditions percolate "upwards" and the obligations percolate "downwards" in search of either satisfying postconditions or the "edge" of the implementation (that is, the interface). Preconditions ceilings are logical barriers to that movement of the precondition "up through" the implementation to the interface. For example, a postcondition of *not P* forms a ceiling for an unsatisfied precondition *P* in its movement up to the interface. The obligation floor functions similarly for obligation as they move "down through" the implementation fragment to the interface, though there is not quite the logical necessity that occurs in the case of preconditions.

An implementation $I =$ sequence $S = S_1 \ldots S_N$ for a program fragment F is *complete* if and only if
- Every precondition in S has either been satisfied or is in the interface of F — that is, all precondition ceilings in S (recursively) are empty
- Every obligation in S has either been satisfied or is in the interface of F — that is, all obligation floors in S (recursively) are empty.
- There are no iteration errors — that is, the preconditions of each iteration are consistent with postconditions of their respective iteration bodies.

One further definition is needed to complete the preliminary groundwork: that for a *self-contained* composition.

An implementation I for a program fragment F is *self-contained* if and only if
- $\mathrm{PRE}(I) = \emptyset$, and
- $\mathrm{OBL}(I) = \emptyset$

An operation (that is, a function or procedure) is the basic usable syntactic fragment in most programming languages.

5 Shared Dependency Specifications

We now have the basis for reasoning about shared dependencies: the definition of what it means to be a consistent interface specification, the definition of what it means for a component to be an upwardly compatible version of another, and the definitions of what it means for an implementation to be complete and self-contained.

In the next subsection, I introduce the structure of a shared dependency specification and propose the method for describing these dependencies. I then define what it means for a shared dependency to be well-formed. Finally, I discuss various ways of satisfying these shared dependencies.

5.1 Form and Method

A shared dependency is a set of partial predicate, data and operation specifications together with a set of partially instantiated interface specifications.

A Shared Dependency Specification SDS =
({ Partial Specifications }, { Partial Instantiations })

The specifications and instantiations are *partial* because they may not contain all the type, parameter, or behavioral information that would be found in a full specification and its use.

The method for defining such shared dependencies is as follows:

- Define the predicates needed for the partial object and operation specifications.
- Declare only those types and objects necessary for defining the constraints on sharing.
- Specify only that part of the semantics (the preconditions, postconditions and obligations) of the operations needed to define the sharing of dependencies.
- Instantiate only the arguments needed to define the relationships between the objects and the operations (use "_" for those arguments that do not participate in the dependency).

A simple example should suffice to illustrate both the method and the specification form. The example shared dependency specification illustrates two operations sharing the use of a particular data structure Q of type Queue, such that operation O1 depends on the state of the shared object Q to be P(Q) and operation O2 provides this state. Only the predicate P, the type Queue, the object Q, and the operations O1 and O2 need to be declared. The operations O1 and O2 are then partially instantiated with the shared object Q.

```
shareddependency Eg1 = (
  declarations {
    P ( queue q ) :: ...;
    type ... queue ;
    var queue Q ;
    O1 ( queue x, ...)
      pre: P ( x )
    O2 ( ..., Queue y )
      post: P ( y )
  }
  instantiations {
    O1 ( Q, _, ...)
      pre: P ( Q )
    O2 ( _, ..., Q )
      post: P ( Q )
  }
)
```

5.2 Well-formedness of Dependency Specifications

There are two important questions to ask of any specification: whether it is well-formed and whether it accurately represents the intent of the designer. The second question is one that all specifiers must wrestle with in the same way that implementors wrestle with the question of whether the code accurately represents the intent of the design. The first question, however, is one that we can address.

The basic intuition, given that we want to concentrate only on those aspects germane to the specific dependency, is that all of the specifications are consistent and that semantic interconnections ought to be "matched up" with just the information available in the shared dependency specification.

Basic consistency is the first consideration for the partial specifications in just the same way that it is the first concern in full specifications. Moreover, the definition remains the same for partial specifications as for full specifications. We note, that for the sake of simplifying the presentation, we consider only the semantics of operations in the discussion below.

There are two ways by which one might "match up" the semantic dependencies. The first way, I call *weak composability* and the second way I call *strong composability*. The difference is in the way that the semantic interconnections are established — that is, in the way in which the semantic dependencies are satisfied.

In weak composability, it is sufficient for each precondition and obligation to be satisfied in some way by the postconditions found in the partial instantiations. That is,

A Shared Dependency Specification SD is *weakly composable* if and only if

- For each Precondition P_i of each Instantiated Interface I_j,
  - there is a set Γ_k such that Γ_k is included in the set POST of all postconditions of all the Instantiated Interfaces except I_j, and
  - $\Gamma_k \vdash P_i$
- For each Obligation O_i of each instantiated interface I_j
  - there is a set Γ_k such that Γ_k is included in the set POST of all postconditions of all the Instantiated Interfaces except I_j, and
  - $\Gamma_k \vdash O_i$

The disadvantage of this form of composability is that it only guarantees that it is possible to satisfy the preconditions and obligations. It does not guarantee that there is any composable sequence that satisfies all of the specified constraints.

The intent of strong composability, however, is precisely to provide that guarantee: there is a self-sufficient sequence in which all the preconditions and obligations are satisfied.

A Shared Dependency Specification SD is *strongly composable* if and only if

- there exists a sequential composition C including all of the Instantiated Interfaces $I_1 \ldots I_N$ such that
  - C is complete, and
  - C is self-contained.

The definition of a well-formed shared dependency specification then matches our basic intuition, using strong composability as the means of "matching up" the semantic dependencies.

A Shared Dependency Specification SD is *well-formed* if and only if
- SD is consistent, and
- SD is strongly composable.

5.3 Sets of Shared Dependency Specifications

We mentioned in the discussion on shared dependencies that components often share in multiple dependencies. One has the choice of specifying these interrelated dependencies as either independent or as integrated specifications. Given that these interdependencies represent system design aspects, perhaps even architectural aspects of the system, the preferred method of specification is to specify them independently and then to combine them.

A combined shared dependency specification is a set of equations and a set of shared dependencies and has the following form.

A Combined Shared Dependency Specification CSDS =
({ Equations }, { SD Specifications })

The set of component equations specify which components in the different shared dependency specifications are to be considered the same components. Applying the set of equations to the set of shared dependencies results in a shared dependency specification in which each set of equated components is merged into a single component. Names are kept distinct in all cases by using the standard dot qualified names in which the name of the specification is prepended to each component name. Merged components are renamed by arbitrarily using one of the equated names. For example,

Eg3 = { Eg1.O1 == Eg2.O3 } applied to { Eg1, Eg2 }

results in Eg3 containing the components of Eg1 and Eg2 that were independent of the equation, and the merged version of Eg1.O1 and Eg2.O3 called (arbitrarily) Eg3.O1.

Having a well-formed shared dependency specification as a result of combining well-formed shared dependency specifications would be a very nice resulting property. However, in merging two separate partial specifications it is all too possible to inadvertently create an inconsistent set of predicates. Moreover, it is very easy to create a non-composable set of operations as a result of the merging.

The best that we can guarantee is that the results of combining shared dependencies will be weakly composable if the original shared dependencies were at least weakly composable.

There is a second reason for combining shared dependencies: creating higher level dependency relationships by aggregating existing shared dependency relationships. Typically, this approach combines independent relationships together. So, for example

Eg3 = { } applied to { Eg1, Eg2 }

yields a shared dependency that has two independent components as parts of the shared dependency Eg3. In this case, we do have a well-formed result returned from applying the empty set of equations to the well-formed two shared dependencies. Both specifications remain consistent, and both remain strongly composed.

5.4 Satisfying Shared Dependency Specifications

We first consider the problem of a component satisfying a shared dependency specification, first for simple satisfaction and then for aggregate satisfaction. We then consider the problem of a composition satisfying a shared dependency specification. Finally, we note that the problems of a composition satisfying a set of shared dependency specifications reduces to the single specification cases.

How a component satisfies a shared dependency specification depends on what the component is. For types we here choose a simple solution: type equivalence (leaving the question of whether it is name or structural equivalence to be answered by the implementation language). Alternatively, one might want to explore the possibility of using type compatibility instead. For predicates, we again choose a simple solution: equivalence of the definitions. For operations, the component must be an upwardly compatible version of the shared dependency component that it is satisfying.

> A component C *satisfies* a Shared Dependency Specification component SC if and only if
> - C and SC are both predicates, C ⊢ SC and SC ⊢ C, or
> - C and SC are both type definitions (or they are both object declarations) and their types are equivalent, or
> - C and SC are both operation specifications and C is an upwardly compatible version of SC.

This definition enables us to satisfy components in a specification in a simple, one-to-one fashion. We may have an operation that combines several of the specification operations into a single component. For this case, we need a slightly richer definition of operation satisfaction.

> A operation O *satisfies*$_2$ an aggregate of Shared Dependency Components A = ($SC_1, \ldots, SC_n$) if and only if

- PI is the propagated interface of a complete sequential composition of the components of A, and
- O is an upwardly compatible version of PI.

Just as in the combining of shared dependency specifications, we required extra information to determine how various parts were related to each other, so we need an equivalent structure here to relate components in the composition to those in the specifications. This required structure is a map from composition components to specification components.

A Map M from Composition Components $C_1 \ldots C_N$ to Shared Dependency Components $SC_1 \ldots SC_M$ is *well-formed* if and only if
- For all C_i, $M(C_i)$ are distinct (that is, no two composition components are mapped to the same shared dependency component or set of components, and
- For each SC_j, SC_j appears in the range of only one composition component, and
- All shared dependency components are in the range of M.

Thus a composition is a set of source components (in the required specification form) and a mapping from those source components to shared dependency components. The composition satisfies a shared dependency specification when all of the source components satisfy all of the specification components.

A Composition C of components $C_1 \ldots C_N$ and Map M *satisfy* a Shared Dependency Specification SD of components $SC_1 \ldots SC_M$ if and only if
- Map M is well-formed, and
- For each C_i, C_i satisfies $M(C_i)$.

The well-formedness of the map guarantees that all the components in the shared dependency will be satisfied either by simple satisfaction or by aggregate satisfaction by the source components in the composition.

We note that we can form a single shared dependency specification from a set of such specifications by applying the empty set of equations to those sets. As we argued, this reduces the set of a single specification with independently related sets of components. We can then apply one large composition to the entire set. Alternatively, we could combine sets of compositions that have been independently applied to their respective shared dependency specifications. To achieve the same results as the first alternative, we would need the additional constraint that all the compositions be disjoint.

6 Summary

In my prior work I was concerned about the syntactic well-formedness of system compositions, the semantic consistency of interface specifications, the semantic interconnections created in system construction, and the semantic relationships between individual interfaces.

Here, I have presented a structure and method for specifying interrelated components that share some semantic aspect of a computation. My claim is that only with this extra information can one properly evolve the components that we use on constructing systems. Not only do we need to know the dependencies, but we also need to know the context of those dependencies. Shared dependency specifications provide a means of describing these contexts. Moreover, it is this sort of shared dependency information that enables us to systematically and effectively evolve our software systems: they provide us with the means of identifying some of the implications of changes to the system and reasoning about those changes prior to testing them.

This gain in understanding of system evolution comes at a cost: the shared dependency specifications tend to be somewhat large and cumbersome. Ameliorating this cumbersomeness is the fact that these specifications could easily be built as an adjunct of the construction and evolution process supported by environments such as Inscape with the environment providing much of the mundane work in capturing these shared dependencies.

It is my claim that the concepts introduced here enable one to effectively reason about both single and multiple component substitution and the effects of those substitutions. Satisfying the shared dependencies, however, is not sufficient in itself to guarantee consistency of a composition. Something like the semantic interconnections provided by Inscape during the construction and evolution of the system are also needed.

References

1. Evan W. Adams, Masahiro Honda and Terrance C. Miller. Object Management in a CASE Environment. The Proceedings of the Eleventh International Conference on Software Engineering, May 1989, Pittsburgh, PA. pp 154-163.
2. Don Batory and Bart J. Geraci. Validating Component Compositions in Software System Generators. Technical Report TR-95-03, Department of Computer Sciences, University of Texas at Austin, February 1995. Updated August 1995.
3. Ellen Borrison. A Model of Software Manufacture. Advanced programming Environments, Trondheim, Norway, June 1986. pp 197-220. Lecture Notes in Computer Science 244, Springer-Verlag, 1986.
4. Geoffrey M. Clemm. The Workshop System — A Practical Knowledge-Based Software Environment. ACM SIGSOFT'88: Third Symposium on Software Development Environments (SDE3), Cambridge MA, November 1988. In ACM SIGSOFT Software Engineering Notes 13:5 (November 1988). pp 55-64.
5. J. Estublier and R. Casallas. The Adele Configuration Manager. In [19], pp 73-97.
6. Stuart I. Feldman. Make — a Program for Maintaining Computer Programs. Software — Practice & Experience 9:4 (April 1979). pp 255-265.
7. A. Nico Habermann and Dewayne E. Perry. Well Formed System Composition. Carnegie-Mellon University, Technical Report CMU-CS-80-117. March 1980.

8. A. Nico Habermann and Dewayne E. Perry. System Composition and Version Control for Ada. Software Engineering Environments. H. Huenke, editor. North-Holland, 1981. pp. 331-343.
9. Gail E. Kaiser. Intelligent Assistance for Software Development and Maintenance. IEEE Software 5:3 (May 1988). pp 40-49.
10. Axel Mahler. Variants: Keeping Things Together and Telling Them Apart. In [19], pp 73-97.
11. K. Narayanaswamy and W. Scacchi. Maintaining Configurations of Evolving Software Systems. IEEE Transactions of Software Engineering, SE13:3 (March 1987), pp 324-334.
12. Dewayne E. Perry. Models of Software Interconnections. Proceedings of the 9th International Conference on Software Engineering, March 30 - April 2, 1987, Monterey CA. pp 61-69.
13. Dewayne E. Perry. Version Control in the Inscape Environment. Proceedings of the 9th International Conference on Software Engineering, March 30 - April 2, 1987, Monterey CA.
14. Dewayne E. Perry. The Inscape Environment. The Proceedings of the Eleventh International Conference on Software Engineering, May 1989, Pittsburgh, PA.
15. Dewayne E. Perry. The Logic of Propagation in the Inscape Environment. Proceedings of the ACM SIGSOFT '89 Third Symposium on Software Testing, Analysis, and Verification (TAV3), 13-15 December 1989, Key West, FL. Software Engineering Notes 14:8 (December 1989), pp 114-121.
16. M. J. Rochkind. The Source Code Control System. IEEE Transactions on Software Engineering, SE-1:4 (December 1975). pp 364-370.
17. Walter F. Tichy. Software Development Control Based on System Structure Descriptions. Ph.D. Thesis, Computer Science Department, Carnegie-Mellon University, January 1980.
18. Walter F. Tichy. RCS — A System for Version Control. Software — Practice & Experience, 15:7 (July 1985). pp 637-654.
19. Walter F. Tichy, editor. Configuration Management. Trends in Software, Volume 2. Chichester: John Wiley & Sons, 1994.
20. P. A. Tuscany. Software Development Environment for Large Switching Projects. Proceedings of Software Engineering for Telecommunications Switching Systems Conference, 1987.

Infrastructure for Wide-Area Software Development

Dave Belanger, David Korn, and Herman Rao

AT&T Laboratories
600 Mountain Avenue
Murray Hill, NJ 07974

Abstract. The Global Research And Development envIronmENT (GRADI-ENT) is a research project, addressing globalization of software R&D. The first effort is to design and implement an infrastructure for wide-area software development. With such an infrastructure, programmers, located on geographically dispersed sites, are able to share source files as if they were in the same location. The system extends the scope of versioning control, found in Configuration Management, from a single site to multiple sites. It allows individual programmers to construct private working areas. Finally, the infrastructure preserves the file system API and requires no modification of commands or the kernel. A prototype running between New Jersey and Taiwan is currently used as a framework for research in configuration management of wide-area software development. This paper reports our experience in designing and implementing the infrastructure.

1 Introduction

To compete in world-wide markets, many international corporations are decentralizing their Research & Development force. The Global Research And Development envIronmENT (GRADIENT) is a pilot project, aimed at addressing issues related to globalization of software R&D and developing infrastructure and methodologies for wide-area collaborations. Currently, GRADIENT includes software researchers located in Murray Hill, New Jersey and in Hsinchu, Taiwan.

Global collaboration introduces four obstacles, not typically found in LAN environments. These are: information and data sharing barriers among machines; communication and interaction barriers among people; bureaucratic barriers among organizations; and cultural barriers among environments. The first effort in GRADIENT is to overcome information and data sharing barriers by implementing an infrastructure for wide-area software development. With such an infrastructure, programmers in widely separated locations will be able to collaborate just as they would if they were in the same location. This paper describes the infrastructure for wide-area software development.

The rationale behind construction of this infrastructure is threefold: provide complete data-sharing facilities; ensure appropriate degrees of programmer and site autonomy; and guarantee uninterrupted access to in-progress sources. Accordingly, three components needed to be added to UNIX-like file systems[1]:

---

[1] Another important component that is absent in UNIX-like file systems is "event notification" [6], which collects file access events and notifies remote and local file-system users or event-action servers [12].

A Repository storing version files, each of which contains multiple versions of one master file similar to those proposed for RCS [19] and SCCS [1]. Having version files replicated at all collaborating sites enables programmers to work with the project even when some sites are unreachable through network.

Version Objects interfaced with the repository such that individual programmers have unique access paths to every version of the projects.

Viewpathing that allows overlapping one file tree with another such that the upper-most file tree contains the virtual union of files from both trees. In effect, it becomes a useful method for users to create a private working area linked to the official-source file tree beneath it.

Together, these maintain incremental versions of projects, not only within individual sites but also among widely dispersed sites collaborating on the same projects. They also allow each programmer to create a private working area free of intrusion or interference from other programmers.

In GRADIENT, these components appear to be embedded in file systems. We believe that overloading file system semantics can improve software reusability and customer acceptability, when compared with the alternative of creating a new API that is incompatible with existing applications. For example, UNIX tools such as nmake [4] and build [3] have demonstrated the usefulness and power of viewpathing in configuration management. This notion has been implemented by adding extra code to each of these tools. We embed viewpathing into the file system and preserve the file system's API so that not only do all tools (e.g., UNIX system commands ls, vi, diff etc.) take advantage of viewpathing without any modification, but they also share the same view of the underlying file system. As another example, with the new versioning repository, users are able to reuse the ls command to browse different versions of a file. And, checking versions into or out of the repository is transparent to file-system users—end users and commands.

The infrastructure is built on top of the Multiple Dimensional File System (n-DFS), which provides a platform for adding new services to the underlying file system [6]. Examples of services include naming services (e.g., viewpathing [9] and semantic naming [7]); monitoring file systems operations and communication [11]; replicating critical files in underlying file systems to remote backup file systems [5]; synchronized replication services among two loosely-connected file systems [16]; accessing Internet-wide file systems [15]; and providing versioning of files [6]. By introducing a logical layer between the operating system and user applications, n-DFS intercepts system calls from applications and then passes them to the appropriate services. The logical layer is implemented as a shared library that an application links to and runs on its own address space. It requires no change in either kernel or applications: it is transparent to both, and it preserves the syntax and semantics of system calls.

We have implemented a prototype of n-DFS, running on Sun OS 4.1, HP-UX, SVR4, Linux, and SGI MIPS. The prototype is running between Murray Hill, New Jersey and Hsinchu, Taiwan. We are using it as a research vehicle to address configuration management in wide-area software development.

The rest of this paper is organized as follows. Section 2 motivates GRADIENT by presenting our vision: *Geography-independent Software Development*. Section 3 describes the infrastructure's architecture, focusing on three components: repository, version objects, and viewpathing. Section 4 then provides an overview of our implementation. Finally, Section 5 offers some discussion and comparison with related projects, and Section 6 concludes the paper.

2 Geography-independent Software Development

Many large software projects are developed at more than one site; each project site develops one or more components of a large system. Sites may be near each other and connected by a high-speed network, or they may be on different continents with low bandwidth network connections. Sites may maintain private source code, but they also may need to share code, libraries, and header files with other sites.

Distributed development is reasonably well understood when the project can be clearly partitioned (e.g., functions such as development and test can be conducted locally on subsets of the system), and when the system can be located in one place with developers connected to a hub. It is harder to grasp where high levels of interaction are required. In most software projects, collaborating sites are loosely connected and poorly integrated. Projects usually choose one site as the primary site, take a snapshot of the source code at the primary site, and ship copies to other remote sites. If changes are made at a remote site, they must be carefully merged back into the source at the primary site, and propagated to other sites. File Transfer Protocol (FTP), UUCP, or even surface mailing of magnetic tapes are often used as transport mechanisms. This transfer process is essentially manual, time-consuming, and requires a high degree of discipline in project management. The situation becomes more complicated when different sites own different components and several sites are making changes in the same components.

On the other hand, as networking facilitates become increasingly ubiquitous, we envision that people, located at widely separated sites, are developing software around the clock for marketing, economic, and technical purposes; we call this scenario *Geography-independent Software Development*. It is one way of taking advantage of distributed development competence. Consider an example in which people in the USA work on core technology and general platforms; people in India port systems to various hardware architectures and software configurations; and people in China (where the market is) tailor systems to local needs (e.g., adding Chinese interfaces). Such multiple-site collaboration requires a well-integrated and tightly-connected infrastructure for sharing data. In contrast to data sharing, however, individual sites may also want to preserve some of their autonomy and minimize interference from and conflict with others. Finally, it is important that people at each site are able to continue to working at acceptable levels even though other sites are temporarily unreachable. Ability of synchronizing data after sites are reconnected is also essential . Hence, GRADIENT has three goals:

- Sharing: Users are able to share data as if it were stored on the same network file system;

- Autonomy: Although collaborating with each other, users preserve their autonomy;
- Availability: Individual sites are able to function regardless of unreliable network connections among them.

Our infrastructure extends versioning control mechanisms from a single site to multiple sites, and replicates shared source at collaborating sites. When a modified version been checked in, the system synchronizes each replica by automatically propagating the *changes* to multiple sites using FTP or UUCP. If conflicts are detected while appending remote changes to local copies, the system notifies project administrators and file owners, and allows files to be rolled back to previous states. Finally, to avoid interference from other sites or users and to preserve autonomy, the system allows individual users to construct their own working areas within the common repository.

3 Architecture

The infrastructure introduces three components to traditional UNIX-like file systems: a repository, version objects, and the viewpath mechanism. The repository maintains version files, each of which is replicated at multiple sites. Version objects allow transparent access to the repository using file system's API. Finally, the viewpath mechanism introduces a third dimension to the file systems[2] by overlapping one directory with another.

Repository

The repository contains sets of *version files*, each of which includes multiple versions of one logical file, all under the same file name. A version is named by one or more version names. Version files are replicated at all collaborating sites.

Implemented as a regular UNIX file, a version file includes a *common base* and sets of *deltas*. Each delta is a compressed, binary data difference that a version relative to the common base. A version is checked into or out of the version file using the corresponding delta. The repository stores the version information: a name, file attributes from the system call stat, and one or more predecessor version names. When checking out a version, the system restores the original attributes of the version, such as ownership, access control modes, and timestamps.

It is important to note that the version's deltas stored in the version file depend only on its common base. The history and branch relationship among versions are determined by predecessor version names associated with each version's delta.

We use a byte-oriented, block-move algorithm to compute and compress the version deltas relative to the base [10]. Because of its byte-oriented nature, version files can be used as repositories not only for textual files such as regular source files, but also for arbitrary binary codes, e.g., executable commands. Since the base and deltas are compressed, the space used to store multiple versions may be less than that of one checked-out version.

---

[2] We consider UNIX-like file systems to be two-dimensional, i.e., breath and depth.

Each version file is append-only and immutable. When a version is checked in, the newly created delta is appended to the end of the version file and hides the old deltas with the same version name; the rest of the version file remains unchanged. Because a version file is immutable, the system is able to retrieve previous versions of the file, although only the latest one is shown in normal operations. Garbage collection operations to remove unused, old deltas are performed on a demand basis.

Version files are replicated at individual sites. When a version is checked into a version file, the system synchronizes the version file by propagating the delta to all collaborating sites, each of which then appends the incoming delta to its local copy of the version file. The system allows each site to set its own policy for appending incoming deltas, thus preserving site autonomy.

Because of propagation delays between sites, different copies of the same version file replicated at different sites may store deltas in different orders. Since all copies have the same common base, and deltas are related only to the base, each site views the same sets of versions for version files. When multiple sites simultaneously check in versions with the same version name, th system notifies project managers and file owners, and stores checked-in site IDs as the deltas' secondary keys.

Version Objects

We have augmented the file system with a new file system object, called a Version Object (VO). A VO behaves like a directory and like a file. Using VOs as the front-end, the repository is transparent to file system users. The operations of checking versions into and out of the version files are completely hidden from file systems' users, and users are able to manipulate versions of logical files just as they manipulate entries in directories.

Currently implemented as a *dynamic* symbolic link, a VO maps the name of a logical file to the desired version of the version file on per-user basis. It is a dynamic symbolic link because the system dynamically replaces the content of the symbolic link with user-defined mapping information; Section 4 describes this in more detail. For example, a user specifies a mapping with the built-in shell command vmap, as follows (The character "$" is a shell prompt):

```
$ vmap   /home/project/src   v2.2/v2.1/v2.0/v1.0
```

where the first argument specifies a file tree and the second argument defines a *version path*. A version path contains an ordered list of version names with the character "/" as a delimiter. When opening for *reading* of a VO in this file tree, the system uses the version path to locate the proper version from the version file and returns the reference to the version; it may actually invoke actions to check the desired version out of the version file. When opening for *writing* of a VO in this file tree, however, the system uses the name before the first "/" in the version path as the current version name. As in the previous example, suppose the version file foo.c contains only versions *v1.0* and *v2.0*. And, the command line

```
$ cp   /home/project/src/foo.c /home/project/src/foo.c
```

creates a new version named *v2.2* that has the same content as the version *v2.0*. In order to improve performance, the system caches versions that have been checked out, and performs check-in operations using batch processing. When its pathname ends with a "/", a VO is viewed as a regular directory with versions as the directory entries. It is possible to browse versions using regular directory commands. For example, the command line

$ ls -l /home/project/src/foo.c/

lists all versions under the version object foo.c as if it were a regular directory, as shown below:

```
-rw-r–r– 2 herman      1641   Apr 15  19:00   default
-rw-r–r– 2 herman      1641   Apr 15  19:00   v1.0
-rw-r–r– 1 herman      2051   Apr 20  17:38   v2.0
-rw-r–r– 1 herman      2060   Apr 25  10:00   v2.2
```

Naming one version of a VO is similar to naming an entry in the directory. For example, the command line

$ diff /home/project/src/foo.c/v1.0 /home/project/src/foo.c

compares the versions *v1.0* and *v2.2* (referenced to by the version path defined by vmap) of *foo.c*.

Finally, merging two versions of one logical file can be done by using the command merge from the RCS package. Suppose the version file bar.c contains versions *v1.0*, *v1.1*, and *v1.2*, and the current version path points to *v1.2*. Versions *v1.1* and *v1.2* are different branches of *v1.0*. The command line

$ merge bar.c bar.c/1.0 bar.c/v1.1

then merges *v1.1* to *v1.2*.

Viewpathing

A user view is created by mounting one file tree on top of another. The result is that the upper file tree virtually contains a union of files in both trees. It is as though each file in the lower tree that was not in the upper tree had been copied to the upper tree. For example, the following command line overlaps the file tree "/home/bob/working" on another file tree "/home/project/src":

$ vpath /home/bob/working /home/project/src

The user can work in this merged file tree. Only the upper layer is writable; All other layers are read-only. Consequently, when the user modifies a file located below the upper layer, the desired file is copied to the upper layer before it is accessed. For example, suppose the directory "/home/bob/working" is empty and the directory "/home/project/src/" contains the file "foo.c". And, the command line

$ vi /home/bob/working/foo.c

copies the file "foo.c" to "/home/bob/working". Files from the lower tree having the same names relative to the root of the tree as files on the upper tree are obscured. However, files on the lower layer can be addressed using the special file name, "...". Taking the proceeding example, the command line

$ diff   /home/bob/working/foo.c   /home/bob/working/.../foo.c

compares "foo.c" on the upper layer with the one on the lower layer.

Wide Area Software Development

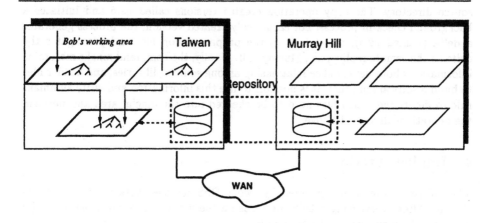

Fig. 1. Infrastructure for Wide Area Software Development

Figure 1 illustrates an example of wide-area software development, where users located at Taiwan and Murray Hill are collaborating on a project. Source code is replicated at both sites. To work on a modification request (e.g., MR7), user Bob at Taiwan initiates a new version (called *v2.5*) based on existing versions *v2.2* and *v2.1* using

$ vmap   /home/project/src   /v2.2/v2.1

He then sets up his own working area by overlapping a newly created and empty directory
"/home/bob/MR7" on the official source area:

$ vpath   /home/bob/MR7   /home/project/src

After that, Bob works on the project in his private area "/home/bob/MR7" using regular UNIX commands (e.g., vi, nmake). All modified and created files are physically located under the tree "/home/bob/MR7". Others users may be working on different MRs on their private areas at the same time, each of which has been set up using vmap to specify the proper version and vpath to construct a per-user working area. Upon finishing the task, Bob checks all changes into official source area, as follows:

```
$ vmap   /home/project/src   v2.5
$ for changed-file in /home/bob/MR7
    do
            cp   /home/bob/MR7/$changed-file   /home/bob/MR7/...
    done
```

The first line defines a new version named *v2.5* in the official source area; The second line copies modified files from Bob's directory to the lower layer, i.e., the official source directory. The copy operation creates versions called *v2.5* and initiates a background check-in process. For each newly created version, the process generates a delta (named *v2.5*), appends it to the proper version file, and propagates the delta to the remote replica, i.e., Murray Hill. Finally, the command nmake maintains information about dependence relationship among sources, libraries, and header files to build a software product. It is possible to use this information and write an nmake rule to determine which files need to be checked into the official area and perform the operations described above.

4   Implementation

The infrastructure is implemented by two *n*-DFS services: viewpathing and versioning. After overviewing *n*-DFS, we focus on the versioning service; the paper [6] describes the viewpath service in details.

4.1   Multiple Dimensional File Systems

n-DFS introduces a *logical layer* between the operating system and user applications. This layer presents applications with the same interface that the underlying system provides. However, it also allows users to *mount* services on nodes (i.e., directories or files) in the name space by maintaining a per-process name space. *n*-DFS intercepts system calls from applications, and then passes them to the mounted services.

    n-DFS provides a set of built-in services that are implemented as regular function calls and reside in the application's address space. No context switch is required to access these services. The viewpathing mechanism is implemented as a built-in service. Users place one directory on top of another using the command vpath. When the system call open is invoked by an application (e.g., vi) to access a file under the directory, *n*-DFS translates the pathname into the corresponding physical pathname by invoking the viewpathing service, and then calls the real system call open on this physical pathname.

    In addition to these built-in services, *n*-DFS also provides an infrastructure for implementing external services supported by external servers that run in different address spaces or even on different machines. To interact with the repository, GRA-DIENT implements a running server (called *VCS*). When the system call open is invoked by an application to access a VO, n-DFS returns the file descriptor of the corresponding version. If, however, the desired version hasn't been checked out yet, the system calls the server VCS to check the version out of the version file before it returns the version's file descriptor.

n-DFS is unique in that the logical layer is realized as a library linked by applications and run in the application's address space. For systems based on SVR4, such as Sun OS 4.1 [18], and most other modern operating systems that provide the concept of dynamic linking of shared libraries, we are able to replace the standard C shared library with n-DFS's library, and applications with dynamic linking may access n-DFS without any change. For systems without dynamic linking of shared libraries or applications with static linking, we need to re-link applications with n-DFS's library. In either case, n-DFS is transparent to the kernel and applications without any modification.

4.2 Versioning Services

To allow file system users transparent access to version files, the system employs *version directories* and version objects. Version directories maintain version names and cache checked-out versions, while VOs provide indirect naming of versions.

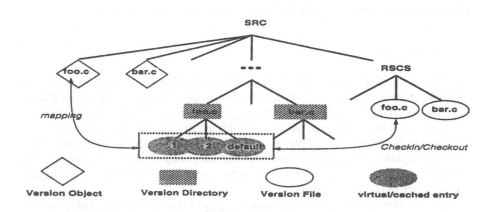

Fig. 2. Version files

Implemented as a regular UNIX directory, a version directory contains entries with available version names. Each entry could be a cached version that has been checked out of the version file earlier (called a cached entry), or a simple hard link to the version file (called a virtual entry). Whenever a virtual entry is opened, the system performs check out operations by calling the server VCS, which replaces the hard link with the real version, and returns the file descriptor of the version. Whenever listing attributes of a virtual entry, the system opens the version file (referred to as the entry's hard link) and returns the version's attributes stored in the version file.

Each VO is implemented as a dynamic symbolic link. Consider an example of source files for the software project illustrated in Figure 2. For the logical file "foo.c", there are

- a VO "SRC/foo.c",
- a version file "SRC/RSCS/foo.c",
- a version directory "SRC/.../foo.c",
- cached entries "SRC/.../foo.c/default" and "SRC/.../foo.c/1",
- a virtual entry "SRC/.../foo.c/2".

The symbolic link of "SRC/foo.c" is "../.../foo.c/*default*", where the last component "*default*" is dynamically replaceable. For example, a user specifies the version name she/he wants to access, as follows:

$ vmap   SRC/foo.c   1

When the user accesses "SRC/foo.c", the system replaces "default" with "1", and therefore
"SRC/foo.c" is pointed to "../.../foo.c/1" instead.

Finally, we list the last component of VO's symbolic link as "default" and have an entry named "default" in the version directory. The result is that users are able to access one version (i.e., "default") even while n-DFS is not running.

5   Discussion

Many research efforts share our philosophy of overloading file system semantics to improve system uniformity and utility, software reusability, and customer acceptability. Apollo's DOMAIN Software Engineering Environment (DSEE) [14] implements versioning files by storing all versions of a file in one file on disk. Digital's Vesta Repository [2] embeds the versioning into file systems to support large-scale software development. Sun's Translucent File Service (TFS) [8] embeds a viewpathing mechanism into file systems. All these projects introduce new functions by modifying the kernel or implementing new drivers.

On the other hand, n-DFS implements a logical layer using the library that is running in the application's address space. As mentioned above, for systems that provide dynamic linking of shared libraries, we are able to replace the standard C shared library with the new library, and applications with dynamic linking may use this infrastructure without any change. For systems without dynamic linking of shared libraries or applications with static linking, we need to re-link applications with the new library. By porting the library to a variety of platforms, we have shown that the library approach is more portable than modifying kernels or implementing new drivers.

Probably, the most closely related work is Atria's ClearCase [13], which implements configuration management functions in file systems. It provides *version object bases* (VOBs) as a common repository and a mechanism (called *view*) that provides per-user views of the repository. Both ClearCase and n-DFS differ in how they are plugged into operating systems, and the degree of transparency they present to existing UNIX commands and tools. That is,

- **Server Approach vs. Library Approach**
  ClearCase's VOB is implemented as a new type of file system and plugged into the Virtual File System (VFS) interface [17]. It uses a runtime server (similar to nfsd in Sun NFS [17]) as the VOB front-end and loads a new module to the kernel. The VOB server runs in the user address space and requires lots of context switch. On the other hand, our infrastructure is built on top of UNIX file systems: Version files are implemented as regular files; VOs are implemented by symbolic links, and most of functions needed to resolve logical pathnames to physical ones are implemented in the shared library. The server VCS is only involved when checking out a version from its version file[3].
- **Degrees of Transparency**
  Both systems use "checkout-edit-checkin" paradigms. However, ClearCase requires users to explicitly issue checkout commands for desired files before editing them. In n-DFS, the checkout process is completely transparent to users. Moreover, we preserve UNIX filesystem API, while ClearCase adds new functions to this API. Some existing UNIX tools and commands that are able to run on n-DFS may have problems on ClearCase. For example, system calls creat() and mkdir() are not allowed to create new files/directories on VOBs. Instead, ClearCase provides a different command (called mkelem). Hence, users need to issue the mkelem command to create a new file element on a VOB before being able to write out the new file in vi.

6 Conclusions

GRADIENT is a pilot project that addresses globalization of software R&D. As the first effort, we are designing and implementing an infrastructure for wide-area software developments. The infrastructure is unique in that it not only preserves the UNIX file system API, but is also implemented as a shared library and sets of services. By linking with a shared library, we are able to reuse most UNIX commands without any modification of commands or the kernel. Currently, a prototype is running between Murray Hill, New Jersey and Hsinchu, Taiwan. We are using it as a research vehicle to address configuration management of wide-area software development.

Acknowledgments

Glenn Fowler was instrumental in the design and implementation of the Multiple Dimensional File System.

---

[3] VCS requires root privilege to restore original attributes of the version, such as ownership, timestamps, and access control modes.

References

1. Eric Allman. An introduction to the source code control system. In *UNIX Programmer's Manual Supplementary Documents Volume 1*. University of California at Berkeley, April 1986.
2. Sheng-Yang Chiu and Roy Levin. The vesta repository: A file system extension for software development. Technical Report 106, Digital Systems Research Center, June 1993.
3. B. Erickson and J. Pellegrin. Build - a software construction tool. *Bell System Technical Journal*, 63(6), July 1984.
4. Glenn Fowler. A case for make. *Software—Practice and Experience*, 20(S1):S1/35 – S1/46, July 1990.
5. Glenn Fowler, Yennun Huang, David Korn, and Herman C. Rao. A user-level replicated file system. In *Proceedings of Summer USENIX*, June 1993.
6. Glenn Fowler, David Korn, and Herman C. Rao. n-DFS: Multiple Dimensional File System. In W. Tichy, editor, *Trends in Software*. John Wiley & Sons Ltd, 1994.
7. David Gifford, Pierre Jouvelot, Mark Sheldon, and James OToole. Semantic file systems. In *Proceedings of the Thirteenth ACM Symposium on Operating System Principles*, pages 16–25, October 1991.
8. David Hendricks. A filesystem for software development. In *Proceedings of Summer USENIX*, June 1990.
9. David Korn and Eduardo Krell. A new dimension for the Unix file system. *Software—Practice and Experience*, 20(S1):S1/19 – S1/34, July 1990.
10. David Korn and Kiem-Phong Vo. Disciplines and Methods. In B. Krishnamurthy, editor, *Practical Reusable UNIX Software*. John Wiley & Sons Ltd, 1995.
11. Eduardo Krell and Balachander Krishnamurthy. COLA: Customized overlaying. In *Proceedings of the USENIX Winter 1992 Conference*, pages 3–7, 1992.
12. Balachander Krishnamurthy and David S. Rosenblum. An event-action model of computer-supported cooperative work: Design and implementation. In *Proceedings of the International Workshop on Computer Supported Cooperative Work*, pages 132–145. IFIP TC 6/WG C.5, 1991.
13. David Leblang. The CM Challenge: Configuration Management that Works. In W. Tichy, editor, *Trends in Software*. John Wiley & Sons Ltd, 1994.
14. David Leblang, Robert Chase Jr., and Gordon McLean Jr. The DOMAIN software engineering environment for large-scale software development efforts. In *Proceedings of the First International Conference on Computer Workstations*, pages 226–280, November 1985.
15. Herman C. Rao and Larry L. Peterson. Accessing Files in an Internet: The Jade File System. *IEEE Transactions on Software Engineering*, pages 613–624, June 1993.
16. Herman C. Rao and Andrea Skarra. A transparent service for synchronized replication across loosely-connected, heterogeneous file systems. In *Proceedings of IEEE the 2nd Workshop on Services in Distributed and Networked Environments*, June 1995.
17. Russel Sandberg, David Goldberg, Steve Kleiman, Dan Walsh, and Bob Lyon. Design and implementation of the Sun Network File System. In *Proceedings of Summer USENIX*, pages 119–130, June 1985.
18. Sun Microsystems, Inc., Mountain View, Calif. *Shared Libraries*, May 1988.
19. Walter F. Tichy. RCS—a system for version control. *Software—Practice and Experience*, 15(7):637–654, 1985.

Distributed Revision Control
Via the World Wide Web

Jürgen Reuter, Stefan U. Hänßgen, James J. Hunt, and Walter F. Tichy *

IPD, University of Karlsruhe, Karlsruhe, Germany

Abstract. Revision control has long been a standard part of software development. With the enormous expansion of the Internet and its increasing use as a means of communicating among geographically dispersed software developers, the need for distributed version control over the Internet has become acute. In order to address this need, the authors have developed a revision control server based on the World Wide Web (WWW) and RCE (an outgrowth of RCS). This proves to be possible and it also highlights the strengths and weaknesses of using the Hyper Text Mark up Language and standard WWW browsers such as NetScape^TM and Mosaic to accomplish this goal.

1 Introduction

Programs for revision control have been available to software engineers for over a decade. The best known examples are RCS[12] and SCCS[11]. Up until relatively recently, revision control was only available locally. Though the network could be used to mount a file system containing revision control archives and archives could be accessed using remote login and ftp, one had to first obtain system access to the appropriate system before one could access an archive. Recently ClearCase[10] has introduced a distributed revision control system that can be used between a number of geographically separated groups. But here again, accessing the archive requires access to the host on which the archive (or versioned object base) resides.

There are many situations where this type of access is not desirable. For example, in a scenario where two companies collaborate on a short term project, they may not wish to grant one another full access to each other's machines. Still, relatively unrestricted access is needed to the the shared source code. Another example is supporting working from home or free-lance software development. Here again, a firm may want to maintain control of the source code without the risk of unrestricted dial-in access.

An obvious solution for such situations is to develop a revision control system based on a client/server architecture. This type of architecture has been quite successfully used for the X Window System and the World Wide Web. It gives all users on the net (including those using dial-in network protocols like PPP

---

* The authors can be reached at (reuterj|haenssgen|jjh|tichy)@ira.uka.de respectively

and SLIP) potential access to the archives without the need to login to the server machine. Access control to the archives can be managed totally independently of any host login process. Thus the desired level of access and protection can be tailored to the individual needs of each development team.

2 Building Blocks

At first glance, this solution seems to require a tremendous amount of effort to implement. A server needs to be developed that supports all aspects of revision control. An interface format must also be developed for communicating between the clients and the server. A client program must be written to present the user interface. Finally, this client must be ported to each machine architecture and operating system where it is to be used. The only way to minimize this development work is to take advantage of already existing tools.

2.1 RCE

At the server end, much work can be spared by using an existing revision control system. There are several revision control systems available, but only one — the Revision Control Engine (RCE) — offers a full fledged API that does not rely on external program invocation. RCE is a descendant of RCS with a number of enhancements, the most important one being that it uses a much better differencing algorithm than RCS[9]. This means that RCE archives are much more compact than RCS archives and binary data can be efficiently stored along side text data. By taking advantage of the RCE API[3], much work can be spared in building a revision control server.

2.2 Using Existing World Wide Browsers

This still leaves the interface format and the client side of the system. As mentioned above, there are two very successful client/server systems that are available on almost every platform: The X Window System and the World Wide Web[5] (WWW). The latter is designed to support the distribution of documents. This is a goal that covers at least half of the client side needs of a distributed revision control system — the selective transmission of data from the server to the client and managing user interaction.

WWW is based on a client/server model where clients request documents from any number of servers across the network. The interface format for WWW is Hyper Text Mark up Language. HTML[2] offers a means of describing documents and user interfaces in a machine independent form. It also contains a mechanism for uniquely locating other documents (servers) throughout the Internet. The client program or WWW Browser is responsible for interpreting HTML, then presenting the result to the user and channeling user responses to the appropriate server.

By combining components from both RCE and WWW one could build a full distributed revision control system. The server can be build on top of the RCE API and must generate HTML and respond to WWW Browser requests. Standard WWW Browsers such as NetScape™and Mosaic can then be used to access the WWW base revision control server. This means the system can take advantage of the enormous base of existing WWW clients. Only small additions on the client side are needed to transfer revisions of data between the client and server.

3 World Wide Revision Control Prototype

The authors have succeeded in building a prototype system named World Wide Revision Control. Before diving into the architecture, here is the user's perspective of the WWRC system in action. This should provide some insight into how it all works. Screen dumps 1 to 4 show different stages of the user dialog involved in checking out a revision. The WWRC Server generates all the HTML pages automatically from the RCE archives. As a popular example of a WWW browser we here use NetScape™. All screen shots are taken from our WWRC prototype implementation written in Modula-3[8] and running on a Sun SPARC 5 under SunOS 4.1.3.

Almost all user actions consist of selecting an item or button by clicking on it. Only adding items to lists or entering text fields (e.g. comments) involves the keyboard at all. The WWRC server handles the actions accordingly and produces a new HTML page as a result[2].

3.1 Login

Before the user can access any archives, he has to give his name and password. The server checks them against its own database and uses them later to tell different connections apart, enforce access rights, etc. This database might be quite different from the system login database. Only once the user is verified, can he make use of the archives belonging to that server.

3.2 Revision archive handling

After login, the user can select an archive and perform various operations on it, e.g. show its log file or its revision graph. To allow easy access to frequently used archives, the user can also define a pickup list from where he can directly choose archives later. Administration functions such as changing the WWRC password, as well as online help are offered here, too.

---

[2] with the exception of the check in/out process which necessitates transfer of other data than HTML files, as described in the Architecture section.

Fig. 1. The WWRC login screen

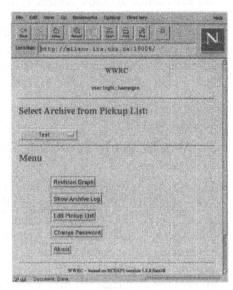

Fig. 2. Archive options

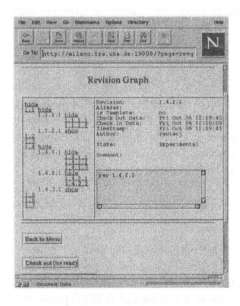

Fig. 3. Revision graph of one archive

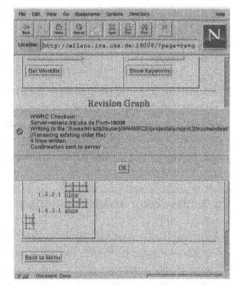

Fig. 4. Successful check out

3.3 Revision graphs

The revision graph view shows the selected archive's revisions. Subgraphs can be hidden or shown again to give a clearer overview. Selecting one revision displays more information on it, such as its time stamps, the author, its state, and commentary about the revision. The graph is displayed as formatted text as shown in figure 3. This saves network bandwidth compared to dynamically generating pictures.

3.4 Check Out

Once a revision is selected, it can be checked out and transferred to the user's machine. How this is done internally using just the WWW browser and a small helper application is the subject of section 5. The user just clicks on the check out button and gets a confirmation of the check out's success.

3.5 Other functions

The functionality described above is just a representative selection. WWRC makes all of RCE's functions accessible over the Internet. Checking in files, adding comments, selecting work files, creating new revisions, etc. are all supported.

4 Challenges

In order to develop this prototype, it was necessary to overcome three problems. How can large amounts of data be transferred automatically, particularly back to the server? How can consistency be maintained with a stateless protocol? How can actions that are inherently separate in HTML be combined to produce a comfortable user interface?

Getting information from a server is the very purpose of WWW, however automatically storing the information in some defined place on the client machine without asking the user for directions is not supported. Also, transferring larger amounts of data from the WWW Browser to the Server is far from trivial. HTML now offers forms for user input, but they are not at all adequate for automatic data transfer in the megabyte range. Therefore, some suitable mechanism for the check in and check out file transfer is necessary.

The WWRC server itself also does not 100% fit the WWW paradigm at first glance. It has to keep some state information for each user, but HTTP[1] is inherently stateless. Also, the server has to perform the RCE functions using the API and generate WWW pages showing archive and control information on the fly.

Furthermore, as a response to a user action such as pressing a form button, the server is limited to just generating one kind of reply: it can either create a new WWW page containing updated information or it can transfer data. This is just like on an ordinary WWW server: one can either follow some link or down load a file, e.g, some PostScript document. In some cases it would be preferable to do both at once.

5 Architecture

A brief look beneath the hood of WWRC will help clarify how WWRC manages to use standard WWW browsers to present the afore described user interface.

To tackle the bidirectional file transfer problem, WWRC uses the concept of helper applications. These are small programs that the WWW Browser calls in order to display those kinds of data it cannot visualize itself. An example is the Browser receiving a PostScript file. After down loading the file, it may start the `ghostscript` application to display it. Adding a new helper application just involves adding the its file type and its calling procedure to the Browser's configuration files. This can easily be done by the user.

The idea of how to perform check in and check out is based on this concept: Upon a check out request, the Server first does a local check out of the file on its machine into a special directory that is unique to each WWRC user. To transfer this checked out file, it then transmits a header stating the file's name and directory position, as well as some administrative information, and finally includes the file contents themselves. The type of this generated transfer file is set to "rceco" which causes the Browser to call the new helper application "checkout" with the transfer file. The application reads the header, determines where in the user's directory tree the resulting file should be created, and writes the file's contents into there[3]. After that, it sends back a confirmation directly to the server stating the file has been received successfully. The server then marks the locally checked-out file as expired to remove it automatically on the next request for an HTML page. In case the transmission failed, this concept still allows the user to request the file once again. Figure 5 illustrates this process.

Similarly, to perform a check in from some user file to the server, the server transmits a dummy file stating which user file to transfer. The corresponding helper application reads the file on the client machine. It then connects itself directly to the server, which puts the file into a special directory there where it is then checked into the server's archive. The server knows into which archive to put the file and to which user it belongs because administrative information from the dummy file is sent back to it together with the file itself. All file paths are taken relative to some root directory on the server and some point in the user's directory tree, so the file structures below that point are the same on client and server.

The server and the helper application have complete control over the connection and the original data on the server is kept until its reception has been confirmed by the client. This means that any protocol can be implemented to handle possible losses of connection during large file transfers or to encrypt data

---

[3] any already existing file is uniquely renamed to avoid overwriting it.

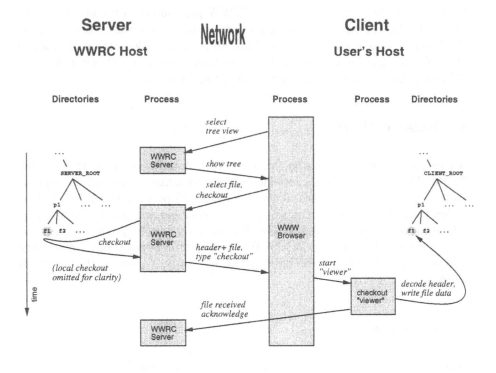

Fig. 5. Internal processes during check out

for transfer. These concepts are well known in the Internet community and could be adapted to WWRC as well; the current implementation prototype does not yet support that functionality.

The second problem, namely the statelessness of the HTTP protocol, can be solved by adding all necessary information to the URLs themselves. In addition to that, the Server keeps an internal database for each user recording information such as the current work file and the user's pickup list. To keep the user from going back in his browser's history of recently accessed pages and perform actions on these pages whose content is out of date, WWRC keeps a time stamp on each page and warns the user when he tries to use outdated forms. The state information is also necessary because the WWRC server process is started anew for each client request. This allows multiple servers to be active at once, rising the throughput of the system, but the server has to know where to resume. This is achieved by combining the user information given in the URLs with the state information database.

For the *either page or data* question we have not yet found an elegant solution that is both platform and browser independent. The problem is that pressing a button, for example to check in a file transmits the data as described above, can cause a file to be transmitted, but the WWW page shown in the browser is not updated. This means that it no longer reflects the state of the archive after the check out. The obvious cure is to add text to the page making the user aware of this behavior and urging him to press a continue button directly after check in. However, this still leaves too many possibilities for errors.

6   Related Work

There are two main aspects to this work: distributed revision control and the World Wide Web as a transport medium for computer supported cooperative work (CSCW). As mentioned above, ClearCase[10] provides for distributed revision control; however, it requires users to have login accounts on the machine where the archives are stored. BSCW[4] is an example of a system that uses the World Wide Web as a basis for CSCW; however, it does not support deltas and revision trees. WWRC is the only system the authors know of that supports both.

7   Conclusion

This paper demonstrates the possibility of using the World Wide Web for distributed Revision Control. The approach taken at the client side is machine-independent and portable — adding a new client architecture just means porting the small checkin and checkout helper applications and making cosmetic changes to the existing Browser's configuration file. Furthermore, the techniques used here may also be used to convert other applications to client-server architectures based on WWW and the Internet.

8   Future Work

While the current system is in a good working condition, as shown above, there are plans to improve usability, efficiency, security, and functionality.

Usability can be enhanced by cleaning up the user interface and integrating user side utility programs. Aside from improving the layout of some of the HTML pages that are generated, provisions need to be added to handle several files at the same time. Also, the integration with the ability to step backwards to previous sides and then forward again needs a bit more support to maintain consistency. Java[7] can be used to replace the helper application and to support other advanced functions in an even more portable manner.

The efficiency can be improved by two means. The server can be made faster by using a daemon to interact with the Web server instead of starting a new large server process for each transaction. Also, data could be automatically compressed to improve the transfer time for check in and check out.

There is a general need to limit access to any revision control system. Though password verification is already present, the data sent over the net is not protected from snooping. This needs to be addressed through the use of data encryption as mentioned above.

Currently, a WWRC version supporting multi-checkouts, i.e. allowing the user to check out a complete set of files, is in development. While concurrent accesses and possible conflicts are handled by the underlying RCE locking concept, the server has to be extended to avoid deadlocks and increase efficiency. For example, the system needs to support the case where two or more simultaneous user requests intersect one another, i.e. they both contain some of the same files. Eventually this list based approach needs to be extended with check out sets and other facilities for managing large projects. Using the system as a communication forum for the developers could help coordinate development in a large project. Configuration management can also be used to make WWRC an effective distributed project management tool.

References

1. HTTP: A protocol for networked information.
   `http://info.cern.ch/hypertext/WWW/Protocols/HTTP/HTTP2.html`, 1993.
2. The HTML 3.0 HyperText Document Format.
   `http://www.w3.org/hypertext/WWW/Arena/tour/start.html`, 1994.
3. *RCE - Introduction and Reference Manual*, API Revision 1.4.5 edition, 1995.
4. R. Bentley, T. Horstmann, K. Sikkel, and J. Trevor. Supporting collaborative information sharing with the World-Wide Web: The BSCW shared workspace system. In *Proceedings of the 4th International WWW Conference*, Boston, MS, December 1995.
5. Tim Berners-Lee. World Wide Web Initiative.
   `http://info.cern.ch/hypertext/WWW/TheProject.html`, 1994.
6. Jacky Estublier and Rubby Casallas. The adele configuration manager. In Walter F. Tichy, editor, *Configuration Management*, pages 99–133. John Wiley & Sons, 1994.
7. James Gosling and Henry McGilton. The Java Language Environment.
   `http://www.javasoft.com/documentation.html`, 1995.
8. Samuel P. Harbison. *Modula-3*. Prentice Hall, 1992.
9. James J. Hunt, Kiem-Phong Vo, and Walter F. Tichy. An empirical study of delta algorithms. *Sofware Configuration Management Workshop*, 1996.
10. Atria Software Inc. ClearCase concepts. Technical report, ., Natick, Mass., 1993.
11. M. Rockhind. The source code control system. *IEEE Trans. on Soft. Eng.*, SE-1(4):364–370, Dec 1975.
12. Walter F. Tichy. RCS: A revision control system. In *Integrated Interactive Computing Systems*. North-Holland Publishing Co, 1983.

The Asgard System: Activity-Based Configuration Management

Josephine Micallef[1] and Geoffrey M. Clemm[2]

[1] Bellcore, 445 South Street, Morristown, NJ 07962–1910
[2] Atria Software, Inc., 20 Maguire Road, Lexington, MA 02173-3104

Abstract. The novel aspect of the Asgard configuration management system is the integration of (1) the use of activities—named objects created by developers to represent development tasks—to define system configurations, (2) the detection of inconsistencies when activities are assembled into new configurations, and (3) dynamic controlled sharing of work products.

In Asgard, a developer specifies the source versions that he wants to see by means of a baseline and a list of activities. A baseline is a fixed set of immutable source versions. An activity is a cluster of versions produced in the course of a specific development task. Activity-based configuration management provides a simple and intuitive way for developers to specify the context for their work, to track project status, and to produce accurate information for system maintainers.

1 Introduction

Many different concepts are discussed under the rubric of "software configuration management": history management, version selection, change tracking, team work, software manufacture, audit and review, release management, process management [11, 4]. In this paper we focus primarily on the following aspects:

- **change tracking**—keeping track of modifications made to each component, including the reason, time, and user who made the change. Traditionally this information was maintained at the individual component level. We argue that the information is more accurate and usable if elicited and associated with "logical changes" being made.

- **version selection**—selecting the right versions of components for development, integration, testing and baselining. An important aspect to version selection is support for composing consistent configurations.

- **team work**—managing simultaneous update of the same component by several programmers, providing "sandboxes" for individual development, and supporting integration of completed work products.

Many user-level requirements of a configuration management (CM) system involve logical changes. Examples of queries one may ask about a system include:

- Find all components that were modified, and the modifications made in each, for a specific change.
- Determine which logical changes a component was modified for.
- Determine what other changes a specific change depends on.
- Determine whether a logical change is contained in a particular configuration.
- Determine which configurations include a particular change.

Despite this, many CM systems in use today are version-oriented rather than change-oriented. They record information on the task being performed, but do not interpret this data other than to answer simple queries. This leads to a major shortcoming that logical change information is often incomplete or inaccurate since the user entering the information derives no direct benefit from it.

In contrast, we place the "activity" that the developer works on at the forefront of the CM system, and center all CM functionality around it. The amount of change tracking information that is elicited from the user is minimal—a developer just indicates his current task when switching to a different work item. Developers have an incentive to provide accurate change information since the same information is used to configure their work context. Examples of how logical changes are used in defining system configurations include:

- Select changes made by a colleague to fix a bug but do not include changes made by the same colleague for a new feature.
- Combine work items completed by the development team.
- Apply a bug fix made in a maintenance release to new development.
- Backout a change that did not pass system test from the release.

In Asgard, a developer (or integrator) specifies the source versions that he wants to see by means of a baseline and a list of activities. A baseline is a fixed set of immutable source versions. An activity is a cluster of versions produced in the course of a specific development task.

One of the attractions of activity-based configuration management is the ability to apply a logical change to a context different from the one where the change was made (as in the examples listed above). Therein, however, lies the source of a serious potential problem: the change may be inconsistent with the new context. Unlike other systems that provide activity-based configuration management [10, 8], Asgard detects inconsistencies in the resulting configuration when the applied change updates some component that was also modified in the new context, or when the applied change depends on other changes that are not included in the new context.

When planning a software release, an attempt is made to partition the changes that are to be included in the release into independent tasks, which are then assigned to individual developers. These changes are worked on in isolation, and combined at scheduled integration milestones in the release cycle. Asgard supports this integration process by a straightforward application of activity-based CM, but in addition informs the integrator about the consistency of the integration configuration as described above. There are often times, however, when tasks assigned to different developers interact and cannot be developed in isolation, requiring closer cooperation among the developers. To support this form of interaction, Asgard allows dynamic controlled sharing of work products among developers by shared activities.

The rest of the paper is organized as follows: An overview of the Asgard system is presented in section 2. The development model supported by Asgard, designed to scale from individual to large team development, is the topic of section 3. Activity-based version selection is described in section 4. Section 5 compares Asgard to other CM systems. We conclude with a brief description of the implementation and direction for future work.

2 The Asgard System

The Asgard configuration management system was developed at Bellcore to support the production of very large-scale software. The design of Asgard was driven by the following goals: support parallel development, be simple and lightweight for developers to use, facilitate early integration, support complex product releases, and minimize errors in producing new configurations. Asgard incorporates the Odin build system [3], which is simpler, more powerful, and more efficient than Make [6] and its successors, especially for large or complex systems.

There are three fundamental object types in Asgard:

- **Workspace**: a private work area for development activities (e.g., editing source files, building executables, integration, testing). Elements (files or directories) in a workspace are either versioned or non-versioned. A versioned element is shared among workspaces while a non-versioned element is only visible in the workspace where the element was created. For versioned elements, the version that is visible in the workspace is determined by the workspace's baseline and list of activities, as described in section 4.

- **Baseline**: a particular configuration of the system (e.g., an intermediate checkpoint, an integration baseline, or a shipped release). A baseline is composed of a fixed, immutable set of versions. In a workspace with an empty activity list, the element versions visible in the workspace are the versions listed in the workspace's baseline.

- **Activity**: represents a development task (e.g., "fix the install script bug", "add command-line editing", "update the test scripts to handle the new foobar command"). The *products* of an activity are the versions created to complete the development task. At most one workspace activity can be marked as the *current* activity. When a new potential version is created as the result of a "check-out" command, Asgard automatically associates the new version with the workspace's current activity. Activities provide the dynamic component of a workspace's view: new activity products are immediately visible in each workspace that contains the activity.

An activity can have nested sub-activities to model the decomposition of a development task. For example, the `add-command-line-editing` activity may

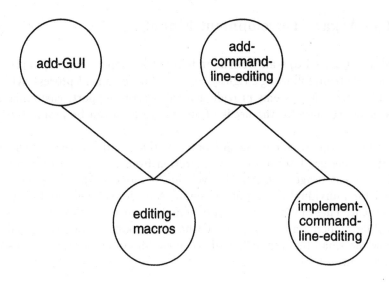

Fig. 1. Activity Decomposition Graph Example

be broken up into an `editing-macros` activity that provides generic editing utilities, and an `implement-command-line-editing` activity, that uses these generic utilities to provide command-line editing.

An activity can have multiple parent activities to model a sub-task that is common to multiple top-level tasks. Continuing with the example above, a graphical user interface also requires editing facilities to enter textual information. The `add-GUI` activity would declare the `editing-macros` activity as a sub-activity, making available all the code that implemented the editing utilities. The activity decomposition graph for the example in the last two paragraphs is shown in figure 1.

When an activity is added to a workspace, all the versions produced in that activity, as well as all its recursively nested sub-activities, become visible. In the previous example, if the `editing-macros` activity is added to a workspace, then only the changes that implement the generic editing facility are visible. However, if instead the `add-command-line-editing` activity is added to the workspace, then in addition, the changes that implement command-line editing are also visible, but the changes made to provide a GUI interface are not.

Developers can easily share work by adding a top-level activity to their workspace, without knowing all the low-level implementation details about how the work was performed (e.g., which files were changed, and which versions of those files to use). The activity decomposition structure is also a useful annotation for system maintenance.

3 The Asgard Development Model

Asgard was designed to scale from an individual developer doing rapid prototyping to a large team following a tightly controlled development process. Although many advanced CM systems provide general process support, customizing the process support layer for the needs of an organization can be prohibitively expensive.

To address this problem, Asgard provides three built-in development models that are designed to allow easy migration from one model to another, or even concurrent usage of multiple development models. The three models are targeted for individual development, small team development and large team development. These models can be used simultaneously to allow, for example, a group of developers on a large project who are working on closely related tasks to follow the small team model, while they coordinate with other groups using the large team model.

3.1 Individual Development

The simplest development model in Asgard consists of the following steps:

1. *Initialize the work context.* This involves choosing the workspace's initial baseline and list of activities. A workspace may need to be created. Typically, a developer has a workspace for all development on a specific product.

2. *Do work.* The developer performs the normal "edit/compile/test" cycle in the selected workspace, with the following additional operations. Before changing a versioned element, the element must be checked out.[3] Before checking out an element, the workspace must have a current activity,[4] which may need to be created if the developer is starting a new task. When an activity reaches a stable point, it can be checked in (i.e., all files checked out for that activity become new persistent versions). The "check-in" command can also be performed on individual files or the whole workspace (in which case all checked-out files are checked in).

3. *Create new context.* At stable points in the development cycle, a new baseline is created. The workspace baseline is then replaced with the new baseline, and activities that have been incorporated in the new baseline can be removed from the workspace's activity list.

Asgard utilizes the check-out/check-in model to maintain a version history of individual elements and to control their concurrent modification. The check-out

---

[3] Note that a workspace provides transparent access to the versions visible in the workspace, so there is no need to check-out an element in order to read it.

[4] Although a workspace can have at most one current activity, a user can effectively work on multiple activities by creating a common sub-activity and making the sub-activity the current activity.

operation creates a mutable version that is a copy of, and is linked to, the version that was visible in the workspace. The check-in operation makes the mutable version immutable. If the predecessor of the mutable version already has successor versions, the check-out operation fails. The user can choose to "force" the check-out by adding the '-f' option to the check-out command, thereby creating a parallel branch that allows concurrent work on the same element in different activities.

3.2 Small Team Development

In a small group where developers are working on related tasks, they often want to see some new changes as soon as they are available but they do not want to see other changes that would disrupt their current work. In Asgard, developers dynamically share work by sharing activities.

Adding an activity to a workspace makes all the versions produced in that activity, as well as its nested sub-activities, visible in the workspace. A developer can add any activity to his workspace, including ones that are owned by other users, as long as he has read permission to the activity. (Asgard objects have read, write, and execute permissions analogous to the standard UNIX permissions.)

Any new work done in an activity is immediately visible in each workspace containing that activity or one of its ancestors. For example, suppose a developer adds a colleague's activity to her workspace. Subsequently, the colleague realizes that he forgot to change a file, so he modifies and checks in that file. The first developer immediately sees the new version of the file—or she gets a conflict if her previously selected version was on a different branch from the one containing the new version (see section 4 for explanation).

3.3 Large Team Development

Asgard provides additional functionality for orderly integration of work performed by multiple developers to allow notification of the integrator when completed work activities are delivered for integration, notification of developers when new integration baselines are available, synchronization of development workspaces with the integrated work, and multiple integration areas to facilitate incorporating an activity in multiple releases.

A workspace has a list of integration areas—workspaces where completed activities are integrated. For clarity, we refer to a workspace where development activities are worked on as a *development* workspace, and a workspace where development activities are integrated as an *integration* workspace. One of these integration workspaces is declared the *primary* integration workspace. The primary integration workspace is used to provide new integration baselines for development workspaces.

Each workspace has a *to-do* activity list. For a development workspace, the to-do list is used to record activities that the user plans to work on. For an integration workspace, the to-do list contains completed activities that have been delivered for integration but which have not yet been integrated. Note that an activity on the to-do list does not affect the workspace's view of source versions.

The integration model supported by Asgard consists of these steps:

1. *Deliver completed work for integration*: The Asgard "deliver" command adds the specified activities to the to-do list of the integration workspace. Email notification is sent to the owner of the integration workspace.

2. *Integrator combines delivered work*: The integrator adds delivered activities to the integration workspace, resolves any resulting conflicts either by performing merge operations, adding missing activities, or deferring some activities for a later integration. Note that the next step, creating a new baseline, cannot be performed until all conflicts have been resolved.

3. *New integration baseline created*: When the integrator is satisfied with the integration configuration, he creates a new baseline. Email notification is sent to the owners of the development workspaces informing them that a new integration baseline is available.

4. *Resync development workspace with new baseline*: When the developer is ready to see the changes made by the rest of the development team, he updates his workspace's baseline with the new integration baseline. This may produce conflicts in the developer's workspace if he has workspace activities that are not included in the integration workspace but which modify the same element changed by an integrated activity.

The following extended example illustrates how integration is set up for a project with on-going work for parallel releases. Developers on the **ws** project are working on new features for the next major release, as well as fixing bugs found in the previously shipped release. Integration workspace **ws-integ** is used to integrate new development activities; integration workspace **ws-maint-integ** is used to integrate maintenance activities.

Developer **jm** uses workspace **jm-dev** to work on new development activities. She sets **ws-integ** as the primary integration workspace for **jm-dev**. When user **jm** delivers completed workspace activities for integration, they are added to the to-do list of integration workspace **ws-integ**.

The same developer **jm** uses workspace **jm-maint** to work on maintenance activities. Since bug fixes need to be propagated to the new release, the **jm-maint** workspace has **ws-integ** as an integration workspace, in addition to the primary integration workspace, **ws-maint-integ**. When user **jm** delivers bug-fix activities from workspace **jm-maint**, they are added to the to-do lists of both the maintenance and new development integration workspaces. Eventually they are integrated into both maintenance and major releases.

Some activities are targeted for a subset of the planned product releases. For example, activity **temp-fix** provides a temporary fix for a problem found in the previously shipped release. Since a better solution is to be implemented for the new release, activity **temp-fix** is only delivered to the maintenance integration workspace.

The copy/modify/merge CM model, exemplified by the nested environments of Sun's NSE system [7], bears a similarity to the Asgard integration model but is less flexible. The flow of changes in the NSE model must follow the environment hierarchy, so changes cannot be shared by sibling environments until they have been committed to the parent. In addition, one cannot selectively commit a subset of the changes from a child environment to the parent environment.

4 Activity-based Version Selection

The version of an element that is visible in a workspace depends on three things: the workspace's baseline, the workspace's activity list, and the element's version graph. Any Asgard operation that changes any of these causes the recomputation of the visible version for each affected element. The version selection algorithm can be described abstractly as follows:

1. Order versions of the element so that if v_2 is a modification of v_1, then $v_2 > v_1$. We say that v_2 *dominates* v_1. A version produced as a result of merging several contributor versions dominates all contributors.

2. Mark versions that are in the workspace baseline, products of a workspace activity, or products of a descendent sub-activity of a workspace activity.

3. Define the *candidate set* to contain all marked versions that are not dominated by any other marked version. If the candidate set contains more than one version, the selection algorithm returns an *ambiguous* selection error.

4. A candidate is *incomplete*, if there is a path through the dominates version graph from the candidate to the baseline version (or an ancestor of the baseline) that passes through an unmarked version.

The version selection algorithm has two possible outcomes: (1) a version of the element is selected, or (2) a version selection conflict is reported for the element. There are two kinds of conflicts: *ambiguous* selection conflicts, and *incomplete* selection conflicts. An ambiguous selection conflict indicates that the set of workspace activities do not uniquely identify a version of the element. The candidate set of versions and the activities that produced them are shown by the Asgard "lsconflicts" command. Such a conflict is typically resolved by invoking the merge command on the conflict element to produce a version that contains all the changes, but it can also be resolved by removing workspace activities. An *incomplete* selection conflict indicates that the candidate version identified by the workspace's baseline and activities includes versions that are products of activities not associated with the workspace. Such a conflict is typically resolved by adding the missing activities, which are shown by the "lsconflicts" command.

When an element has a conflict, no version of that element is selected in the workspace. This means that any attempt to access the element, such as for editing or compiling, will fail with an error message from the operating system (e.g., "No such file or directory"). In interactive mode, the Asgard prompt indicates

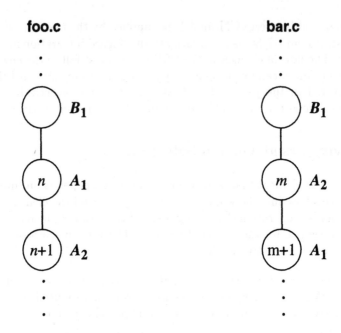

Fig. 2. Scenario for Incomplete Selection Conflict

whether the workspace has conflicts or not: a :-) is used when there are no conflicts, while a :-(is used when there are conflicts.

The reason for reporting an incomplete selection conflict rather than simply selecting the candidate version, ignoring included changes not explicitly requested, is that to do so would result in erroneous configurations. Consider the two elements shown in figure 2. If the workspace has baseline B_1 and an activity list consisting of just A_1, then version n of foo.c and version $m + 1$ of bar.c would be selected. But the change made in bar.c version m in activity A_2, which is included in the selected version of this element, depends on version $n + 1$ of foo.c, which is not selected! In Asgard, version n is selected for foo.c and an incomplete selection error is reported for bar.c. The user can add activity A_2 to the workspace, or produce a version of bar.c that does not include the change made in A_2.

An alternative we considered instead of reporting an incomplete selection error is to automatically add the missing activities to the workspace. Since adding an activity may result in additional incomplete candidates, this operation may need to be repeated. We rejected this alternative because the decision to include a change in a configuration should be made by the user.

5 Related Work

The technical contribution of the Asgard configuration management system is the integration of three features that are critical to effective team development: (1) activity-based configuration specification, (2) detection of inconsistent configurations, and (3) dynamic update of workspaces by shared activities. Other systems have provided some of these features. Table 1 compares Asgard to four representative CM systems.

Software Management System's Aide-De-Camp system [10] is the only commercial product that provides activity-based version selection. Aide-De-Camp allows you to combine arbitrary activities (which they call "change sets") without any consistency constraints. For example, if two change sets both insert a line of text after a specific line in a file, the result when the two change sets are selected depends on which change set was installed first. Aide-De-Camp does provide a turnkey development model, Model 209, which detects conflicting changes to the same physical region of a file, but Model 209 significantly constrains activity-based version selection. Aide-De-Camp provides no support for dynamically updating a file version when the file is changed by another user; the user must do an explicit "adc-write-file" command to obtain the new version of the file.

Change-oriented versioning is used in the EPOS research project [8, 9]. The EPOS system extends the Aide-De-Camp model by introducing the concept of an "ambition", which is the list of activities (which they call "options") for which a given change is applicable. Being able to specify more than one option in an ambition allows an EPOS user to declare that a change should be visible if and only if the user selects the particular option combination specified in the ambition. This particular kind of consistency is not provided by any of the other systems, but EPOS does not detect the types of conflicting changes detected by Asgard. One drawback of the EPOS method of defining configurations is that there is no notion of a baseline, so every option ever used to modify the desired version must be listed. Also, EPOS does not implement dynamic sharing of changes among multiple workspaces.

Atria Software's ClearCase product [1] provides rule-based version selection. To select a version of an element, the rules are evaluated sequentially until an applicable rule is found, in which case the version identified by that rule is selected. If no rule applies, then no version of the element is selected. Activity-

Table 1. Comparison of Asgard to other CM systems

	Aide-De-Camp	EPOS	ClearCase	Workshop System	Asgard
Activity-Based Version Selection	X	X			X
Consistent Configurations		X		X	X
Dynamic Views			X	X	X

based version selection cannot be simulated by ClearCase's version selection rules. To see this, consider again the example shown in figure 2. If the workspace has baseline B_1 and activities A_1 and A_2, then if the rule for selecting A_1's products appears before the rule for selecting A_2's products, versions n of foo.c and $m + 1$ of bar.c are selected, which is incorrect. But if the rule ordering is reversed, then versions $n + 1$ of foo.c and m of bar.c are selected, which is also incorrect. In ClearCase, there is also no notion of an inconsistent configuration. ClearCase supports dynamic views in that a new version that is produced in some view is immediately eligible for selection in other views.

The Workshop System [2], like Asgard, has activities (or "jobs") as the central CM objects. Unlike activities, jobs can only be used to select an existing version of the system, not to compose new configurations. Since new configurations are explicitly created by the user, and the user has to resolve any conflicting changes before committing the new configuration, no inconsistent configurations can be generated. The Workshop System provides dynamic updates from the global database to user workspaces and tools when a file version changes.

Other CM systems provide some support for logical changes, primarily by recording which file versions were produced for a logical change. For a comparison of the capabilities of several commercial configuration management systems, the reader is referred to the excellent article by Peter Feiler [5].

6   Implementation

Asgard is implemented as a layer on top of ClearCase. Asgard objects—workspaces, baselines, and activities—are stored in an object-oriented database (ObjectStore, from Object Design, Inc.). The version selection algorithm attaches labels to selected versions, which are then used in simple ClearCase configuration specification rules. Error rules are used to hide elements with a version selection conflict. Each workspace has an "update daemon", which performs version selection when commands in other workspaces affect that workspace's view.

7   Conclusion

Asgard has been used by 3 development groups at Bellcore. It has been used for its own development for the last two years. The size of the groups ranged from 5 to 20 developers, with our largest group spread over three Bellcore sites. Initial training consisted of an hour long overview of the system, followed by a two-hour introduction to the Asgard command set. User feedback has been very positive.

We are exploring several directions for future work:

- Composite baselines: Large software project consists of several subsystems, each of which may consist of hundreds or thousands of modules. It is necessary to break up baselines along subsystem boundaries rather than having a monolithic project-wide baseline. This is the appropriate granularity for selecting versions in other subsystems since they change more or less independently of each other, yet only some subsystem versions work with other subsystem versions.

- Information filtering/scoping: The number of objects managed by the system may get very large over time, especially if the development group is large. A mechanism to select only those objects that are "interesting" to a developer is necessary—both from a user-interface perspective as well as from an algorithmic complexity point of view.

- Process tracking and control: Activities are the logical connection between a CM system and bug-tracking and project scheduling systems. Asgard activities have fields to provide this connection, but actual integration with commercial tools has not yet been implemented.

References

1. Atria Software, Inc. *ClearCase Reference Manual*, 1994.
2. Geoffrey M. Clemm. Replacing version control with job control. In *2nd International Workshop on Software Configuration Management*, pages 162–169, Princeton, New Jersey, October 1989.
3. Geoffrey M. Clemm. The Odin system. In *Software Configuration Management: Selected papers / ICSE SCM-4 and SCM-5 workshops*, number 1005 in Lecture Notes in Computer Science, pages 241–262. Springer-Verlag, October 1995.
4. Susan Dart. Concepts in configuration management systems. In Peter H. Feiler, editor, *3rd International Workshop on Software Configuration Management*, pages 1–18, Trondheim, Norway, June 1991.
5. Peter H. Feiler. Configuration management models in commercial environments. Technical Report CMU/SEI-91-TR-7, Software Engineering Institute, Carnegie Mellon University, March 1991.
6. S.I. Feldman. Make—a program for maintaining computer programs. *Software— Practice & Experience*, 9(4):255–265, April 1979.
7. Masahiro Honda. Support for parallel development in the Sun network software environment. In *2nd International Workshop on Computer-Aided Software Engineering*, pages 5–5 – 5–7, 1988.
8. Anund Lie, Reider Conradi, Tor M. Didriksen, Even-Andre Karlsson, Svein O. Hallsteinsen, and Per Holager. Change oriented versioning in a software engineering database. In *2nd International Workshop on Software Configuration Management*, pages 56–65, Princeton, New Jersey, October 1989.
9. Bjorn P. Munch, Jens-Otto Larsen, Bjorn Gulla, Reider Conradi, and Even-Andre Karlsson. Uniform versioning: The change-oriented model. In *4nd International Workshop on Software Configuration Management*, pages 188–196, Baltimore, Maryland, May 1993.
10. Software Maintenance & Development Systems, Inc. *Aide-de-Camp Administrator's Guide*, 1994.
11. Walter F. Tichy. Tools for software configuration management. In Jurgen F.H. Winkler, editor, *International Workshop on Software Version and Configuration Control*, volume 30 of *German Chapter of the ACM Berichte*, pages 1–20, Grassau, West Germany, January 1988. B.G. Teubner.

Experience Report on the Maturity of Configuration Management for Embedded Software

Antti Auer and Jorma Taramaa

VTT Electronics,
Kaitoväylä 1, P.O.Box 1100, FIN-90571 Oulu, FINLAND
E-mail: {Antti.Auer, Jorma.Taramaa}@vtt.fi
www: http://www.ele.vtt.fi

Abstract. The growth of software applications and the need to maintain application-specific software packages have forced industrial organisations to develop their configuration management processes. Configuration Management (CM) is often developed as part of the whole software process, but CM may also be developed, e.g. from the viewpoint of product management. Our experiences indicate that CM is indeed not usually integrated in product management and does not support multi-product, application-specific software production. In Small and Medium size Enterprises (SME) CM is often limited to occasional ad hoc practices. This situation suggests that systematic procedures for evolving industrial software configuration management schemes are needed.

We have developed an incremental approach to building CM environments in cooperation with several industrial embedded systems manufacturers. In this paper, we describe the approach and the experience of using it in a number of applications. The experience is based on cooperation with companies for which practical solutions have been developed taking into account their different maturity level of CM.

1 Introduction

Embedded computer programs are built-in control software for such high-value-added products as telephone switching and production control systems, measurement devices and instruments, communication devices, home electronics, and automated machines. Embedded software plays a central role in most modern electronics products [7].

During the last few years the complexity of embedded software has remarkably increased. The size of software often amounts to hundreds of thousands of lines of code. Table 1 shows the evolution of the size of software in subsequent generations of mobile phones as an example. Products based on embedded software are typically used for a long time and require several modernisation cycles. A questionnaire concerning the maintenance of embedded software indicated that the current software generation will in many cases be used for the whole of the nineties [15]. The average age of embedded software was about seven years, but some pieces of the software had been used more than for twenty years. In some applications such as telephone switching systems, [21] the lifetime of products may be even longer.

Customers expect repair and maintenance services from product manufacturers. Mechanical parts, hardware, sensors and actuators of an automated machine may have to be replaced several times [16]. The software that controls such parts often must then also be changed. In addition, some software-controlled product features may need optimisation and tuning to accomodate to a new environment because the machine may be resold and relocated several times.

Table 1: Increase of software size in mobile phones [10]

System type	Generation	Example system	Software size
Analogue	1st	Nordic mobile phone system (NMT)	some Kbytes
Analogue	2nd	NMT	tens of Kbytes
Digital	1st	Global system for mobile telecommunications (GSM)	hundreds of Kbytes
Digital	2nd	GSM	about 1 million bytes

During the last few years customer-oriented product development has become an important competing strategy. Companies developing embedded software can solve some of the customer-specific product tailoring problems using existing software development methods, tools, and environments. In the longer run, however, more effective approaches are needed that provide better means for taking into account application-specific requirements [14].

Indeed, software production problems have forced industrial organisations to assess the disciplines used to manage the software process in practice [4]. Configuration management (CM) appears to be one of the software process activities that require improvements. It has been even regarded as the foundation of software development environments [5]. Although CM and its basic functions have been well known since the early eighties [3, 19], the comprehensive and systematic industrial usage of CM methods has been quite limited. Difficulties are caused if all CM functions are taken in use at the same time. There is need for incremental improvement. This concern has been called "CM adoption", by taking technical, managerial, process-related, organisational, cultural, political, people-related and risk-related aspects into account [6].

2 Management aspects in software production

2.1 From version control to configuration management

Version control (VC) provides a means to maintain specific instances of software products developed for use in different environments [3]. One of its practical benefits is saving of the archive space, because versions are stored based on their incremental changes rather than full copies. One example of the VC tools used in SMEs is PVCS [9], others are SCCS [13] and RCS [20]. A very common practice is that the VC tool is used differently in separate software development projects of the same company. This will, in practice, introduce new problems when parts of the software are needed in other projects, or when the CM process is being improved.

The second step is to integrate VC to an automatic assembly system that contains configuration builders such as compilation and linking. Automatic assembly requires management of a variety of different revisions of files with a configuration builder. The most common method of dealing with multiple versions is to add version labels to a set of file versions and to compile the whole set by a batch command. In Unix environments solutions using makefiles are common.

From the viewpoint of embedded software, the main benefit of using an automatic configuration builders is to control the complex compilation process. In some cases the software must be pre-processed through three or even four compilers using different parameters.

The next step is often to create a mechanism for maintenance, i.e. the integration of CM and change management. A typical change management system is an in-house data base where change requests are recorded. Often the data base structure is not well-organised and does not support the comprehensive system viewpoint. Usually, the change data base is handled separately and not integrated to any defect tracking system. Change management is a specific task that is often conceptually separated from CM activities. However, in the most advanced CM environments it is included as an inseparable part of the CM scheme [18].

Software maintenance requires change control for specific maintenance functions, such as problem understanding, change localisation, solution analysis, and impact analysis. These functions involve specific application management problems in addition to general configuration management concerns. Therefore, application management is a wider concept than CM [1].

Practical software assembly systems have been developed, because models of software processes can be relatively easily linked to CM systems. CM tools that include implicit process models have actually played quite an important role when advanced CM mechanisms have been integrated in state-of-the-art software engineering environments. There are already some commercial CM systems available that include implicit process models, such as PVCS, CaseWare, ClearCase, Aide-de-Camp, and PCMS [9].

2.2   From configuration management to product management

Embedded systems manufacturers have to take into account the fact that software is just one of the implementation technologies of these systems being developed [16]. It is common to handle CAD and CAE data bases manually or using a document management tool, such as Lotus Notes, ComputerVision or Sherpa[1]. Integrating CM and such tools is a challenge for tool developers.

The next step of CM is to apply it to product families sharing the same software and hardware components. The problem is to build multiple product versions from the same CM data base. According to our experience, this is very difficult to manage with commercial CM tools, especially if a company has committed to a gradual extension of its CM system. The usual solution is to build an in-house data base application based on some commercial solution, such as SQL, Delphi, or MS-Access, to keep track of products, product variations, platforms, operating systems, parameters, etc. that are specific to certain products and product families. One of the main problems of commercial CM tools in this regard is their lack of compatibility with standard data base formats, such as SQL, which would facilitate relations between components.

3   Development model for configuration management

We have developed an incremental approach to building CM environments [17], which has been evaluated and applied in cooperation with several industrial embedded systems manufacturers [16, 18]. One of the key aspects of the approach is a systematic roadmap from simple software configuration management practices to total product management methods (Figure 1).

---

[1] In some occasions these are called product data management systems (PDM).

We have made some corrections and extensions to the lower steps of the previous version of the diagram. Based on our experience, the incremental approach to CM has to be split to smaller steps: basic CM, standardised CM, basic product management, and automated CM. The major reason for these steps is the division of different configuration items (CI) which will be connected incrementally to the product configuration. The basic product configuration indicates that all product documentation is linked to the configuration, which will be then extended by assembly automation, process and change aspects.

In practice, the incremental improvement of CM starts with the assessment of the CM process to determine the current practice (Table 2). In addition to configurations and product data, the assessed aspects include delivery, customer and error data. These aspects indicate relations to logistics functions, which have typically taken a minor role in CM.

After assessment the level of CM maturity is defined. This is usually assisted by standard evaluation procedures, such as CMM [8, 12], Bootstrap [11] and Trillium [2]. In case of Trillium, we extracted roadmaps 6.5 (Configuration Management), 6.6 (Re-Use), 8.1 (Problem Response System) and 8.5 (Customer Engineering) for the assessment. The assessment is repeated regularly to measure process improvement from the CM point of view. The key idea is to define the ideal process model needed in a particular company.

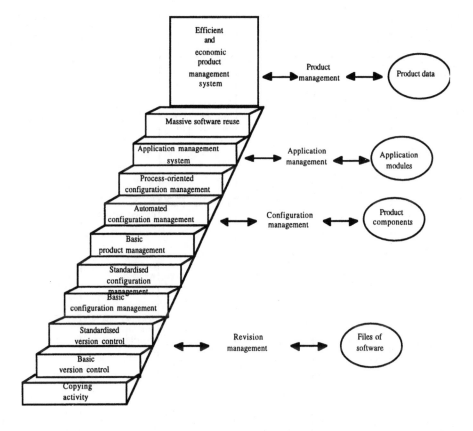

Figure 1: Steps in the development of the different management aspects.

The next step is to find out practical means to achieve a specific level; first in pilot projects and then in all projects through standardisation. An usual approach is to start from upper left corner of Table 2 and then develop simultaneously all subprocesses diagonally. This approach helps to integrate and develop all subprocesses towards total product management. This may take time, although we have experiences that a company can proceed from the first CMM level to the third level within six months in the CM process, using our development model.

Table 2: Evaluation of the maturity of CM.

	Configuration items (modules)	Product data	Delivery Data	Customer Data	Error records
No product management 0	No archiving Backup system possibly allows to return to some older versions One "latest" version	Manual building of products One "latest" version	No information stored on deliveries Invoice & bookkeeping the only source of delivery information	Invoice and bookkeeping the only source of information	No error lists
Copying activity with manual versioning 1	Manual archiving using ZIP or XCOPY Source code for main delivery versions are stored in a common project directory	Lists of product component descriptions	Manual delivery file on paper	Manual customer files on paper	Manual error lists
Basic version control 2	Product has its own archive All source revisions retained and accessible	Change information documented manually Batch files used in builds Release is produced automatically from version controlled code	Computerised delivery register Order handling & invoicing systems (purchase order systems)	Computerised customer register	Error data base Error number counting metric
Standardised version control 3 Traceability over module, product and error data	Archive organised into components Components designed to be reused within one project Advanced version control concepts such as version labels and promotion groups in use Design documentation and user documentation under version control	Products build using make Make file under version control All releases and test versions are produced automatically from version controlled code	Delivery database Delivery data contains information about products delivered	Data base contains delivery info All customer contacts are recorded Customer data base contains links to the delivery data base	Error base with errors linked to source file Errors are reported and collected directly to specific product and module versions.

	Configuration items (modules)	Product data	Delivery Data	Customer Data	Error records
Basic configuration management 4		Make file dependencies reach all the way to version control		Service request concept formalised	
Standardised configuration management 5	Project management documentation and quality documentation under version control	Automated dependency generation	All deliveries to each customer can be traced down, to individual source code modules		Errors linked to specific revisions of source files Error classification system in use -> feedback to inspection & testing & coding
Basic product management 6	All versions of build tools retained All documentation under version controlled data base	Build environment configurations in makefiles Build configuration separated from makefiles Build configuration data base Build record data base (stores source file revisions used in each build)	Delivered products can be fully rebuilt later		Errors linked to specific revision of all affected documentation such as source files, change requests, specifications, etc. Error reports are used to optimise the residual error level and testing
Total product management 7-11	Components are reusable across several products Whole product is configured automatically	Automated configurable builds Build configuration tool all builds are uniquely identifiable	Delivery data base with links to build records and build configuration records Information about customers' environment stored	Service request contains link to all affected source, design and product management files	Error reports are used to optimise the software process
Global product management 12	Components are reusable across several companies	Automatic configuration of third party products			

4 Experience

We have cooperated with companies which had very different maturity levels of CM in the beginning ranging from simple manual revision control to full-automatic CM systems with on-line configuration change and linkage control. In general, the companies use commercial CM tools as much as possible. This has made it possible for them to concentrate on company-specific CM methods.

The companies assessed is described by Table 3 which is based Table 2. The arrows between the names in Table 3 describe the development of different CM aspects. The company name by italics indicates our assessment where the company was in CM at the end of this project.

The companies on the lowest maturity level (steps 0 and 1) have problems on managing software production, when the amount of software and the number of projects increase. Typically they are companies developing instruments and machine automation where strategic knowledge has been based on other technologies than software engineering, e.g. measurement and control technology. The role of software has emphasised new user interface solutions, which have become common in several embedded computer systems. The software in these products is only part of the product and it is often unchangeable. This sets strict requirements on quality of software. The minimum target maturity level was therefore set to 3 in all categories. After the project the companies could automatically build maskable software from VC archive.

Table 4 describes the CM aspects of Trillium which were used when assessed 'Electronics company-1' and the development of its CM practices. The boldfaced sentences of Table 4 indicate the practices implemented after CM development on the CM level 3, Standardised version management. The first improvements can be especially achieved by evolving repository which is essential for VC activities.

The companies starting from the next maturity level (steps 2-5) have had to plan for other improvements, since markets have required several alternatives for the customised versions of their products. This requires quite a good architecture of the embedded software. As a solution we developed a data base system, which is used to control component configurations. In this situation, the delivery data have to be related to the CM practices. In this way it is possible to keep the consistency of the configuration. The basic aspects of software engineering are typically under control, although the major technological skill is in other technological disciplines, e.g. advanced measurement technology and signal processing. The better position of the CM issues is indicated by the organisation of the CM activities, because there is typically a named person responsible for them.

The companies with more advanced CM solutions develop products where the importance of software has been significant from the beginning. Therefore, the value of the basic CM solutions has been understood well. Typically the companies are working with automation and telecommunication applications. Some companies on the highest maturity level (steps 6 and 7) have developed an efficient software production system based on massive reuse. This has required the use of data bases linked to CM, facilitating the building of new applications.

A problem for companies which deliver their own software as part of a larger information system is the management of the other commercial software with respect to computing and communication platforms. This involves management of compatibility information between components, platforms and networking.

The main issue for the companies working on the product management level is the relation to logistics aspects. The value and possibilities of software have been understood well. The relation to other product technologies is partly undefined. In addition, several companies are developing organisation-wide information systems. These set requirements for such common matters as documentation and identification of the software products. In addition, a computerised implementation of a logistics system is often slightly different for software development units concerning different identifications. This contradiction can require changes in the items used by the R&D and the logistics functions. The definition of the items is missing and the role of software engineering is not clearly seen in this activity.

The treatment of error data indicates the relation to change management. In many cases the change management aspects have been regarded as so large activity that its improvement has been left outside. It has been made separately, however, relating to the CM aspects.

The main problem in SME companies is non-standard CM processes which may block the development of CM, documentation and change management methods. Therefore, the maturity level of CM reflects the maturity level of the software process or even the maturity level of the whole software production.

Table 3: The results of the evaluation of CM practices and their development.

	Configuration items (modules)	Product data	Delivery Data	Customer Data	Error records
No product management 0	Electronics company-1	Electronics company-1	Electronics company-1		
Copying activity with manual versioning 1	Machine/Process automation company-1	Machine/Process automation company-1			
Basic version management 2		Machine/Process automation company-3	Machine/Process automation company-1		
Standardised version management 3	*Electronics company-1* *Machine/Process automation company-1*		Telecommunication company-1 Machine/Process automation company-3 Telecommunication company-2		
Traceability over module, product and error data	Telecommunication company-1 Machine/Process automation company-3	*Electronics company-1*			
Basic configuration management 4	*Telecommunication company-1*, 2 and 3 Machine/Process automation company-2	Telecommunication company-1, 2 and 3 Machine/Process automation company-2	*Telecommunication company-1* and 3 Machine/Process automation company-2		
Standardised configuration management 5					
Basic product management 6	*Telecommunication company-3*	*Telecommunication company-1*			
Total product management 7-11		*Machine/Process automation company-3*	*Machine/Process automation company-3*		

Table 4: List of CM items of TRILLIUM ([2], pp. 79-81).

CM perspectives	The CM aspects to be evaluated
SCOPE:	
6.5.2.1	Source code is under Configuration Management (CM) control.
6.5.2.2	All projects and product (internal and external) documents are under CM control.
FUNCTION:	
6.5.2.3	A board having the authority for managing the project's product baselines exists or is established
6.5.2.4	There is a function responsible for coordinating and implementing CM for the project.
FUNDING:	
6.5.2.5	Adequate resources and funding are provided for performing the CM activities.
PLANNING:	
6.5.2.6	A CM plan is prepared for each project according to a documented procedure.
6.5.2.7	A documented and approved CM plan is used as the basis for performing the CM activities.
REPOSITORY:	
6.5.2.8	A CM is established as a repository for product baselines.
6.5.2.9	The product repository ensures secure storage of configuration items and secure and controlled retrieval of current and previous versions of configuration items.
6.5.2.10	The product repository ensures the secure and controlled retrieval of current and previous baselines.
6.5.2.11	The status of configuration items/units is recorded according to a documented procedure.
6.5.2.12	The product repository maintains records of the status and change history of all configuration items and baselines.
TRACEABILITY: ...	
CHANGE CONTROL: ...	
BASELINES: 6.5.2.16	Baseline(s) are created and released formally.
6.5.2.17	Product baseline audits are conducted according to a documented procedure.
REPORTING: ...	

5 Conclusions

This paper presents an incremental approach to developing CM, illustrated as steps from simple CM procedures to product management methods. When maintaining software, modules developed using various languages, methods, and tools must be managed. Typically, the software to be maintained has been developed over the period of several years, even tens of years. Resources in the most cases are limited. All these things favour an incremental approach to developing CM. A single step in such an approach results in a visible baseline where a company can assess the need of further work and more advanced tools. The risks of failing in the development of CM practices can be effectively limited.

In the incremental approach it is essential to understand the state-of-the-practice of CM in the company, the domain of application of the software to be developed or maintained, and the role of software developers in the context of all product technologies, because all these constrain the CM tools that can and should be obtained. The CM investments are typically long-term decisions and it is difficult and costly to withdraw them.

Acknowledgements

The work presented in this paper has been carried out in the LEIVO (Management of Customised Versions of Embedded Software) project. LEIVO was funded by the Technical Development Centre of Finland (TEKES) and a number of Finnish automation, electronics and telecommunications companies including ABB Industry, Elektrobit, Honeywell, Kone Elevators, Nokia Cellular Systems, Polar-Electro and X-Net. In addition, we would like to thank our colleagues at VTT Electronics, Dr. Veikko Seppänen, Mr. Doug Foxvog and Ms. Heli Puustinen for their contribution.

References

[1]   AMES, *AMES - Application Management Environments and Support*, Esprit 3 Project 8156, Technical Annex, Version 3.0, November 1995.

[2]   Bell, *TRILLIUM - Model for Telecom Product Development & Support Process Capability*, Version 3.0, Bell Canada, December 1994.

[3]   Bersoff, E.H., Henderson, V.D., Siegel., S.G. *Principles of Software Configuration Management*, Prentice-Hall, Englewood Cliffs, New Jersey, 1979.

[4]   Buckley, F.J. *Implementing Configuration Management - Hardware, Software and Firmware*, IEEE Computer Society Press, Los Alamitos, California, 1996.

[5]   Dart, S. *Past, Present and Future of CM Systems*, Technical Report of Software Engineering Institute CMU/SEI-92-TR-8, 1992, 28 p.

[6]   Dart, S. Adopting An Automated Configuration Management Solution, *the Seventh International Workshop on Computer-Aided Software Engineering CASE'95*, Toronto, Ontario, July 1995, an Invited Paper, 15 p.

[7]   Davis, A.M. *Software Requirements - Analysis & Specification*, Prentice-Hall, Englewood Cliffs, New Jersey, 1990.

[8]   Humphrey, W.S. Characterizing the Software Process: A Maturity Framework, *IEEE Software*, 5(3), 1988: p. 73-79.

[9]   Ingram, P., Burrows, C., Wesley, I. Configuration Management Tools: a Detailed Evaluation, *OVUM report*, 1993.

[10]   Karjalainen, J., Mäkäräinen, M., Komi-Sirviö, S., Seppänen, V. Practical Process Improvement for Embedded Real-Time Software, to be published in *The Journal of Quality Engineering*, 1996: 13 p.

[11]   Kuvaja, P., Similä, J., Kraznik L., Bicego A., Saukkonen S., Koch, G. *Bootstrap: Europe's Assessment Method*, Blackwell, Oxford, UK, 1994.

[12]   Paulk, M.C., Weber, C.V., Curtis, B., Chrissis, M.B. *The Capability Maturity Model: Guidelines for Improving the Software Process*, Carnegie Mellon University Software Engineering Institute, Pittsburgh, Pennsylvania, 1995.

[13]   Rochkind, M.J. The Source Code Control System, *IEEE Transactions on Software Engineering*, 1(4), 1975: p. 364-370.

[14]   Rosenthal, S.R. *Effective Product Design and Development*, Business One Irwin, Homewood, Illinois, 1992.

[15]   Taramaa, J., Oivo, M. Evaluation of Software Maintenance of Embedded Computer Systems, *International Symposium on Engineered Software Systems*, Malvern, Pennsylvania, May 1993, Published by Scientific Publishing Co., Singapore: p. 193-203.

[16]   Taramaa, J., Lintulampi, R., Seppänen, V. Automated Assembly of Machine Control Software, *Mechatronics*, 4(7), 1994: p. 753-769.

[17]   Taramaa, J., Seppänen, V. A Roadmap from Configuration to Application Management. Proceedings of the 3rd International Conference on Software Quality Management, Seville, Spain, 3-5 April 1995. In: *Quality Management. Software Quality Management III* vol. 1, Ross. M., Brebbia, C.A., Staples, G. and Stapleton, J. (eds.). Computational Mechanics Publications: p. 111-120.

[18]   Taramaa, J., Seppänen, V. and Mäkäräinen, M. From Software Configuration to Application Management - Improving the Maturity of the Maintenance of Embedded Software, *The Journal of Software Maintenance*, 8(1), 1996: p. 49-75.

[19]   Tichy, W. Design, Implementation and Evaluation of a Revision Control System, *Proceedings of the International Conference on Software Engineering*, Tokyo, September 1982, pp. 58-67.

[20]   Tichy, W., RCS - a System for Version Control, Software - *Practice and Experience*, 15(7), 1985: p. 637-654.

[21]   Weider, D., Yu, D., Smith, P., Haung, S.T. Software Productivity Measurements, *AT&T Technical Journal*, May/June 1990: pp. 110-120.

Experiences with the Use of a Configuration Language

Bjørn Gulla[1] and Joe Gorman[2]

[1] Telenor R&D, N-7005 Trondheim, Norway. bjorn.gulla@fou.telenor.no
[2] SINTEF Telecom&Informatics, N-7034 Trondheim, Norway. joe.gorman@delab.sintef.no

Abstract. This paper reports on some practical work undertaken to assess the use of a formalised *configuration language* to support industrial system development and evolution. The language and supporting analysis and system generation tools are the main result of the PROTEUS[1] project. The work described is based on practical application of the PROTEUS approach in Stentofon, a Norwegian industrial company producing customized internal communications systems.

Keywords: Software configuration management, system evolution, configuration language, system modelling, system building.

1 Introduction

To respond to business and environmental changes and customer specific requirements, industrial software systems must evolve. As a system evolves, different kinds of variability are introduced in the system, thus creating system families. Developers use a range of different techniques and representations to manage system evolution and variability.

The PROTEUS project has investigated support for system evolution. A key result of the project is the *PROTEUS Configuration Language* (PCL), which allows definition of system models that include information on all sources of variability within a system. Together with associated tool support, PCL allows construction of detailed system models which can be used not only to provide a clear picture of all system variants, but to act as a basis for system generation as well.

In order to demonstrate the practical applicability of the PROTEUS approach, the paper is centred round one of the trial applications used in the project: the intercom products developed by Stentofon. Stentofon participates as an application company in PROTEUS, i.e. stating requirements, validating specifications and evaluating developed methods and tools in operational divisions.

---

[1] PROTEUS is project no. 6086 in the European research programme ESPRIT. The goal of the project is to provide methodological and tool support for system evolution. PROTEUS started in May 1992 for a period of three years and has a budget of 9,6 MECUs. Participants are CAP Gemini Innovation (F), Matra Marconi Space (F), Debis Systemhaus(D), SINTEF (N), Lancaster University (UK), Intecs (I), CAP Sesa Telecom(F), and Hewlett Packard (F). Stentofon (whose practical experience with PROTEUS tools is reported in this paper) are subcontractors to SINTEF.

Section 2 and Section 3 describe this industrial context and highlights why evolution support is an important problem area in Stentofon's product development. Section 4 describes the PROTEUS approach. The integration with the current development process in Stentofon is then discussed. Finally, Section 6 provides an assessment of how successful the approach has proven to be in its practical application in Stentofon.

2 Industrial Context: the Stentofon Intercom Product

2.1 Stentofon

Stentofon is an industrial company based in Trondheim, Norway. Their principal business is the production of customized internal intercom systems. They design and supply both the hardware and the software elements of these systems, and are a market leader in this area.

Stentofon has been in this business for many years, and has a significant share of the world market for this type of product. As a result, they have a large number of installations around the world - and many of these are different variants of the intercom product. Good hardware reliability also means that many older systems are still in use. In addition, it has always been - and continues to be - an important element of company strategy that Stentofon provides *customized* solutions for the special needs of individual customers. Combined with the large number of installations, this means that the company is responsible for the maintenance and further development of a very large variety of systems.

The large variety of systems produced by Stentofon, combined with the fact that new product development is always necessary to maintain a competitive edge, means that support for evolving systems is very important at Stentofon. Although evolution applies to both the hardware and software parts of the product, the issues discussed in this paper will be restricted to the software components.

2.2 Tool Chain for Software Development

The tool chain used at Stentofon is summarised in Figure 1. It is mainly based on use of the ITU[2] design language SDL [10], supported by a methodology [4] developed in the SISU[3] programme. Software development work is carried out on a host environment consisting of a network of workstations; code developed on that platform is then re-generated for various target platforms consisting of the hardware systems developed by Stentofon.

SDL is a high-level language with a graphical syntax which facilitates communication amongst system designers and between them and the customer. It is

---

[2] ITU stands for International Telecommunications Union (formerly known as CCITT).

[3] SISU is a Norwegian national research and development programme (1988-1996). Its main goal is to increase the effectiveness of software production for the real-time software industry in Norway.

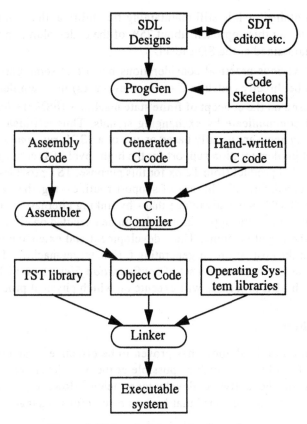

Figure 1. SDL tool chain used at Stentofon

highly suitable for expressing the functional design of real-time software systems of the type developed by Stentofon, and provides a clear picture of system structure and behaviour. For editing and analysing SDL descriptions, Stentofon use the SDT toolset [17] from Telelogic. The support offered by this toolset is satisfactory for these tasks, but there is very little support for handling variants of SDL systems.

SDL is not a "programming" language, and there are many different strategies one might choose to implement designs expressed in SDL. There is no single, obvious strategy for producing implementations from SDL descriptions. Nevertheless - to support evolution - it is best to work at as high an abstraction level as possible, without being too concerned about implementation strategies. The Stentofon approach to this problem is to *transform* SDL designs to C code, in such a flexible way that the system designer can describe/select the transformations that are appropriate as the system evolves. For this purpose, the ProgGen tool [7][8] from SINTEF DELAB is used. ProgGen has two inputs: the SDL description to be transformed and a set of *code skeletons* which allow the designer to describe the exact strategy for transformation to C to be used in a particular case. By using this automatic but flexible code generation, the advantages of working at the SDL level can be maintained, while still maintaining flexibility at the programming language level. Using this approach, about 75% of the code volume in the Stentofon systems is maintained at the SDL level.

However, various practical considerations mean that some parts of the software have to be directly coded in C or (in a few cases) in assembler.

SDL is based on the concept of finite state machines (FSMs) which execute in parallel, and communicate by exchanging signals. Thus, efficient implementations of SDL systems are usually based on use of an SDL *run-time system* providing low-level implementation support for the high-level SDL concepts. Stentofon uses the TST [18] product from Telox for this purpose. TST provides an SDL run-time system consisting of a library of support routines, together with extensive test facilities. TST has the advantage that - by linking alternative versions of the support library - the same application code can be executed on either the host machine or on the target machine. Thus, development and extensive testing can be carried out on the host before re-generating for the target machine. In order to use TST, it is necessary to provide a set of *configuration files* which include information like which SDL processes will execute on which physical processors.

2.3 Variability

The tool chain described above has proven to be effective at Stentofon, and the advantages of working as much as possible at the SDL level are appreciated by all members of the software development team. However, there are many different types of "source code" that have to be carefully managed:

– SDL designs
– ProgGen skeletons for describing the process of C code generation
– C code - hand-written
– Assembly code
– TST configuration files
– declaration of the system building process, currently represented by a set of shell script files and makefiles
– "foreign" libraries, e.g. TST, AMX etc.

As the system evolves, variants of all of these item types are produced, and inter-dependency relationships between them also increase in complexity. In order to make effective use of the various tools of the development platform, it is vital that support be provided to control these sources of variability.

3 Evolution Support Needed by Stentofon

This section describes the problems concerning evolution that Stentofon identified *before* the PROTEUS project started. In each sub-section, we describe the nature of the problem, the requirements for improved support and "Today's approach" i.e. how the problems are currently being handled *without* support from PROTEUS.

In Section 5 we assess the extent to which these problems have been solved or alleviated by using the PROTEUS approach.

3.1 General Requirements

Stentofon require support for two main **types** of system evolution:

- evolution over *time* (e.g. corrections, product enhancements, adaptations for new platforms etc.)
- evolution arising from *customizations* carried out for specific customers

The support provided must handle *versions* and *variants* of all the item types involved in the tool chain described in Section 2.2 on page 2. In particular, it has to be able to deal with:

- stable system versions: systems already delivered to customers
- versions under development (including test and debug variants)
- variants for different platforms (host/target)
- variants produced to fulfil the needs of specific customers

A basic requirement is to provide **visibility** of the overall system structure, clearly indicating which parts of the system are common and which vary. For variants it must be possible to express that the choice for one item might depend on the choice of variant for some other items.

Another key issue is support for the *system building* process. Since this process is to a large extent determined by the system structure, consistency between these must be ensured. The build process should:

- be completely automated, through tool support
- result in executable code that is at least as time and space efficient as that previously produced using a less automated generation process
- be reliable: *all* necessary re-compilations etc. needed for a new variant must be carried out using the correct versions of files, compiler flags etc.
- be fast: unnecessary build operations must be avoided

Today's approach: Existing support for evolution falls far short of the requirements described above. There is no globally documented, detailed overview of existing system variants, so "visibility" is poor. RCS [20] is used for version control of the various types of source files, and Make [6] is used for partial automation of the system building process. But the support provided by these tool does not fulfil the requirements here described.

3.2 SDL Composition Structure

Systems described in SDL are essentially built up of *processes* and *procedures* which are composed in a hierarchical *block* structure. In developing evolving systems, Stentofon often wish to reuse particular processes, procedures and block hierarchies; these elements need to be composed to produce a given system variant. However, the version of the SDL language used by Stentofon lacks support for modularisation[4], and composition must be carried out using various ad hoc facilities provided by the SDT editor tool.

This composition problem is particularly important because the SDL level is the "top" level of the system, and many other components used to generate an executable system are dependent on the SDL composition structure.

Stentofon require tool support which facilitates composition of SDL processes etc. into complete SDL systems. Systems composed in this way must then be able to be used as the basis for the automated system generation process, in full confidence that all dependencies with other item types (C code, ProgGen skeletons etc.) will be taken into account.

Today's approach: SDL composition is carried out using the SDL editor provided in the SDT tool; this involves a considerable degree of user interaction, and makes it very difficult to see which variants of which SDL components are composed together in different system variants.

3.3 Complexity of System Generation

The system building process used at Stentofon involves many complex dependencies between the various item types that are involved in the process. These have to be taken into account when deciding which tool invocations are necessary, as do other sources of variability such as the correct compiler flags etc. that are needed when generating a particular system instance.

The process is made more complex due to use of the ProgGen tool: there is a large number of ProgGen skeletons (several hundred), and it is essential that the skeletons used during system generation are appropriate for the system variant being produced. Skeletons must be selected according to which translation strategies are required for the various SDL concepts, distribution and run-time organization of the application, the hardware configuration and non-functional requirements (time/space).

Given the general requirement that system generation should be completely automated, tool support is required which takes account of these complexities and ensures consistent choices.

Today's approach: System building is performed using a mixture of makefiles and shell scripts. The "implicit" rules provided by Make have proven not to be sufficiently powerful to handle the complexities of the system generation process, and a considerable amount of manual maintenance of makefiles is necessary. This is both time-consuming and potentially error prone. It has also led to a situation where the flexibility offered by the Proggen skeleton mechanism has not been fully exploited because of the complexities of selection of skeletons during system generation.

---

[4] Stentofon use SDL/88. A more recent version of the language - SDL/92 - provides much improved support for modularisation, and also supports object orientation. Stentofon plan to move to this version of SDL.

3.4 Run Time System and Operating System Considerations

Some important sources of variability are dealt with at the run-time support and operating system level. For particular system variants, customizations are needed in order to make most effective use of the basic hardware/software platform on which the system will run.

A case in point is the *distribution* of the software: which SDL processes will run on which physical processors? This is dealt with by producing appropriate low-level *configuration* files for the TST run-time support system.

Tool support is required which will remove the need to maintain such low level files, and allow such considerations as software distribution to be dealt with at a higher abstraction level.

Today's approach: No tool support: all run-time and operating system dependencies are dealt with by manual procedures.

4 The PROTEUS Approach

The objective of the PROTEUS project is to provide support for system evolution. The project is developing methods and tools for (1) domain analysis, (2) adapting existing design methods (SDL, HOOD, MD) to support evolving systems, and (3) modelling system structure and software system building. The following sections provides an overview of the main constructs of the configuration language and its supporting toolset.

4.1 PROTEUS Configuration Language (PCL)

PCL[15][21] is a formalism for system modelling, configuration definition and software system building.

As systems evolve, large numbers of system and component versions with slightly different properties are created. A *system model* is a description of the items in a system and the relationships between them. Such a model uniquely identifies the comprising components, their properties, structure and possible variability, and tracks their evolution. Its purpose is to capture knowledge about a system and its domain in an easily understandable and concise manner.

The system model in PCL is based on the *family* notion, first introduced in the system modelling language INTERCOL[19]. A family represents a logical entity which may occur in different variations in particular systems (being essentially the same as a version group). The family description encompasses all potential variability of the entity.

A specific member (version) of the family is determined by removing ambiguity in the family description. We call this operation *binding*, and it is one of the core functions of the tool set supporting PCL usage. Information about a specific family member is expressed in a special kind of PCL description known as a *version descriptor*.

PCL is a new language, and there is currently no "method" advising who is responsible for updating which PCL descriptions, how often, or at which stages in the system development process. Such a method must grow from experience in using the language. However, it is envisioned that *family descriptions* will be maintained primarily by technical software designers, while *version descriptors* should ideally be the responsibility of sales and marketing staff, who know the specific requirements of individual customers.

4.2 System Modelling Facilities

In PCL the family construct is used for modelling the logical entities in the system. A model is organized as a layered composition structure at the logical level. Entities may be part of other entities, and may also have sub-components. In the parts section the logical composition structure is declared. The following example shows ASVP[5] – one of the sub-systems in the Stentofon application.

```
family ASVP
    parts
        software => ASVP-software;
        hardware => ASVP-card;
        documentation => ASVP-docs;
    end
end
family ASVP-software
    parts
        sdl => svp;
        manual => asvp-manual-c-s;
        sdl-support => sdt-standard;
        sdl-trans => pg-skeletons-c1;
        run-time => (tst-interface, tst);
        oper-sys => amx;
    end
end
```

In the example above, the ASVP entity is composed of ASVP-software, ASVP-card and ASVP-docs. The decomposition of ASVP-software is further indicated: Parts may of course be shared among subsystems, relations which must be kept track of during change impact analysis.

Note the use of *slots*, i.e. the identifiers to the left of "=>". Slots act as place-holders for information and are a general PCL mechanism. Since families may be defined by inheriting from other families, slots can be used to identify which parts to override in forming a new system variant.

A family may represent any kind of entity: hardware objects, software artifacts or even combinations. PCL facilitates multi-dimensional classification in user-defined term spaces. There is also a relationships section for declaring other kinds of relationships between entities and a general relation type definition facility.

---

[5] ASVP is an abbreviation for AICE Stored Voice Playback.

A set of *physical objects* may be associated with a family. Physical objects is the PCL term for tangible objects existing in the real world and for software artefacts making up a system. They are called physical objects to distinguish them from the logical notions which exist only within the PCL model.

```
family AICE_COMM
   attributes
      IMPL_DIR : string;
      manual : boolean := true;
   end
   physical
      p1 =>  "aice_comm.spr";
      p2 =>  "AICE_COMM_def.h"
             attributes workspace := IMPL_DIR; end;
      p3 =>  if manual = true then
                "AICE_COMM_proc.c"
                attributes workspace := IMPL_DIR; end
             endif;
   end
end
```

Three physical objects named "AICE_COMM.spr", "AICE_COMM_def.h" and "AICE_COMM_proc.c" are associated with the AICE_COMM entity representing an SDL process. Classifications and attributes may be declared for physical objects just as for families. All physical objects here are software objects, i.e. files, which is the default unless classified otherwise. The workspace attribute is a special attribute recognized by the PCL tools which indicates where in the file system this file should reside.

Attributes are used to characterize a family and its potential variability. Attributes are typed and may be of type integer, string, or a user-defined enumeration. There are two kinds of attributes. Information attributes state properties common to all members of the family. They are declared by using the "=" assignment operator.

```
family hwif-manual-c
   attributes
      language : string = "C";
   end
end
```

Variability control attributes indicate possible variability among the members of a family. Default values may be assigned to such attributes with the ":=" operator, but these may be overridden at binding time.

```
family ASVP-software
   attributes
      target : target_type;
      speed : speed_type := fast;
   end
   ...
end
```

Attribute assignments can refer to the values of other attributes in the composition hierarchy, thus allowing propagation of key values to distinct attributes.

Particular members of the family are identified by determining values for all variability control attributes. For example, if binding attribute **target** to **emulator-stripped** and **speed** to **fast**, a unique member of **ASVP-software** is established. Each variability control attribute defines a dimension of variability as illustrated in Figure 2. Variability control attributes can in principle be selected independently, although there might be some disallowed combinations. Although there is (currently) no dedicated language construct, such constraints are easily expressed using conditional expressions.

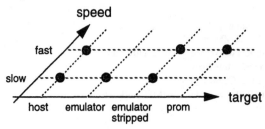

Figure 2. Two dimensions of variability and some possible family members

Note that attributes denote *conceptual* variability – they do not say anything about how that variability is realized. PCL covers a wide range of types of variability, for example structural variability, version selection of associated physical objects, and differences in processing tool parameters. The example below illustrates *structural* variability, i.e. a family whose members have different composition structures. This is expressed by embedding **if-then-else** phrases in the description. Such phrases use expressions based on attribute values. Alternatives can also be viewed graphically; this is illustrated by Figure 3 which shows how the following PCL description is displayed by the *PCL Browser* tool.

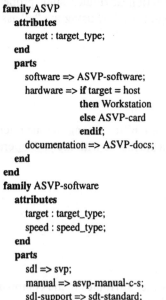
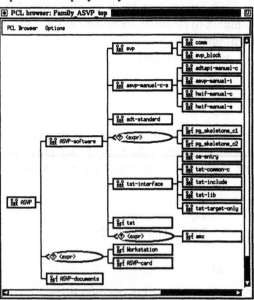

```
family ASVP
    attributes
        target : target_type;
    end
    parts
        software => ASVP-software;
        hardware => if target = host
                    then Workstation
                    else ASVP-card
                    endif;
        documentation => ASVP-docs;
    end
end
family ASVP-software
    attributes
        target : target_type;
        speed : speed_type;
    end
    parts
        sdl => svp;
        manual => asvp-manual-c-s;
        sdl-support => sdt-standard;
```

Figure 3. PCL Browser view of top levels of ASVP

```
        sdl-trans => if speed = fast then pg-skeletons-c1
                     else pg-skeletons-c2
                     endif;
        run-time => (tst-interface, tst);
        oper-sys => if target <> host then amx endif;
     end
  end
```

In descriptions of large systems, it often happens that several family descriptions share a similar structure and content. In Stentofon's AICE system, for example, one family description is required for each SDL process in the system. It would be tedious to have to write (basically) the same PCL description once for each SDL process; it would also be difficult to maintain all the descriptions. To avoid such problems, PCL provides a comprehensive *inheritance* mechanism. Thus, for Stentofon's AICE system, one can capture the *common* information in an "sdl-process" family, and highlight what is *unique* to each individual process in separate family descriptions all of which inherit from "sdl-process".

A *version descriptor* determines a particular member of a family by assigning values to variability control attributes. Such assignments override potential default expressions occurring in families.

```
  version v-ASVP-host of ASVP-software
     attributes
        target := host;
        speed := slow;
        HOME := "/users/arvid/";
     end
  end
```

During binding the version descriptor is applied to the family and sub-families recursively, producing a bound family hierarchy. All attributes are treated with equal priority during binding. Incomplete version descriptors (i.e. values are not computable for all variability control attributes) results in a partially bound family, corresponding to a partially bound configuration [23]. Tool support provides diagnostic information if the version descriptor leaves attribute values undefined, or if selection constraints are violated.

File versioning is supported through a two-tier repository approach. The contents and descriptions (sets of attribute name-value pairs) of file versions are managed by a special tool called the Repository. Otherwise, descriptions of file versions would soon make the system model impractically voluminous and hard to use. *Version selection* is the process of determining a consistent set of versions for all elements in a system. PCL supports intensional version selection [2][1][13]. Based on a query stating desired properties, the best matching version (if any) for each file is computed by the Repository by inspecting the available versions and their characteristics. This process is controlled by the PCL system model, since the submitted query is constructed by including certain attributes from the PCL model. Available operations include literal attribute matching, regular expression matching, negation, minimal and maximal values, and priorities.

4.3   System Building Support

For modelling software system building processes [3], PCL includes the **tool** construct. It allows declarative specifications of generic steps in the building process by defining the signature, behaviour and possible variability of software tools. See for example [21] for a typical definition of a C++ compiler.

In order to apply tools, files must be classified. There are some predefined classifications, e.g. hardware, software, primary, derived. A PCL user may add sub-classes to any defined class, or even define new classification dimensions, offering an extensible mechanism. The principal dimension is **type**, which is used during system building analysis. Different file types are declared as sub-classes of **software** in this dimension.

```
class sdl-process-src inherits sdl-source
    physical name ++ ".spr"; end
end
```

Here, **sdl-source** is an (indirect) sub-class of **software**. The **physical** section defines a pattern which will be matched against file names to automatically determine file type classification if none is declared explicitly.

Below is an excerpt from a **tool** declaration in the Stentofon model. This derivation step transforms SDL processes into C source code. The **tool** has several input and several output arguments. Note how the names of the output elements are not necessarily derived from names of input elements.

```
tool grpr_fsm_pg
    attributes
        SDL-Comp-Path : string;
        IMPL_DIR : string;
        fam_name : string;
        ...
        analyze_cmd := ...; // complex expression
        preproc_cmd := ...; //
        proggen_cmd := ...; //
    end
    inputs
        sdl => sdl-process-src;
        prd : multi => sdl-procedure-src-wo-state;
    end

    outputs
        c-h => c-header(IMPL_DIR++"/"++fam_name++"_def_pg.h");
        c-s => c-source(IMPL_DIR++"/"++fam_name++"_pg.c");
        res => text(IMPL_DIR++"/"++basename(sdl)++".res");
    end
    scripts
        build := analyze_cmd ++ preproc_cmd ++ proggen_cmd;
    end
end
```

There are similar rules for transforming other kinds of SDL entities (SDL system and SDL procedure with state). These rules are similar to some extent, and this fact is exploited in the PCL code currently used in Stentofon. Common aspects

(attributes and outputs slot definitions) are declared in an abstract tool entity
sdl_compile from which the actual tools inherit.

Due to strong demands from the application companies, system building support in PROTEUS is realized by generating standard makefiles, which are interpreted by the Make program [6] for actual system (re)generation. Figure 4 shows a part of the derivation graph for an **ASVP-software** variant. The generated makefiles may optionally include Repository coupling, i.e. automatically invoke check out of correct versions of files.

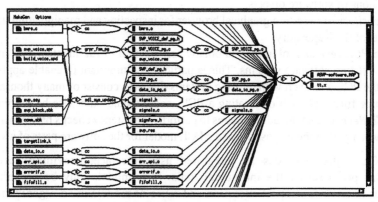

Figure 4. MakeGen screen dump

4.4 Tool Support

A comprehensive toolset to support the creation and use of PCL models has been developed. Figure 5 presents an overview of the core PCL tool set.

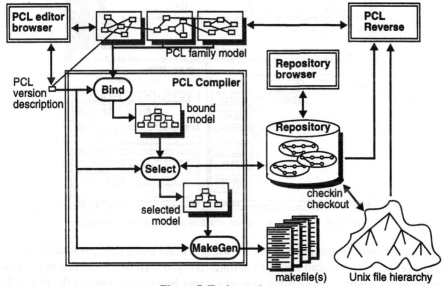

Figure 5. Tool overview

- *PCL compiler* is an interactive tool for management and analysis of PCL models. Primarily it supports the three fundamental operations for PCL models, namely binding, version selection, and makefile generation. Partial and interactive binding are both supported. Check in and check out of software subsystems are possible either through PCL compile or the Repository browser.
- *PCL editor/browser* is a graphical structural editor for entering and browsing PCL models.
- The *Repository* manages the contents and descriptions (attribute annotations) of versions of software objects.
- *Repository browser* is a graphical browser for inspecting and manipulating the contents of the Repository.
- The *PCL reverse* tool allows automatic construction of rudimentary PCL models for existing software systems. This is particularly important to enable application of the PCL approach with existing systems that may consist of many thousands of source files. (The job of creating a PCL model would otherwise be prohibitive). *PCL Reverse* also includes features to perform consistency checks between a workspace, a part of the Repository and a PCL model for the software parts of a system.

The PCL toolset includes an integrated user interface, providing access to functions provided by the individual tools. PCL models may be organized in libraries in order to support evolution and reuse of models in an organization.

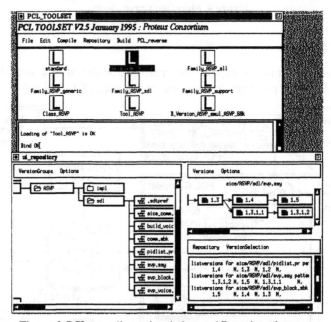

Figure 6. PCL compiler main window and Repository browser.

The tool set is implemented in C++ using X11R5 and the OSF/Motif^{TM} toolkit. It is available for Sun and HP workstations. BMS, a selective multicast implementation provided by CAP Gemini, is used for tool integration, both of the PCL toolset itself and for integration with external design tools. In Stentofon a Repository running on top of RCS [20] is used.

5 The PROTEUS Approach Applied in Stentofon

In this section we discuss how the PROTEUS approach may be integrated into Stentofon's development process. The discussion is organized according to the requirements for evolution support listed in Section 3.

5.1 General Requirements

Overall system *visibility* is provided by the PCL system model. Descriptions of all relevant parts and their inter-dependencies are possible, for e.g. SDL parts, hand-coded software, documentation, hardware elements. Elements are classified in a company-defined schema. The system building process is controlled from the same descriptions, ensuring consistency between the model and the actually generated system.

The PCL system model allows representation of all potential variability in a system, highlighting which parts are common and which differ between variants. In Stentofon a number of different mechanisms for achieving software variability are used, e.g.:

- varying system composition
- component selection, i.e. different files and libraries
- component version selection (revisions and branches)
- conditional compilation [24]
- tool selection and ordering of invocation
- tool parameters/switches, e.g. for selection of code generation skeletons, target platform, debug support, optimization
- configuration files for the run-time system

PCL allows expressing and controlling variability of all these kinds with a single mechanism, namely attributes. A single PCL attribute may control several kinds of variability. Dependencies between variability selections may also be expressed.

5.2 SDL Composition Structure

The SDL decomposition structure is reflected in the PCL model. Each SDL system, block, process and procedure is described by a PCL family construct, which includes references to the SDL source and associated handwritten-code (if any). Initially this PCL fragment is created by running ProgGen on the initial SDL model with an appropriate set of skeletons. After subsequent *structural* changes at the SDL level, these must be incorporated into the system model by a manual merge step using the PCL editor. This task typically involves inserting conditional expressions over attributes and possibly introducing new attributes.

For structural changes in the hand-written code, i.e. creation or removal of files, a similar procedure is followed, but now PCL reverse may be used to produce the PCL fragment to merge into the existing model.

To generate a particular system instance, a user states the desired properties related to functional characteristics, non-functional aspects, implementation choices etc. in the form of a version descriptor. During the instantiation process the best matching SDL component versions are selected, possibly forming an original combination of versions. The SDT tool [17] will report possible inconsistencies during system analysis and allow manual editing to resolve conflicts if necessary.

5.3 Complexity of System Generation

PCL allows all knowledge related to the system building process to be stated in one formalism and be represented in one place. Complex derivation steps far exceeding the expressiveness of implicit Make rules[6] are handled. Manual maintenance of makefiles and shell scripts is avoided by automatically generating appropriate makefiles for each particular system instance.

To ease maintenance of the system model itself, *derived* relationships are supported in PCL. Dependencies which can be derived from files, e.g. #include dependencies between C source code files, need not be represented in the system model. Rather, by declaring depend scripts for tool entities, such dependencies can be extracted automatically during the system building process.

Variability in the SDL-to-C transformation is solved by including a model of the ProgGen skeleton set as a subsystem of the system model. Skeleton files are versioned and managed by the Repository. Variability in this subsystem is then characterized and disambiguated just as any other variability in the system model.

5.4 Run Time System and Operating System Considerations

The run-time organization of an application is possible to model in PCL. PCL includes predefined relations which are taken into account during system analysis, allowing a high-level declaration of distribution aspects and usage of the underlying platform. Since hardware elements are already included in the model, this fits naturally into the framework.

The current Stentofon PCL model does not yet cover distribution variability. However, during evaluation in another PROTEUS application company (Garex), automatic generation of appropriate TST low-level configuration files from a PCL model has been achieved, using the general tool construct.

6 Evaluation

6.1 AICE

This section summarises experiences from applying the PROTEUS approach in Stentofon. Table 1 shows the number of files, total number of lines of code, and number of versions per file for AICE, one of Stentofon's new products. There were in total 721 manually maintained files, and over 8000 versions of these. Note that all *generated* files (C files generated from SDL, Make dependency files, object code files etc.) are omitted in this overview.

Table 1. Size of Stentofon's AICE application

Type of source	No. of files	LOC	Versions per file
SDL	141	181421[a]	5–300
C	238	93500	10–100
Assembly	14	5266	10–100
ProgGen skeletons	288	3481	2–5
Foreign libraries	2		3–5
Configuration files	11	918	5–50
Makefiles, shell scripts	27	17224[b]	10–100

a. LOC for SDL source is approximated by the number of bytes in GR files divided by 30.
b. Five of these makefiles (14.263 LOC) are for recreation of old configurations.

Table 2 gives the size of the PCL model of the AICE application. When using the PROTEUS approach, 'Makefiles, shell scripts' and 'Configuration files' in Table 1 can be eliminated, since equivalent files are generated from the PCL model.

Table 2. PCL model of the AICE application

Type of source	No. of files	LOC
Generic[a]	3	500
System specific[b]	7	1700

a. Common to all SDL-based systems in Stentofon
b. Of this, ca. 75% was initially generated by ProgGen and PCL Reverse

Due to time limitations and some practical problems, only a single release (but several variants) of the AICE system is covered by the current PCL model. The effort required to construct the PCL model was unfortunately not measured.

6.2 Evolution support

It has been claimed that the detailed system modelling required by PROTEUS-like systems is very time consuming [11]. Also, it is not obvious how real-life pragmatic system evolution affects the stability of PCL models. In order to investigate these issues, a separate case study was performed [9]. A medium sized software system (70 KLOC) written in OMT and C++ was modelled in PCL. As the system evolved over the following six months, the PCL model was enhanced to incorporate the new releases. The time used in the PCL modelling effort was carefully monitored.

Initially, a complete PCL model for the first official release (V2.3) of the system was created and verified (Column 1 of Table 1). Supported system variants were included into the model, covering different hardware platforms, operating systems, development sites, debugging support and linkage conventions (Column 2). Column 3 to 5 in Table 1 address three subsequent external system releases.

The first two rows of Table 1 show the number of source files and lines of code for the software system. Numbers for the associated makefiles are listed separately. The next row gives the size of the complete PCL model. Note that the system building specification was much simpler here than in the AICE model, since only simple tools like uil, omtool, CC, yacc, and ld were used. The makefiles generated from PCL were about the same size as manual ones, depending a bit on whether check-out rules and dependency extraction was included or not. In the last row the time used for constructing and verifying each PCL model revision is listed.

Table 3. System size, model size, and modelling effort [9]

	V2.3	+variants	V2.4.1	V2.6	V2.6.1
Source files	194		205	212	212
(LOC)	59.9K		62.7K	69.5K	70.2K
Makefiles, scripts	26		29	29	29
(LOC)	1087		1210	1262	1262
PCL model (LOC)[a]	780	873	900	920	922
Effort (hours)[b]	19.6	7.0	6.0	1.8	1.8

a. Of this, ca. 60% was automatically generated by PCL Reverse.
b. The model author was familiar with both the PCL formalism, the PCL toolset and major parts of the modelled software system.

When considering evolution and model stability, we note that the increase in PCL model size (+5.6%) is less than the increase in system size, both in terms of number of files (+9.2%) and in LOC (+17.2%). When further investigating changed lines (not shown in Table 1), we found that 37.9% of the source code was changed from V2.3 to V2.6.1, while only 11.3% of the PCL model was modified when enhanced to cover the additional releases.

The total modelling experiment required 107 hours, which involved constructing the PCL model, documenting the procedure, and collecting metrics. We observe that the dominant part concerns creating the complete initial model (26.6 h). Incorporating later releases into the model is quite cheap, even if substantial system changes were done. The PCL Reverse tool was used pervasively, both to create the initial PCL model and to extend and verify the model as the system evolved.

6.3 Experiences

The evaluation has been based on three main criteria: (1) support for evolutionary development, (2) support for design-oriented development, and (3) flexibility of approach. Among the more advantageous experiences we can mention:

- PCL allows a number of tasks to be carried out at a higher abstraction level than before. Many highly inter-dependent details around the system and in the associated system building process are now automatically taken care of based on intensional specifications.
- Constructing a *total* system model covering all aspects of a system has been a favourable experience. Knowledge previously distributed and unavailable (person dependent) is now made visible and represented in a formal model. This information is also useful e.g. for internal communication and training. Modelling of system variability is however still somewhat incomplete.
- The choice of building the Repository on top of an existing version management system worked well at Stentofon. Several years of evolution history became instantly available, and could be presented in a convenient graphical form.
- "High" expressiveness of PCL is a vital factor for the success of PCL. It allows concise models, which are easy to understand and maintain as the system evolves. Intensional mechanisms are essential to handle the size and complexity of real systems.

Problem areas and deficiencies observed are:

- A crucial problem is to ensure consistency between the system model and the actual system. Structural and even some non-structural changes require that the system model is updated. Tighter integration between the design tool and the PCL model is one possibility, and this is being explored by other partners in PROTEUS. At Stentofon the use of ProgGen and PCL Reverse was been reasonable successful.
- A more practical obstacle in the experimentation has been the lack of availability, stability and maturity of the PCL toolset. The tools were originally released for a platform not available in Stentofon's development department.
- PCL is a language that must be learned. The absence of courses and suitable pedagogic textbooks has so far hampered training.[6] The lack of a comprehensive PCL *method* is another problem that must be addressed. Guidelines for how to apply PCL to best support system evolution are clearly needed.

---

[6] Tutorial material now exits, but it was not available at the time the evaluation work was carried out.

– The file version selection mechanisms currently supported by the toolset lack some expressive power.
– The system building process could be further optimized by not utilizing Make. More accurate processing would require explicit management of derived elements as in [12][5].

7 Related Work

With regard to system modelling support, PCL tries to incorporate the best ideas from the module interconnection language (MIL) tradition [14][19] and from the more database-oriented approaches to software configuration management, e.g. [1][12][13].

Compared with earlier MIL approaches, the novel features of PCL may be summarized as incorporation of descriptions of hardware items and dependencies thereof, inheritance mechanism, embedded variability expressions, extensibility (classification schemes), and integrated tool support for system building and version management. See [16][21] for further discussion and comparison of PCL with other MILs.

The main difference between the PROTEUS approach and database-oriented SCM systems is the explicit logical system model apparent in PCL. A visible, human readable representation provides a basis for discussion, communication, and reasoning, opposed to the implicit models often hidden deep inside database systems. In addition, the structure of a logical system model tend to remain more stable than physically (file) based models. Many types of pragmatic evolution, such as renaming, splitting or joining of files, may be represented as variability in physical mapping, avoiding cluttering up the logical structure.

As for software system building support, a primary concern has been to achieve separation of knowledge about system building tasks from knowledge about any particular system[22], beyond the capabilities of Make [6] and Odin [5]. On the other hand, it is important to be able to control and customize the building process for particular components or subsystems through the system model.

8 Conclusions

Software is a valuable organizational asset. As organizations find themselves having to respond more and more quickly to business and environmental changes, it is important that the collective expertise and knowledge about a system can be pooled, formalized and recorded.

Using PCL to support system development and evolution through the use of complete system models is a promising approach to this problem. Experience at Stentofon shows that it requires a significant effort to build such models, but that the benefits in terms of improved visibility and automation are also substantial.

The initial experience reported here is sufficiently positive that Stentofon intends to continue this evaluation work, and it is quite likely that they will eventually decide to adopt PCL in all their software development projects.

The potential *economic* benefit of the evolution support provided by PROTEUS has not been assessed by the work reported here. It is an important issue, and future work based on longer-term evaluations should be planned.

The feasibility of applying the PCL approach to very large legacy systems is another issue requiring further investigation, though initial experiences with the *PCL Reverse* tool are promising.

Acknowledgements

The work described in this paper is carried out in the scope of PROTEUS, project number 6086 in the European Commission ESPRIT research and development programme. The work carried out in Norway has been partly funded by the Norwegian Research Council (NFR). We would like to acknowledge the contributions made by current and previous members of the project, and especially Arvid Strømme and Tor Arne Grindal of Stentofon for their patience in assessing the numerous PCL descriptions and tool versions introduced during this work. Thanks also to Professor Reidar Conradi of NTNU and Richard Sanders and Jacqueline Floch of SINTEF Telecom&Informatics for many valuable comments.

References

1. N. Belkhatir and J. Estublier. Experience with a Data Base of Programs. *Proceedings of the 2ⁿᵈ ACM SIGSOFT/SIGPLAN Software Engineering Symposium on Practical Software Development Environments*, pages 84-91, Palo Alto, CA, December 9-11, 1986, December 1986. ACM SIGPLAN Notices 22(1), January 1987.
2. Yves Bernard, Michel Lacroix, Pierre Lavency and Marlene Vanhoedenaghe. Configuration Management in an Open Environment. *Proceedings of the 1ˢᵗ European Software Engineering Conference*, pages 35-43, Strasbourg, France, September 1987. LNCS 289, Springer-Verlag.
3. Ellen Borison. A Model of Software Manufacture. *Proceedings of the International Workshop on Advanced Programming Environments*, pages 197-220, Trondheim, Norway, June 16-18, 1986. LNCS 244, Springer-Verlag.
4. Rolv Bræk and Øystein Haugen. Engineering Real Time Systems. Prentice Hall, 1993. ISBN 0-13-034448-6.
5. Geoffery M. Clemm. The Odin Specification Language. *Proceedings of the International Workshop on Software Version and Configuration Control*, pages 144-158, Grassau, January 27-29, 1988. B.G.Teubner, Stuttgart.
6. Stuart I. Feldman. Make, A Program for Maintaining Computer Programs. *Software—Practice and Experience*, 9(4):255-265, April 1979.

7. Jacqueline Floch. Supporting Evolution and Maintenance by Using a Flexible Automatic Code Generator. *Proceedings of the 17th International Conference on Software Engineering*, pages 211-220, Seattle, WA, April 23-30, 1995. ACM Press.
8. Jacqueline Floch, Joe Gorman and Ulrik Johansen. ProgGen User's Guide 3.0, and ProgGen Skeleton Author's Guide 3.0. ProgGen tool documentation provided by SINTEF DELAB, N-7034 Trondheim, Norway, 1994.
9. Bjørn Gulla. Constructing a PCL model of the PCL V2.x toolsets. Technical Report P-WP-A224b-BG036-SIN.1, 70 pages, PROTEUS consortium, August 1, 1995.
10. ITU. Specification and Description Language SDL. Recommendation Z.100, CCITT ITU, Geneva, 1993.
11. Michel Lacroix and Jacky Estublier. SCM Systems Session. In J. Estublier, editor, *Software Configuration Management*, page 215, LNCS 1005, Springer-Verlag.
12. David B. Leblang and Robert P. Chase, Jr. Parallel Software Configuration Management in a Network Environment. *IEEE Software*, 4(6):28-35, November 1987.
13. Anund Lie, Reidar Conradi, Tor M. Didriksen, Even-Andrè Karlsson, Svein O. Hallsteinsen and Per Holager. Change Oriented Versioning in a Software Engineering Database. *Proceedings of the 2nd International Workshop on Software Configuration Management*, pages 56-65, Princeton, New Jersey, October 25-27, 1989. ACM SIGSOFT Software Engineering Notes 17(7), November 1989.
14. Ruben Prieto-Diaz and James M. Neighbors. Module Interconnection Languages. *Journal of Systems and Software*, 6(4):307-334, November 1986.
15. PROTEUS consortium. PCL-V2 Reference Manual. Technical Report P-DEL-3.4.D-1.9, 85 pages, September 2, 1994.
16. Ian Sommerville and Graham Dean. A configuration language for modelling evolving system architectures. Submitted for publication.
17. Telelogic. SDT User Manual. Telelogic, Sweden.
18. Telox. TST User Manual. Telox, Norway.
19. Walter F. Tichy. Software Development Control Based on Module Interconnection. *Proceedings of the 4th International Conference on Software Engineering*, pages 29-41, September 1979. IEEE CS Press.
20. Walter F. Tichy. RCS - A System for Version Control, *Software—Practice and Experience*, 15(7):637-654, July 1985.
21. Eirik Tryggeseth, Bjørn Gulla and Reidar Conradi. Modelling Systems with Variability using the PROTEUS Configuration Language. *5th International Workshop on Software Configuration Management*, Seattle, WA, April 24-25, 1995. In J. Estublier, editor, *Software Configuration Management*, pages 216-240, LNCS 1005, Springer-Verlag.
22. Richard C. Waters. Automated Software Management Based on Structural Models. *Software—Practice and Experience*, 19(10):931-955, October 1989.
23. Douglas Wiebe. Object-Oriented Software Configuration Management. *Proceedings of the 4th International Workshop on Software Configuration Management*, pages 241-252, Baltimore, Maryland, May 21-22, 1993.
24. Jürgen F. H. Winkler and Clemens Stoffel. Program Variations in the Small. *Proceedings of the International Workshop on Software Version and Configuration Control*, pages 175-196, Grassau, January 27-29, 1988. B.G.Teubner, Stuttgart.

Introducing Configuration Management in an Organisation

Sissel Kolvik

Technical Documentation, Stentofon AS, 7005 Trondheim, Norway
e-mail: sissel stentofon.no

Abstract Introducing configuration management in a company is a complex issue with many aspects. Both technical and organisational as well as human aspects have to be considered. Stentofon AS has just completed a project on introduction of configuration management in our organisation, and we would like to share some of our experiences with others. We did this work as a part of the SISU project, a Norwegian national research, development and technology transfer program. We participated in this project together with the industrial company TrioVing, and the research institute SINTEF DELAB. As a result of this work, we have established procedures for configuration management, changed some of our existing procedures and defined some tasks that need to be done in the near future. For the last couple of years the company has also made an effort to achieve ISO 9001 certification; we succeeded at this in November 1995.

We have focused more on procedures than on tools, and we have made a step-wise approach to the issue, starting to establish configuration management for one major new product. We also want to put emphasise on the process in the company and the human aspects of the issue. It is important to establish configuration management thinking in the organisation, and you need to involve a lot of people, use quite a lot of time in discussions, and you must have the patience to argue and compromise without losing sight of the overall goal - a good configuration management system that everyone can benefit from.

1. Introduction

1.1 Stentofon AS

Stentofon AS is an industrial company based in Trondheim, Norway. Our principal business is the development, production and marketing of internal communication (intercom) systems. We design and supply both the hardware and the software elements of these systems.

Stentofon has been in this business for many years, and we have a significant share of the world market for this type of product. Good hardware reliability also means that many older systems are still in use. In addition, it has always been - and continues to be - an important element of company strategy that Stentofon provides customised solutions for the special needs of individual customers. Combined with the large number of installations, this means that the company is responsible for the maintenance and further development of a very large variety of systems.

The large variety of systems combined with the fact that new product development is always necessary to maintain a competitive edge, means that many versions of all types of product components must be maintained over long time periods. There is therefore a clear need for configuration management procedures at all levels in the organisation.

1.2 The SISU Project

The work described in this article was carried out as a part of SISU, a Norwegian national research , development and technology transfer program. The main goal of SISU is to increase the effectiveness of software production for the real-time software industry in Norway.

The project was started in 1988, and its first phase ("SISU I") concluded in 1992. The project was regarded as highly successful by both the national funding authorities and the industrial participants. It was therefore decided that the program should be continued until 1996 ("SISU II").

The high proportion of industrial firms in SISU means that it is a rather practical program, with the industrial participants having high expectations. They want useful and effective technologies, customised to their needs.

In the course of SISU I configuration management (CM) was identified as being an important area, contributing significantly to productivity in software development.

Initial work on fairly brief tool evaluations 1 was followed by development of a configuration management "scenario" 3 to be used as a basis for more thorough tool evaluations. This was followed by a comprehensive, long-term assessment of the PCMS tools at Siemens 2.

Later work involved integration of configuration management tools with development tools4, and approaches to the gradual improvement of configuration management practices in companies 6. There was also a realisation that improvements in configuration management require the active support of managers in a company, and accordingly a "management seminar" was arranged to highlight the importance of configuration management 5.

Towards the end of SISU I, the focus was moved away from tools towards a methodology for product maintenance. This resulted in a comprehensive document being produced, describing in some detail a general methodology for product maintenance in the life cycle of a product 8. A course on this methodology was also arranged 7.

The main issues that were highlighted in this methodology were organisational aspects, versions and variants, change control, configuration management, and re-use of software components . There were rather detailed descriptions on change control and a number of suggested forms that could be used.

When the SISU II project started in 1993, it was decided that it would be worthwhile to look closer at configuration management. The methodology 8 developed in SISU I was regarded as being a good starting point, but being rather too generic to be *directly* applicable in a specific industrial context. It was therefore decided to start a project whose main aim would be to *really introduce* configuration management in an industrial setting.

The result of this decision was the SISU project "Introduction of Configuration Management at Stentofon and TrioVing". The project started in May 1992 and lasted until December 1995, and results of that project are presented a final report 9. The participants of this project were the industrial companies TrioVing and Stentofon, and the research institute SINTEF DELAB.

1.3   CM adaptation at Stentofon

At Stentofon we decided to start the work on configuration management because:

- The need for configuration management was already identified in the development department through experiences with software and hardware development and maintenance. By participation in the SISU project further attention had been drawn to the issue. Management finally decided that configuration management should be a part of the company policy.

- It was a company policy to achieve ISO 90001 certification.

2. Starting point

2.1 Assumptions

When we started on the work to introduce configuration management at Stentofon AS we established some main assumptions as a basis for further decisions in the project.

1. There was no room for large investments in an overall configuration management tool. The main effort in the project should be put into establishing useful procedures with support of the tools we already had. New tools should be recommended and introduced only where absolutely necessary. The procedures should be a part of Stentofon Quality Manual 11.

2. We had a fairly good change control procedure for circuit boards, mechanics and cables. We did not want to change this dramatically, but it needed brushing up and adjustments.

3. With our large product range in mind we soon realised that if we were going to implement configuration management on all our products at the same time, the task would be too overwhelming. There would be the danger of creating chaos instead of improvement. We therefore decided that configuration management should only be introduced for new products delivered after 1.1.95.

4. Configuration management should not only concern software. The whole product was to be considered, including hardware, mechanics, cables, software and documentation.

5. Introducing configuration management should be done through participation in the SISU II project. Management and participants in the project looked upon the SISU project as a useful way of having a source of expertise and a forum for discussions.

6. The work of achieving the ISO 9001 certificate should be carried out by Quality Management in parallel with the work on configuration management, but independently of the SISU project.

2.2 The main goal of the project

The main goal of the project was to introduce an effective configuration management into the company. The configuration management would be considered effective if it supported:
- Methods to apply rapid yet safe changes in products
- Handling of a considerable variety in the product base
- Handling of a large number of products and customers

In addition to this main goal, several sub-goals were identified:

1. The configuration management methodology developed in SISU I 8 should be customised to the needs of the company

2. The relevant requirements in ISO 9001/9000-3 concerning Configuration Management, discussed in one of the reports in the SISU project 10, should be taken into account in order that the company could be ISO certified

3. The methodology should be adopted within the company, with enthusiasm from management, the quality assurance manager and system developers

4. The experience gained in this project should be effectively communicated to other companies participating in SISU, in order that they can benefit from the lessons learnt

3. Results

We feel that we have reached our main goals with the project. We cannot say that we have achieved the perfect result, but we have introduced the main aspects of configuration management into the organisation, and we look upon the results so far as a good starting point for further improvement and adjustments.

We cannot say that everyone is enthusiastic about the procedures, but there is a general acceptance that it is necessary and will be helpful for us.

The results of introducing configuration management at Stentofon can be set up in 8 main points:

3.1   Configuration Management Plan

We have established a generic Configuration Management Plan for Stentofon 11 is at Stentofon, without saying too much in detail about how the principles are practised. The plan is included in the QA manual in the company.

3.2   Procedures

The procedures in our QA manual 11 have been reviewed, and some changes and add-ons have been made. Three new procedures have been established: One for configuration management in general, one for establishment of a configuration management plan for each project and one for registration of dependencies. Major amendments had to be made to procedures concerning numbering and identification, version control and change control.

3.3   Test project for CM

We introduced configuration management as a special topic into our largest project at that time: the development of our new generation of intercom system, the AlphaCom. We have used this project as a test case to introduce and use configuration management. The product has now been released, the two first baseline have been established and further development and changes are done according to the established procedures. A configuration management plan for the project has been written, stating in detail how the different issues concerning configuration management are to be carried out. This project configuration plan is established as a template for later projects.

3.4   Numbering and versions

To have a structured numbering and version scheme is the basis of any configuration management. We have given special attention to this issue, and the existing procedure for numbering and versions was adjusted and extended 11. Version control turned out to be a headache, as our tool for material administration was not very willing to let us do this in an elegant way. For the software components the situation turned out to be somewhat better, as we already had a reasonably good tool for control of software files in the UNIX environment, using the RCS version control tool. For the PC environment we have introduced a tool for version control of software files called· SourceSafe, which seems quite promising to us. We clearly see that the system we have established is not as good and complete as we would like it to be, and improvements in tools for version control and material administration is one of the main issues for future improvements.

3.5   Change Control of Software and Documentation

We already had a pretty good procedure for change control of hardware and mechanics. It was not at all a perfect system, but it worked. We introduced change control of documentation and software into this procedure 11 without changing it dramatically. We also introduced a more structured way to register questions on improvement and new features, and established a mechanism to make decisions on such questions.

3.6   Registration of Incompatibilities

One of our main problems has been to keep track of incompatibilities between the different components in our old systems. Such incompatibilities always exists in systems which for a long time have been subject to changes and improvements. The knowledge was present in the organisation, but mostly in the heads of senior staff. It was considered an impossible task to look back and register in detail all the incompatibilities in our existing systems. If we could establish a good way of keeping track of this for the new product, that would be a major achievement and appreciated by everybody. We realised that if we could establish a good method at this point, it would become easy to sell the idea of configuration management to the organisation. Everybody realised the problems that had evolved for our existing product range and would welcome a method that could help us to keep track in the new product.

We have managed to establish a procedure 11 for how to register incompatibilities between the different parts of the AlphaCom product. A baseline listing has been defined and a simple matrix has been set up. The baseline lists all items and their version at the time of the establishment of the baseline. In the matrix all items are listed and for each incompatibility which turns up between two or more items, a number is entered in the matrix and a text file explains what the impact of the incompatibility is.

An example: To use the system's French voice messages, you must have version xxxx or later of one of the circuit boards. In the matrix number y is entered in the cross reference box between the voice messages (listed as an item) and the circuit board (listed as another item). The numbered text list explains this in writing. For a start it works without any extensive computer support , but the need for database support is obvious and will be introduced. The procedure requires that the product manager register the incompatibilities as they evolve and requires that you have a structured way to introduce changes and handle errors for all parts of the system.

3.7 Effective use of Existing Tools

The existing tools we had to use in our work with configuration management were:
- RCS for version control of software files
- IMPCON for parts lists
- SID (Stentofon Identification program) for item identification, and add-on to IMPCON

The RCS tool was established as a good tool for version control of software files, and we did not change the way it was used.

IMPCON is a VMS based system for control of parts lists, and also provides the company's economic and administrative programs. We had to look very closely at this program to find possible ways to register and keep track of versions. We would very much have liked to have replaced it, but a replacement would have been expensive and a time-consuming process which may have slowed down the process of implementing configuration management. We found solutions to the problems, but some of them are not very elegant and requires quite an amount of additional work for those doing the registration in the database. Our work with configuration management clearly showed some of the shortcomings of the IMPCON system, which added up with others already known, and management has now decided to replace the system within 2 years. We are at the moment in the middle of an evaluation process for a new system.

The SID tool is very closely linked with the IMPCON. We decided to use the existing numbering system and expanded it to include item numbers for software and revised the numbering scheme for documentation. With a replacement of IMPCON coming up, we will also have to look at our identification tool and methods.

3.8 Impact of Configuration Management on Quality Administration at Stentofon

A number of the procedures that were updated as a result of this project had earlier been a part of the company's general QA procedures. Thus we had to make sure that the suggested changes were accepted by the quality management and implemented into the QA system. New procedures also had to be implemented into the QA manual 11.

The company wanted to achieve the ISO 9001 certification and has set this as a main goal for the QA manager in 1995. ISO 9001 establishes certain requirements concerning configuration management 10 which we had to take into consideration.

Some of the main elements of quality management are also central points in configuration management, such as
- importance of a controlled process
- approval of documents and deliveries

Stentofon AS achieved the ISO 9001 certificate in November 95. The fact that we managed to establish and use new procedures for configuration management was one of several factors that contributed to this.

4. Experience with introducing Configuration Management

Introducing configuration management into an organisation that has a set of established routines, long traditions and a complex product spectrum is no simple and easy task. It is easy to get lost in all the different aspects of the matter, easy to get overwhelmed by the task and easy to say that "this is all very well, but I don't think it will work for us". It is important to be aware of the complexity of the task and the human aspects involved, otherwise the solutions may turn out to be good theory, but not useful in everyday life. We would like to share some of our experiences on the process with you.

4.1   CM is a quality task

A good starting point when setting out to introduce Configuration Management in a company is to establish Configuration Management as an important QA task. You should involve the Quality Manager in the company, discuss the matter and ask for advice and co-operation. As the introduction of Configuration Management most certainly will include establishing new routines and procedures you will need to work closely with the QA people in your company. Improving change control and keeping track of versions and compatibility's in your product will as a whole improve the stability and thus the quality of your product.

4.2   CM is a complex task

Establishing configuration management involves a lot of people. You need to look at how you work, look at your routines and change them if necessary. You must be willing to discuss changes and to have your own ideas evaluated by others. You have to consider the impact of the suggested changes for all parts of the organisation. This means that you must know how things have been done - and why - to be able to suggest good alternative solutions. So get to know your organisation. Show respect for the work that has been done - there is probably a good reason why things have become the way they are.

4.3   CM takes time

Configuration management must be put on the agenda and you must be allowed to spend time on it. As the changes involves different parts of the organisation and a lot of people, you need to spend a lot of time finding out how things have been done and why. You need to know this before you can suggest any changes. You need to spend a lot of time taking to people, selling the idea of configuration management and making them contribute with ideas and suggestions for improvement. This is very time-consuming - but should not be considered a waste of time. The organisation needs some time to discuss and accept the changes.

4.4   CM involves a lot of people

You need to co-operate with all parts of the organisation. At Stentofon we decided to include all the parts of the new product in the configuration management. This meant that you had to discuss the matter with at lot of people. The need to establish responsibilities for the different aspects of configuration management became obvious. In an everyday situation with a lot of other things to do, it was necessary to sell the idea of configuration management thinking to the whole organisation.

4.5   Decisions and management support

There is the danger that discussions may kill the issue. There must be a limit on who you involve and how far to stretch the discussions. Decisions have to be made even if the solutions are not perfect or complete. Support from the management level in all parts of the organisation is vital to get on with the work.

4.6   Compromise

One of the major aspects in having a successful process in the company is the ability you have to compromise. You may consider yourself the expert and have many ideas on how things should be. Others may be just as sure about their own ideas. Involvement of the organisation is essential. You need to listen to ideas, protests and arguments and ask people to help find good solutions. If you can make people understand the need for the new routines, you will all be able to compromise and find solutions that may work.

4.7   No ready-made solutions

Each company has its specific problems. You have to know what configuration management really means, and then you have to look at your own organisation and find out what to do. Depending on existing routines, organisation structure, complexity of the products and available resources, the implementation of configuration management will be different from one company to another.

4.8   Role of SISU

It is unlikely that we would have come as far as we have without being a part of the SISU project and Stentofon AS has had considerable benefit from this project. The main points to mention are:

1. Configuration management has been put on the agenda and we were allowed to spend time on the project

2. The generic methodology 8 from SISU I was helpful in the start-up period, where we struggled to define and limit the work.

3. It was necessary to have other people as discussion partners. It has been very useful to have people from different companies with different background in the project. Working with people from TrioVing and SINTEF DELAB has added valuable input during the work and made it easier to get a good understanding of the issue and the problems and how to get on with the work.

4. We never lost sight of the more general aspects of the matter. That could easily have happened it we had worked by ourselves.

5. Taking part in the SISU project made it easier to establish a platform inside the company for "configuration management thinking". Once the commitment had been made to join the SISU configuration project, management was very eager to see that there was some results coming out of it, (especially as SISU provides less than 50% funding of project costs!)

6. When it came to the work with the configuration management details, the SISU project could not contribute with "ready-made" solutions suitable for our

organisation. We had to discuss and decide matters within the company. Attending SISU meeting made you sharpen your attention to the matter, and it contributed positively to concentration and motivation.

5. The way forward

We have just started using the new routines for configuration management. There are a number of tasks concerning this issue that have been defined and recognised within the organisation, but which have not been fulfilled. The main tasks within the next year will be:

5.1   Training the Organisation

The new methods and procedures have to be introduced into the organisation in a structured way. We have had a training session with the project members of the of the AlphaCom project. One person has been assigned the responsibility of configuration management in this project. There has also been some introductory lessons on configuration management for the different parts of the organisation, and this work will go on till everyone has been informed.

We all have to help each other in this starting phase to carry out our work according to the new procedures. If someone forgets (most of us will), and slips back to old ways of doing things, we have to help out to get things right without grumbling and criticism.

5.2   Establish Configuration Management plans for new projects

One of the new procedures states that each project shall establish its own Configuration Management Plan 11. This plan shall be based on the overall Configuration Management Plan 11 for the company. Such a plan has been written for the AlphaCom project. This plan is an appendix to the procedure and can be used as a template for other projects. This has up to now not been done for any of the newer projects, so this has to be checked on by quality management, and the project managers will probably need some help on this issue.

5.3   Establish tool support for registration of dependencies

The method for registration of dependencies has been established 11. As the complexity of the AlphaCom product increases and incompatibilities evolve, we will need better tool support for this. We need to have a look at possible solutions and either buy a suitable tool, or work on development of a customised database solution.

5.4   Establish better archive structures and more complete version control

Today we use our existing tool for material administration to register versions of the different components in the system. As earlier mentioned, this is an old tool which does not handle version control in a graceful manner. For software files and document files we have good version control in the UNIX environment; we also have version control for software files on PC. We do not have any tool support for version control of document files in the PC environment. We are at the moment looking into new IT solutions for the company, and an important issue is to find a system that can give us a structured archive and good version control for all types of data. It is possible that we can find a tool which also provides us with the functionality we need for the registration of incompatibilities.

5.5 Reporting status for configuration management

In the Configuration Management Plan, we state that there should be a way of telling the organisation the current configuration status for a product. We have not yet spent much time considering how the information available should be presented to those not deeply involved in the project. There is a need for engineering, sales and marketing staff to have an easily understandable presentation of the dependencies between the different parts of the product, and a list of the incompatibilities that they have to watch out for. This will be evaluated together with the tool evaluation mentioned above, and will hopefully be completed within a year.

6. Conclusions

Finally here is a list of headlines that you should keep in mind if you want to introduce Configuration Management into your organisation:
- Introduce Configuration Management as a QA task
- Management support is essential
- Involve all parts of the organisation - sell configuration management thinking
- Limit the task from the beginning
- Compromise and make decisions
- Routines must survive changes in the organisation
- The results must be so detailed that people understand what to do
- Training the organisation is important
- Use external resources if possible for discussions and advice
- Be patient and keep up faith!

7. Bibliography

1. Terje V. Arnesen, Evaluering av Produktforvaltningsverktøy (Evaluation of tool for product management and maintenance) SISU report SISU-88008.

2 O. Andeassen, Evalueringsresultater PCMS - SISU Configuration Management Scenario (Evaluation results PCMS) SISU report SISU-89009

3 Joe Gorman and Svein Hallsteinsen, Configuration Management Scenario, SISU report SISU-9002

4 Svein Hallsteinsen, Integration of Configuration Management Tools with Development Tools, SISU report SISU-90013

5 Arne Ramstad et al, Lederseminar i produktforvaltning (Management seminar in product management and maintenance) SISU report SISU-90002

6 Ole Solberg, Skrittvis forbedring av konfigurasjonsstyring (Improvement in configuration management -step by step) SISU report SISU-91003

7 Ole Solberg, Kursmateriale for "Metodikk for produktforvaltning" (Course material in "Methods for Product management and maintenance") SINTEF/DELAB / SISU 1993-08-26

8   Ole Solberg et al, Metodikk for produktforvaltning (Methodology for Product management and maintenance) SISU report SISU-92007

9   Joe Gorman et al, Configuration Management: Introducing procedures in two industrial companies, SISU report L-1211-13

10 Joe Gorman, Rune Christensen, Sissel Kolvik, How to relate to ISO 9000-3 in the work with Configuration Management, SISU report P-1211-1

11 Stentofon Quality Manual

12 Sissel Kolvik, Konfigurasjonsstyringsplan for Stentofon , (Configuration Management Plan for Stentofon), SISU report L-1211-11

13 IEEE, IEEE Guide to Software Configuration Management, ANSII/IEEE Std 1042-1987

An Odyssey Towards Best SCM Practices:
The Big Picture

Taek Lee, Peggy Thomas, Vivienne Lowen

Xerox Corporation, 701 S. Aviation Blvd. Mailstop: ESAE-229, El Segundo, CA 90245
tlee@cp10.es.xerox.com

Abstract. The success of an SCM team depends on procedures and processes in place and not solely on the tools identified for use. This paper describes what happens AFTER a tool has been selected. It identifies processes and tools that support these processes for one Xerox organization. It also describes what hurdles other organizations will have to face to achieve similar results.

1   Introduction

Odyssey is a major software project currently consisting of about 450 KLOC. About 45 developers submit an average of 400 checkins per release. Inter Program Development Configuration Management (IPDCM) is the configuration management team that supports Odyssey as well as several other organizations and projects. Consisting of three people, it is a competent and empowered team. One senior full time IPDCM member is dedicated to this project. Other CM team members are capable of providing backup support as necessary. Management is supportive of the configuration management team and requires their representation at program meetings.

The configuration management processes instituted by the team are relatively tool independent, having been reused through three tool transitions in five years. Experience demonstrated that the processes were applicable despite tumultuous changes caused by adopting new CM tools. With minor effort, homegrown support tools later identified in this paper were modified to be compatible with newer commercial tools. The net result is that the CM processes remained stable despite the changes of CM tools in use. We found that documented procedures and automated high-level scripts are key enablers to process reuse.

2   CM Requirements and Implications

In 1994, a task force comprised of volunteers met to define a development model to support the next generation of projects. Members were charged with investigating GNU Autoconf, Imake, and a generic #include feature of Make as candidates for the build tool. The tools needed to support the following requirements:

- concurrent development on multiple UNIX platforms
- concurrent development of multiple releases and variants
- standardization
- portability
- reliability
- dynamic generation of dependencies

Information was sought from various sources, including the USENET Configuration Management newsgroup. Imake was eventually selected for having best met the necessary requirements. GNU Make was also chosen to complement Imake due to its portability and availability on most UNIX operating systems.

One of the key requirements that the new Imake usage policy addresses is standardization. Rather than let developers be creative and ad-hoc with their makefiles, standard Imake templates were proposed, with central makefile rules managed by the CM team. Central rules allow for easy expandability throughout the project, from identical project compile flags to the incorporation of lint checks, memory checks, etc. For example, a debuggable variant was originally supported, followed by an optimized variant, then a code-coverage enabled variant. Creativity was relegated to the source programs themselves, not the makefiles. This practice was acceptable to the developers, who actually welcomed the transfer of makefile responsibility to the configuration management group. Mastering complex makefiles was not something most developers desired. Development managers have observed that productivity is considerably enhanced by the new procedures and tools.

At the same time, various directory structures were discussed. A choice was made based on efficiency, scalability, and ease of use. The selected directory structure was a product of an evolution of several projects, with refinements added incrementally over a period of three years and augmented by input from various companies and references. The standard structure allowed developers to find what they needed quickly and surely. It would not have been possible to implement the Imake system as effectively without the uniform directory structure. We feel the standard directory structure was crucial to our success.

3 CM Process

The Odyssey SCM Plan was written to meet the IEEE Std. 1042-1987 specification. It defines actual SCM activities such as work products identified, changes to baselines are controlled, etc. in full detail. The focus of this paper will be upon the tools and processes originally described by the SCM Plan which support these activities (identified by *italics*.) The following enumerated items describe the process flow. Many of these support tools/processes are evolutions from past projects.

1. Developers read the *IPDCM TeamWare Users Guide*. This helps them 1) get familiar with the SCM tool TeamWare, and 2) provide training in basic functions such as create workareas and perform checkouts and checkins. A practice repository has been established to support this training. When ready, developers create an actual workarea for their project.

2. Developers read the *Imake Users Guide*, which explains how to create Imakefiles/Makefiles, and how to use them to build programs and libraries. Definitions of the build environment are provided, along with a list of supported makefile targets. Templates for building libraries, programs, subsystems, etc., in addition to various shell scripts, exist to support Imake usage.

   This guide contains only enough information to allow a developer to be productive. For more ambitious souls, a reference book on Imake is also provided.

3. Developers add standard SCCS keywords to their source and header files, per *IPDCM SCCS Keywords* document. This also includes a standard copyright message that gives all source file headers a similar appearance.

4. Developers code and test.

5. Developers follow the *IPDCM Checkin Procedures* when they are ready to check in. This document provides step by step instructions customized for the TeamWare SCM tool. An important part of the checkin process is the use of checkin comments by the submitter. Checkin comments have a standard format, where certain fields are parsed automatically and used by several reporting scripts. These reports are described in detail throughout the rest of this paper. It is imperative that the SCM tool supports comments, as comments are the cornerstones of our process. Most modern CM tools do support comments. Comment fields are updated from time to time, depending on new program requirements.

6. The TeamWare tool is customized to notify the CM team and the *Electronic Filing Assistant* program of all checkins via email. Each checkin notification contains various information about the checkin, including the standard checkin comments. All members of the CM team are first alerted of a checkin in this manner. We feel automated notification triggers are an important feature of commercial CM tools.

7. The *Electronic Filing Assistant* stores each checkin notification mailnote as a file into a centrally located directory. For example, a checkin notification mailnote is shown in Figure 1. All checkin messages, integration messages, and any other pertinent mail messages are filed appropriately and automatically. These files are then sorted, transferred, parsed, etc. by shell scripts. Checkin notifications provide a good history and metrics of all checkin activities that occur for each release. These files are themselves configuration items that get regularly controlled and archived. Implementing the *Electronic Filing Assistant* was a major milestone in the tracking abilities of the CM team. Easily expandable, it has been used to track additional configuration items that are widely distributed throughout the Odyssey project, such as release notes and project bulletins.

8. The *Get AR Status* script checks for code inspection and/or AR[1]/CR[2] approval, if appropriate. The *Get AR Status* script creates a list of ARs for the current release, and evaluates whether or not they have been inspected, checked in, integrated, built, and/or approved.

AR/CR status can also be obtained from the *List of AR/CR Reports*, which are sent by the CCB[3] to the *Electronic Filing Assistant* and stored as files in the baseline. These reports capture the weekly list of CCB approved CRs. If the checkin meets the entrance criteria, the CM team processes the checkin, e.g. building as requested, and sends an integration message stating that the checkin has been integrated. As a matter of policy, the CM team builds and unit tests all the official software. Developers never check in derived objects; the CM team is entrusted with the build responsibility. Standard integration messages are created via the *Create Integration Mailnote* script. This script

---

[1] AR: Action Request, i.e. problem tracking ID
[2] CR: Change Request
[3] CCB: Change Control Board

sends mail to the submitter, recipients as specified in the CC: comment field, *Electronic Filing Assistant*, and the CM team. Integration messages incorporate the integrated checkin information. Thus even the integration messages are saved on-line. The *Create Integration Mailnote* script also transfers the checkin notification file to a "processed" directory. The CM team sorts the processed checkin notification files by release.

```
% cat subsys2.component1.BL3.POSTPA_NewJobNotify.checkin
Event:  putback-to
Parent workspace:  /server/cm1/BL3
(montezuma:/cmpart1/cm1/BL3)
Child workspace:  /home/jpark/odyssey2
(afs:/u25g/jpark/odyssey2)
User: jpark


Comment:
Submitter: jpark
CC:  netcon
Subject:  CHECKIN:
subsys2.component1.BL3.POSTPA_NewJobNotify.checkin
INSPECTION DATE: N/A
DESCRIPTION: Changed the name POSTPA_AddJob to
POSTPA_NewJobNotify and ran purify.
UNIT TEST: Done
SUBSYSTEM: subsys2/component1
CM:  cd subsys2/component1/src; make debug unittestdebug


Files:
update: subsys2/component1/src/postpa1_procs.c
update: subsys2/component1/src/postpa.c
update: subsys2/component1/src/postpa_utils.c
update: subsys2/component1/src/postpau_main.c
```

Figure 1: A checkin notification mailnote

9.   When ready to release, the CM team generates releases via the *Create Project Releases* script. This script generates a Bill of Materials itemizing the release content, and stores releases out on the network. *Create Project Releases* also generates a nearly complete release message in a standard format.   This script builds complete or update releases in the form of compressed tarfiles. It also checks for several other release factors.   This script is adequate for the engineering releases that the CM team conducts.

The following reports are generated at this time:

> *ARs Numeric Report* - reports, in sorted order, a cumulative set of ARs fixed for ALL releases.
> *ARs Fixed Report* - reports, in sorted order, ARs fixed by each release date.

These reports give the program team an additional glimpse of the ongoing development activity.   They are usually cross-referenced with the reports obtained from the problem tracking system.

Details and complete CM related information and examples can be found in the Odyssey SCM Plan. All developers are expected to use the SCM Plan as reference.

4 Benefits

Enhancing the build function to include unit test allows for the demonstration that the source code compiles without errors and passes a rudimentary unit regression test. All modules are required to provide complementary standardized, portable unit tests. The CM team always compile the modules and run the unit tests on all applicable platforms, then parse the output for any errors. Each unit test is required to post an overall pass/fail status at the end of its output. The addition of code coverage enabled unit tests and the subsequent *Baseline Status Reports* foster an environment where developers feel compelled to achieve high levels of code coverage. These advances are made possible by the underlying centralized Imake usage policies. Several reports are provided for Odyssey:

- *Lines of Code Report* - Reports total lines of source code (Figure 2), broken down by subsystem or component. It also counts lines of comments and blanks in a source program. This report is circulated to management and developers, and is used as input to generate other project metrics. Graphs of this data are used to project program growth.

```
==================================================
LinesOfCode in SUBSYSTEM subsys1
==================================================
Directory: /server/cm1/BL3/subsys1
   SrcFiles:    79       SrcCode:   23431 + SrcComments: 7095        =
   SrcLines:    30526
   TestFiles:8   TestCode:2679 + TestComments: 399   =              TestLines:
      3078
TotalFiles:87   TotalCode:26110 + TotalComments: 7494               =
TotalLines: 33604


Directory: /server/cm1/BL3/inc/subsys1
   SrcFiles:    57       SrcCode:    4070 + SrcComments: 9780        =
   SrcLines:    13850
   TestFiles:1   TestCode:5 + TestComments: 17        =              TestLines:
      22
TotalFiles:58   TotalCode:4075 + TotalComments: 9797                =
TotalLines: 13872



==================================================
LinesOfCode in SUBSYSTEM subsys2
==================================================

Directory: /server/cm1/BL3/subsys2
   SrcFiles:    58       SrcCode:   17783 + SrcComments: 4867        =
   SrcLines:    22650
   TestFiles:46   TestCode:18469 + TestComments: 2323               =
   TestLines:   20792
TotalFiles:104          TotalCode:   36252 + TotalComments: 7190    =
TotalLines: 43442
```

Figure 2: Lines of code report

- *Checkin List Report* - Reports checkin names by release date. This report is circulated to management to help monitor project activity.

- *Checkin Statistics Report* - Reports total number of checkins per release, divided between updated and new files. This report is circulated to management.

```
* * * * * * * * * * * * * * * * * * * * * * * * * * * * * * * * * * * * * * * *
    /server/ipdcm/blines/BL3/./cm/doc
    BaselineStatus.BL3.950822
* * * * * * * * * * * * * * * * * * * * * * * * * * * * * * * * * * * * * * * *
```

__SUBSYSTEM:__	subsys2					

__COMPONENT__ *developers*	*OS1*	*build*	*utst*	*OS2*	*build*	*utst*
comp1	*Pass*	*Yes* *joe*	*Pass*		*Yes*	
comp2	*Pass*	*Yes* *smith*	*Pass*		*Yes*	
comp3	*Pass*	*Yes* *jane*	*Pass*		*Yes*	
comp4	*Pass*	*Yes* *doe*	*Pass*		*Yes*	
comp5	*Pass*	*Yes* *jack*	*Pass*		*Yes*	
comp6	*FAIL(both)MF*	*Yes* *jill*	*FAIL(both)CD*		*Yes*	
comp7	*Pass*	*Yes* *joe*	*Pass*		*Yes*	
comp8	*Pass*	*Yes* *smith*	*Pass*		*Yes*	
comp9	*Pass*	*Yes* *jane*	*Pass*		*Yes*	
comp10	*Pass*	*Yes* *doe*	*FAIL(opt)CD*		*Yes*	
comp12	*Pass*	*Yes* *jack*	*Pass*		*Yes*	
main	*Pass*	*Yes* *jill*	*Pass*		*Yes*	

...
* = no optimized unit test available
CD = core dump
MF = memory fault

Figure 3: Baseline status report

- *PureCoverage Summary Report* - Reports code coverage results of each file organized by subsystem and component. This report is circulated to management and all developers. This report spurred policies regulating code coverage goals for all modules. Modules falling below the coverage guidelines are flagged in the reports. Coverage-enabled variants are required to collect this data, but this is simple to create thanks to the centralized Imake build structure.

- *Baseline Status Report* - Reports compilation and unit test status for all modules as shown in Figure 3. They are broken down by variants (debug/optimized) and by platform. Status is pass/fail, with failures having an attached footnote identifying the type of failure:

5   Corporate Commitment to Continuous Improvement

In 1994, Xerox Corporation made a commitment to improve its software management capabilities with respect to the Software Engineering Institute's (SEI) Capability Maturity Model (CMM). One of the key elements of meeting this objective requires satisfying the Key Process Area (KPA) for SCM.

An extra benefit of having a well-defined CM process is the ability to meet the SCM KPA. The CM team was recently certified as having met the four goals of the SCM Key Process Area. The Odyssey SCM Plan and other documents referenced in this paper demonstrated that the team's goals were aligned with those of the KPA. In addition, the CM team invited SCM representatives from throughout Xerox to participate in the first Odyssey SCM Plan audit. This was the first SCM audit within the company. The audit details such as agenda, SCM Plan, checklist, and other handouts are available on-line via World Wide Web to assist other programs conducting audits. The CM team feels that its direction is consistent with corporate commitment to improve its software management capabilities with respect to the CMM.

6   Considerations For Other Organizations

The identified configuration management processes are being applied to many other projects currently active in various departments supported by the CM team. It has been a lot of work, but there is still much room for growth. The SCM Plan audit revealed that most activities are followed, but identified several key configuration items that still need to be aggressively controlled. Previously, documents in proprietary Xerox formats were excluded from formal control. Basic procedures have been instituted to address these outstanding issues. Extensive control over documents is a future area targeted for advancement. A major strength identified from the audit is the repeatability of the CM team processes via automation and documentation. Now that the feedback has been incorporated, the next step for the CM team is to process the outstanding action items.

New projects that the CM team supports will benefit from all of the current infrastructure. Most tools and reports can be reused on new projects. Work is still required to retrofit legacy projects to the new standards before IPDCM tools can be applied. For instance, without the standard directory structure and use of centralized Imakefiles, many of the processes described earlier would not be applicable. Currently there is an ongoing task of converting about a dozen legacy projects, spanning several million lines of code, to the new infrastructure. The conversion process is on schedule.

The platforms presently targeted by the CM team for development include only UNIX operating systems. All the scripts are written in Bourne and C-shell. Porting to other operating systems such as Windows NT will require work. However, it would be relatively easy to identify what needs to be ported. Since the processes are clearly documented, they should be adaptable to any new platform. The CM team has demonstrated in the past that its processes are relatively CM tool independent which should ease porting. All of the IPDCM tools and processes are openly available to anyone within the corporation. Reuse among various organizations within Xerox should enable others to quickly obtain IPDCM tools and processes. Several software process improvement initiatives have been started to facilitate the sharing of these processes. One barrier to reuse could be the difficulty in mastering the Imake system. However there are many references available, and IPDCM can serve as a competency center in this area for the other organizations.

7 Conclusion

Three major milestones were identified: 1) implementation of the Electronic Filing Assistant, 2) selection of the standard directory structure, and 3) the establishment of the centralized Imake usage policies. The CM team has been able to leverage off this infrastructure to make significant productivity gains. The gains reflect not only the CM team's productivity, but development productivity as well. Also of note should be the evergreen nature of the processes and tools. Program requirements always change, but a good infrastructure allows easy support of any new requirements. Good infrastructure also allows for easy dissemination of information, for example hypertext based documentation and reports. The results have been well worth the effort. It is the intent of this paper to have provided the readers with an understanding of the types of work involved, and a scoping of the effort required. If there are any questions, please contact the authors.

Best Practice for a Configuration Management Solution

Susan Dart

Dart Technology Strategies, Inc.
1280 Bison, Suite B9-510, Newport Beach, CA. 92660. USA
E-mail: sdart@earthlink.net

Abstract. This paper captures best practice in attaining a configuration management (CM) solution. Some buyers of CM tools assume that installing a new tool will automatically solve their CM problems. But this "silver bullet" expectation is not met without effort since there is more to attaining a good CM solution than merely buying the tool. Key practices that enabled successful companies to implement the best possible CM solution, are presented here. It turns out that the best solution is a combination of having the most suitable CM technology, sensible deployment strategies, a culture that is amenable to change and growth, and people that are knowledgeable about CM activities. Understanding best practice is vital for companies considering a better CM solution - it allows leveraging from previous experiences so that they can more easily, effectively, cheaply and painlessly attain their corporate CM goals. Unfortunately, some companies fail because of poor practices. Yet, every company should succeed. The best practices presented here are designed to help companies avoid typical pitfalls in the procurement, evaluation, strategic planning and deployment of their CM tools.

1 Introduction

Configuration Management (CM) technology has advanced considerably over the last decade. Such advancement has enabled many companies that previously had no automated CM, or that had their own "home grown" tool, to effectively address their needs using commercial CM tools. This paper explores how companies avoided major pitfalls by following "best practices". Best practice fundamentally boils down to two key areas:

1. Procurement: the process of evaluating, choosing and buying the right CM tool, and

2. Deployment: the process of adopting and implementing the tool throughout the organisation (whether it be for one project or for the entire company).

Unfortunately, most companies do not follow best practice. As a result, what they achieve is a degree of success which can be classified as good, bad or ugly adoption of a CM solution. And the degree of success is typically independent of the CM tool chosen.

2 The Good, the Bad and the Ugly Adoption of a CM Solution

Good adoption occurs when a company has been successful, effective and optimal in the procurement and deployment of its CM solution. "Successful" means it has achieved it goals. For example, the quality of its products has improved and the number of bugs found in field releases has been reduced.

"Effective" means a full spectrum solution was attained: all the targeted user groups are using the CM tool in a meaningful way and its usage has become part of standard practice. "Optimal" means it achieved the success in an efficient manner: minimal "change pain" was incurred and the deployment happened as quickly as possible with little impact on the production schedule. (Note that the best practices come from companies that achieve this level of success.)

Bad adoption occurs when a company has only been partially successful, ineffective and not optimal in its procurement and deployment of a CM solution. "Partially successful" means it didn't achieve all goals: there was insignificant change in product quality and there was no change in the number of bugs found in released baselines. "Ineffective" means a piece of the desired solution was attained: only a few users, perhaps only the pilot group, are using the tool and not all the capabilities of the tool are being used. Also, perhaps only a pilot project was completed and full deployment was not attempted. "Not optimal" means there were too many road-blocks along the way: there was significant resistance and a high level of "change pain". The deployment was progressing too slowly and time was wasted. (Note that most companies generally fall into this category.)

Ugly adoption occurs when a company has failed to attain a CM solution: no change happened and the new CM tool was shelved, meaning it was never used by any group. The company believed in the "silver bullet" approach - a tool, that when installed, magically and instantly provides a total CM solution for the company. These companies end up cycling through every tool in the marketplace in the constant quest for the silver bullet but consequently, shelve all the tools, having wasted much time, effort and money. It doesn't have to be this way though!

2.1 Overview

By understanding what constitutes best practice, companies are able to achieve good adoption of a CM solution, assured of having bought the right tool and of having deployed it effectively.

This paper discusses CM today. It looks at a key decision that companies need to make when buying a CM tool: whether they want an enterprise-wide CM solution or a project-oriented CM solution. As part of understanding best practice, the drivers or catalysts that force a company to address a new CM solution, are presented. Then a discussion follows that highlights the best practices for procurement and for deployment. The paper concludes by summarising the major lessons learned by companies.

3 CM Technology Today

CM tools have matured over the last 10 years. The amount of functionality, their quality, their usability and their platform coverage has been improved. No longer are CM tools just a version control vault for source files. They are now extremely powerful, sophisticated and reliable providing all the necessary automation required to implement an enterprise-wide CM solution.

The leading CM tools are built on commercial database systems and are integrated with third-party tools thereby providing a true software development and maintenance environment for developers, testers, quality assurance groups, product release groups and managers.

As the technology evolves, so does the definition of CM. In a broad sense, CM is thought of as a discipline for managing the evolution of software systems: all the data and its engineering are safely and reliably governed. At the automation level, CM is:

1. Efficient version control for all types of data

2. The manufacturing and building of code

3. Release management for families of baselined products

4. Change management for bug tracking, problem fixing, enhancements and patches

5. Workflow management for automating processes and data management

6. Team engineering for co-ordinating and synchronising team work across distributed workspaces

7. Dependency tracking of related data

8. Audit control on all CM activities

9. Report generation and status accounting of work under development or released.

In fact, today, a CM solution can be thought of as "groupware" for a company's development and maintenance activities. The report [1] provides the industry's most comprehensive analysis and evaluation of client-server CM tools.

4 Benefits of a Modern CM Solution

Companies are finding they require a better CM solution because of:

- The desire to use better technology

- Unacceptable pain level with existing solution

- Overwhelming cost of maintaining homegrown system

- A need to meet various internal and external quality standards (such as ISO 9000, SEI CMM, Bootstrap, etc.)

- The consequences of corporate mergers: multiple CM systems

- The goal to maintain a competitive edge by being more productive and responsive to the marketplace.

A modern CM solution can provide companies with many benefits such as:

- **Productivity enhancements**, especially for developers who can focus mostly on the creative part of their work (code development) as opposed to chores (setting up their own workspace, tracking down people to find when they should merge code changes, sitting in on meetings to communicate status and filling in forms)

- **More opportunity for growth** with capabilities not possible before, such as the ability to have variant releases for multi-platform products and propagate changes across them and to be able to ship patches to specific customers

- **Visibility** into the state of the software development and maintenance activities as well as to all the changes and data items; history of all items such as who made a change, when, how, why and what changed

- **Better forecasting** of release dates because the change cycle time becomes measurable and hence, more predictable

- **Change impact analysis** to help determine how much effort is involved in a change and hence, how much time it will take

- **Fewer bugs** in field releases; many bugs found in releases (such as having the wrong patch or missing a patch or having not been through testing) could have been avoided if CM were in place. Some companies find that 50% of the bugs found in their field releases by customers could have been avoided had proper CM been in place.

- More **independence** for a company. There is less reliance for a company on a single guru i.e., instead of the CM knowledge being in one person's mind, it is disseminated throughout the organization via the CM tool; this reduces some risk for the company

- Enables **concurrent engineering** e.g., optimize productivity across a team (developers, testers, build managers, change engineers, release managers.) Each team member can work simultaneously and not hold up each other's work. For instance, some developers can be fixing bugs while others are creating new code while testers are testing certain bug fixes in test releases while quality assurance staff are doing quality checks on QA baselines while build managers are building the latest test baselines

- This then can significantly **reduce cycle time** for a change and hence a release

- Enables **distributed development** so that teams can work on related changes at different geographical sites

- **Better quality releases**: because of the repeatability, there's the guarantee that all the necessary steps, such as build and integration testing or Quality Assurance have been carried out on the releases. There are no surprises and less opportunity for the introduction of errors.

- CM enables a company to **leverage** its development activities providing strategic corporate benefits. A company can expand its product lines because it now knows how to manage parallel or variant releases of it software and propagate changes properly

- A company with effective CM, can **be more responsive to its customers needs** since change cycle time is more predictable. The company can better meet its software release schedules.

- A **cheaper way of doing CM** where each step takes less time and manpower because of the automation so there's less opportunity to introduce errors. This can provide a project with more slippage time i.e., time that, in the past, would have been spent on doing horrendous code merges and can now be spent on more productive activities such as adding more enhancements.

With the decision to buy a commercial CM tool, a company also needs to decide upon the scope of their CM solution: enterprise-wide or project-specific.

5 Choosing the Scope of a CM Solution

Companies that buy commercial CM tools choose either a "centralised approach" or a "decentralised approach" for their CM solution. A centralised approach means the company is looking for an enterprise-wide CM solution: everyone in the company will use the same CM tool -- it becomes a corporate standard. Whereas, a de-centralised approach means each project group or department or site in the company will look for its own CM solution: each group will probably use a different tool based on its own preferences.

An **enterprise-wide CM solution** implies that the capabilities of the CM tool must meet the requirements of all groups within the company, such as requirements for developers, CM managers, project managers, documentation staff, testers, build managers, QA staff, quality engineers, release managers and process managers. The solution involves automating processes that represent the interactions of these people with each other and between the various groups. With such a solution, the focus is on process improvement.

A **project-oriented CM solution** implies a more limited set of requirements for a CM tool: typically, the needs of developers and the build manager are the main concern with some problem tracking support thrown in. Such a solution involves limited process support as well as team work. Process improvement is not a major focus, although it may be a side-effect.

Figure 1 highlights some differences between each approach. Of course, some companies can't decide which approach to choose: they need to do a "proof of concept" pilot project where they get to know the tool and its capabilities before deciding.

5.1   Project-oriented CM solution

In a project-oriented CM solution, a particular group changes over to a particular CM tool. Since each project could end up with a different CM tool, the CM solution appears piecemeal: everyone has their own approach to CM. Since the target user population is likely to be smaller as well as the number of roles and responsibilities. This kind of CM solution typically takes a shorter amount of time compared to the enterprise-wide one.

Procurement tends to happen "just-in-time": when each department considers itself ready for a new CM solution. The initial cost in terms of time tends to be cheaper since there are fewer people and issues involved in attaining sponsorship for the group's procurement. And since the set of requirements for the tool are smaller, the evaluation process tends to be shorter. But, the long-term costs regarding maintenance, systems administration and inter-department workflow, tend to be higher.

Deployment focuses on one project and is typically very developer-oriented. Since deployment is treated as a "one-time event" for the company, it generally relies on the vendor's services to ensure smooth deployment and expends minimal effort on a formal adoption strategy.

5.2   Enterprise-wide CM Solution

In an enterprise-wide CM solution, the goal is a full spectrum CM solution. Since many groups need to be rolled out to the new solution, more time is required than would be for just rolling out one group as in the project-oriented case. Often the capabilities of the tool need to be adapted or customised to suit the many needs and processes of all groups.

Procurement happens as part of a top-down corporate planning process. Because of the need to get corporate-wide sponsorship, buy-in, and commitment, there is an initial higher cost to the company in terms of time. And because the tool must meet the needs of all groups, the evaluation period tends to be longer since more tools are evaluated in more detail and by more people.

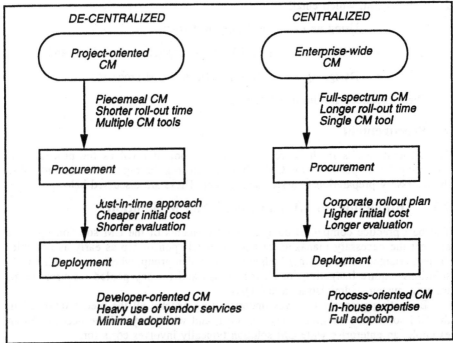

Figure 1: Project-oriented and Enterprise-wide CM Solutions

Deployment generally involves a formal, corporate-wide adoption strategy. The company develops its own in-house experts on deploying, implementing and customising the tool for all of the groups. Considerable process development is included such as capturing the entire software workflow throughout the company, from the creation of every data object through its release and its subsequent maintenance.

5.3   The Better Approach

Which approach is considered the better? Each provides its own benefits and trade-offs, as highlighted in Figure 1.The choice really depends on the company's needs, its long-term strategic goals, the availability of resources, its budget and its reasons for change. Whichever approach is chosen, the company needs to see it through maturation. Companies will end up doing bad or ugly adoption of a solution if they profess to want an enterprise-wide CM solution but execute actions more in line with a project-oriented solution.

6   Best Practice in Attaining a CM Solution

"Best practice" means the key processes, methodologies and activities that enabled companies to achieve the best possible CM solution. Best practice can be thought of in terms of procurement and deployment:

1 . Procurement, which entails:

- Budgeting for all elements of the CM solution
- Evaluating the most appropriate CM tools, and
- Preparing for the deployment.

2 . Deployment, which entails:

- Using an excellent deployment team
- Following a simple, risk-based adoption methodology, and
- Designing and automating effective CM processes.

These practices are discussed below.

7   Procurement

Procurement results in the purchase of a CM tool: it involves the processes of budgeting for all pieces of the CM solution, choosing the right CM tool, and doing the necessary preparation to assist deployment. These are discussed below.

7.1   Budgeting for all elements of the CM Solution

The best practice companies budget for all elements of the CM solution up front and get the necessary management and financial sponsorship as early as possible. Project-oriented solutions only budget for their own group, whereas enterprise-wide solutions require budgeting for all the groups and for any pooled resources (e.g., training, systems administration and QA).

Budgeting properly involves understanding exactly all the pieces involved in the CM solution, how much they will cost, and when they will be needed. As an example, an enterprise-wide CM solution typically involves costs for:

- The CM tool - including all its associated parts e.g., the core functionality, the problem tracking part, the distributed code management part, the build manager capability, repository

- Vendor tool training - there are typically several kinds of classes: novice training, build manager training, train-the-trainer, training for each part of the tool, customisation training, process design training, adoption training

- Consulting services - technology transition support, risk management, metrics development, process design, standards certification, code reengineering

- Customisations to suit specific needs

- Integrations of CM tool with the existing environment and its tools

- Maintenance - upgrades and patches

- Vendor hot-line support, and

- Corporate pooled resources - training group, systems administration support for the CM tool, internal hotline for user questions.

The best-practice companies streamline their procurement processes. More importantly, they budget for all the expenses up front (even if it's an incremental purchase and the money is paid out over time). And they are not afraid to ask the vendor what the real costs are likely to be. During procurement, it is important that the company have an initial, corporate roll-out plan in mind. This is helpful to the vendor and company in meeting the incremental procurement needs.

7.2 Evaluating the Most Appropriate CM Tools

Companies evaluate tools before choosing the right one for them. The keys to successful evaluations are:

1. Having a properly skilled evaluation team

2. Having a realistic and comprehensive set of requirements

3. Designing useful evaluation criteria based on that set of requirements, and

4. Running meaningful evaluation tests.

An ineffective evaluation typically consists of purchasing several trade magazines that have articles about CM tools and then choosing the one that has the most glowing review. This is a terrible way to do an evaluation because it doesn't take into account the needs of the company and its people, and it assumes that all meaningful details were addressed in the trade magazines (which is generally not the case). An effective evaluation is comprised of the following:

- The Evaluation Team is chosen

- The evaluation methodology and selection criteria are designed

- A set of requirements, categorised by priority, is developed

- All possible sources of information on CM tools are read (trade magazines, comparison reports, online bulletin boards, CM mailing lists)

- An initial set of candidate tools is examined

- Typically, two final candidates are chosen

- Detailed evaluation tests are run in-house with the candidates

- Reference companies are interviewed for their tool experiences

- Based on the results of the above and the evaluation criteria, the better candidate is chosen.

The following sections discuss important aspects about the Evaluation Team, creating a set of requirements, and doing the right kind of preparation for deployment.

7.2.1 The Evaluation Team

The Evaluation Team includes various representatives of the user community (developers, testers, QA people, technical leaders, build managers, and project managers). Additionally, each provides their perspective and ensures their needs are captured in the evaluation criteria. They each provide their experiences and skill sets and together, can provide a balanced evaluation of a tool and discern its potential for the company. As a minimum, it is important that the Team have an understanding of the current CM workflow. Good Evaluation Teams maintain an objective viewpoint when evaluating tools and have an evaluation plan.

A smart Evaluation Team will leverage from the vendor by obtaining examples of case studies, comparisons to find out weaknesses in the competitor's product and deployment guidance such as the pitfalls other customers have experienced. They realise that the vendor provides a wealth of experience based on its previous customers in following best and worst practice.

7.2.2 The CM Requirements

A set of prioritised requirements is developed by the Evaluation Team based on feedback from their colleagues, in particular, the eventual users of the tool. The priorities are "must have", "would be nice to have", and "wish list".

When developing requirements, it is particularly important to analyse the existing CM solution to understand what works along with its pains or weaknesses. These "pains" form the best requirements. Companies struggle with developing a list of CM requirements. A simple way of defining a requirement is to turn a "pain" into a "vision statement".

For instance, a "pain" is "we have no idea what goes into a build and hence, is shipped to a customer". Turning this into a vision statement results in "we would like to know every piece of code, tool, option, flag, library, environment variable, etc. that participates in a build of a configuration item so that at any point in time we know exactly which pieces were involved in a build by looking at a list or making a query and similarly, we can tell which pieces were shipped to each customer".

The Evaluation Team does a thorough analysis of cause-and-effect of the weaknesses of the current CM solution so that a real understanding of the problems exist. For instance, given the problem, "we miss deadlines", they look at the root cause which could be: "we have no CM workflow defined so it is constant chaos which means there are no repeatable processes making it impossible to forecast release cycle times."

Best-practice companies use various categories of requirements: functionality, usability, performance and scaleability.

Functionality Requirements

These are the features provided by the tool. Typical functional aspects include: build issues, team engineering, structure and relationship support, versions of all kinds of objects, controlling access, status visibility and reports, audit trails, process mechanisms and workflow management.

When evaluating tools against the requirements, unfortunately many companies focus on tool features. That is, they do the evaluation by creating a table of features and having a column for each CM tool in the marketplace. Then, each column is ticked or crossed based on the existence of that feature. This is partially useful in culling out the initial set of candidates, but beyond that, it is not an effective way of choosing the final tool. That's because each vendor uses different terminology, has different architectures and concepts. Much more is needed to properly differentiate.

Usability Requirements

These make the CM tool easy to use including: intuitive interface, simple set-up and installation, straightforward migration of legacy code and CM information, minimal change in usage model, clear understanding of methodologies, straightforward concepts, minimal learning time and easily customisable.

Performance Requirements

These make usage of the tool feasible including: having acceptably fast times for manipulating large volumes of data, command response, check-out time, builds, work area updates and synchronizations, and customisations.

Scaleability Requirements

These address the ability of the solution to scale to meet the large number of users and large volumes of data, as well as the large number of platforms distributed around the world. It also includes the potential for growth -- the CM solution needs to evolve as the company's needs evolve. The tool's repository needs to scale up to easily add new users, roles, access rights, and more complex objects

7.2.3 Preparing for the Deployment

The best practice in preparing for the deployment entails correctly setting user's expectations, aligning people's goals, cultivating champions, and setting up a Deployment Team. It is analogous to a public relations event for releasing a new product.

Setting expectations involves communicating realistic messages. It is particularly important to communicate to the company when deployment will begin, how it is likely to happen and what can be expected from the new tool. Groups should be solicited for pilot projects and the company reminded of the reason for the change. It is a good time to demonstrate the tool to all groups so that they get a "look and feel" for the new tool. All these help to set reasonable expectations.

Another key message concerns **aligning goals**: ensuring that the business goals set by management are in line with the development teams' goals, is vital. It is important that the goals be understood by all parties in order to avoid unnecessary resistance and to be certain that the implementers and users of the CM solution (mostly the developers, testers, QA people, technical leads) are deploying the solution as planned by management. At the same time, the plans from management need to realistically support the work of the development teams. It is only through communication and making all the goals visible that all parties will be in tune. The goals need to be reinforced, which is done by providing the appropriate amount of, and calibre of, resources for deployment. **Technical and managerial champions** should now be cultivated since they will be major players in the deployment. The **sponsor** needs to actively "network" with peer management to slowly develop management commitment.

8 Deploying the CM Solution

Best practice in deployment involves having an excellent Deployment Team following a risk-based adoption methodology and implementing workflow that integrates the processes of all the users.

8.1 The Deployment Team

Deployment is treated as a project in itself. Thus, plans are developed, risks are mitigated, schedules and milestones are set based on the adoption strategy. A Deployment Team is needed to implement the adoption strategy.

The Deployment Team will lead, manage and implement the change. It consists of representatives from each user group. A representative is the champion for their group. Each reflects and addresses the needs and opinions of their groups. The Team has a Leader whose role is equivalent to that of a project manager. As a whole, the Team needs to have a broad set of skills. These skills include: excellent communication and group facilitation, conflict resolution, analytical, strong technical experience especially in CM and software development and maintenance, negotiation, public relations, leadership, intestinal fortitude, and a sense of humour.

The team needs a member, ideally the Leader, who has "boundary spanning" skills: can communicate effectively up and down the corporate hierarchy with developers and with management. To function efficiently, the best-practice companies put the Team through team-building activities in order to develop trust and confidence in each other.

8.2 The Risk-based Adoption Methodology

The best practice companies have found that the essence of successful deployment is following a risk-based adoption strategy. Risk management enables all the correct, strategic deployment decisions to be made. It provides a way for management and developers to rally around the deployment in a constructive manner by addressing the risks -- risks are the critical success factors for deployment. Mitigating the risks is the best avenue of eliminating most resistance to change.

The adoption strategy consists of five phases:

1. Analysis and Planning

2. Process Refinement

3. Piloting

4. Rolling Out

5. Process Improvement.

For a project-oriented deployment, the adoption strategy is scaled down, as is the size of the Deployment Team.

Analysis and Planning

The purpose of this phase is to do all the necessary preparation, strategizing, analysis and scheduling required to begin deploying to all groups. The result of this phase is a Corporate Adoption Plan consisting of all the steps, goals, milestones, success criteria, decision making issues, strategies, and schedules to enable deployment across the company. Also, from the analysis work, a Corporate Risk Management Plan is written. This plan describes all the risks, mitigation strategies, questions, and contingency plans needed for managing the critical success factors.

Process Refinement

This phase is used to understand the existing CM processes, and to refine them or define new ones. The CM Process Model document captures the processes at a level of abstraction that is meaningful to all users and the CM Process Implementation Plan documents how the processes will be automated to achieve effective workflow.

Piloting

This phase is used to mitigate the risks. Multiple pilot projects are designed where each addresses a certain number of the known risks. The details of each pilot project are captured in the Pilot Plan. The results of each pilot project are used to resolve the risks or to put in place the contingency plan, as well as fine-tune all the preparation required for each group's roll-out, such as the type of training needed.

Rolling Out

This phase consists of systematically rolling out each group to the new CM solution. Few problems and surprises are encountered due to all the risk mitigation activities of the previous phase. All preparation and tasks required for each group's roll-out are captured in each Group's Roll-out Plan.

Process Improvement

This phase is geared to capturing lessons learned from the deployment. From those lessons, plans for continuous improvement are made.

8.3   CM Processes

Automating processes enables effective and safe CM workflow management. The key processes that best-practice companies address are:

- Corporate process: the company-wide standard for product development

- Software development and maintenance process: software flow throughout the company; for each project team, capture all steps from code creation through to delivery of changes to the customer

- Change management process: how bugs, problems and enhancements are tracked, reported and fixed

- Testing process: the different levels of testing carried out (unit, integration, system, QA)

- Quality Assurance (QA) process: the certification of the quality of the products, and

- Help Desk and Call tracking process: customer hot-line support.

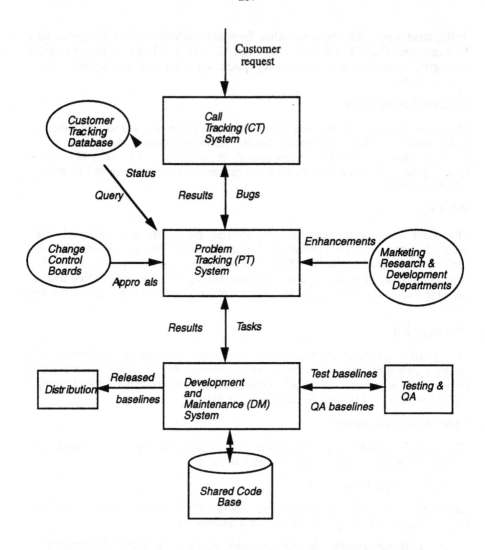

Figure 2: Integrated Processes Making Up A Complete CM Solution

Companies that strive for a totally automated CM solution have all these processes integrated, thereby providing a complete workflow/groupware-like solution, as shown in Figure 2. This simplified figure shows a high-level architecture for how various processes (and tools) are integrated.

A customer request is fed into the Call Tracking (CT) system. The CT system analyses the request to determine if it is a bug or whether the hot-line staff are able to answer their request. The Problem Tracking (PT) system manages the workflow of a bug and enhancement requests. A bug is fed into the PT system from the CT system. The enhancement requests often come from the Marketing and the

Research and Development (R&D) side of the company. Approvals for changes typically come from the Change Control Board.

Fixing the bug or developing the enhancement is broken down into tasks to be done by the developers. These tasks are fed into the Development and Maintenance (DM) system (typically called a CM system). The DM system manages the workflow of those tasks as well as the data from the shared code base/file system. It works with Testing and QA tools to ensure the appropriate validation of baselines and passes the approved baselines to the Distribution system which is responsible for deploying the baseline into the field at various sites.

Each of the systems feed back into each other to keep information synchronised. All the systems mentioned are typically sold as third-party tools. These are integrated where possible so that information within the systems can be fed into other systems, such as to customer databases and project management tools.

8.3.1 The Corporate Process

The corporate process is the company's standard for how new products are developed. For instance, for a new product to come into existence, the following major events usually occur:

1. Market research and analysis is done to determine the viability of the new idea or the need for a major release

2. Requirements are developed

3. The product is designed

4. The product is coded

5. Integration testing is done to ensure all elements of that new product function together as a whole

6. System testing is done to ensure that all elements of that new product work with all elements of dependent products and libraries

7. QA testing is done to certify the product passes company quality standards

8. The product is shipped to alpha test customers for initial customer reactions

9. The product is shipped to best test customers for final customer testing

10. The product is made available for general release to the entire customer base.

Because the corporate process effectively sets the workflow for a product and new releases of it, it must be aligned with all the other processes that make up the CM solution. That is, it influences the design of the other processes. The major processes that are influenced by the corporate process are problem tracking and development.

8.3.2 CM Problem Tracking Process

The PT process reflects the workflow of bugs and enhancements. At any point in time, the status of any bug or enhancement is visible to the user of the system. Figure 3 shows a simplified PT process for a bug report or a change request.

A bug report or change request is entered into the PT system. Depending on the kind of bug or its severity or the site responsible for analysing it, it will be forwarded to the appropriate PT database. Once in a database, it goes through a review process, such as the Change Control Board (CCB). The CCB may decide to reject it or to defer until a later point in time. Otherwise, it is assigned to a developer or several, to be fixed. This results in tasks being fed into the DM system for those developers. Once those tasks are completed, the DM process feeds back into the PT process so that the bug report or change request can be resolved and concluded. Some companies have simpler processes, some more complex; it depends entirely on the company's needs.

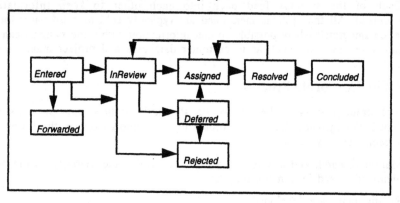

Figure 3: A Typical Problem Tracking Process

8.3.3 CM Development Process

Best-practice companies automate their development, maintenance, testing, QA and distribution processes as much as possible via the DM system. The tasks that are fed into the DM system are assigned to developers, typically by email notification. Each developer works on a piece of code in an isolated and protected manner from other developers but in a manner in which they have visibility into each other's work and can merge and integrate their changes. The automation is designed to optimise the amount of parallel development and concurrent baselines. A typical process for a piece of code is shown in Figure 4.

A piece a code starts out in a working state where a developer is creating or changing it. From there, the developer can checkpoint it in order to baseline a personal copy or can integrate that code with other developers' code once unit testing is done. This enables integration testing of each team member's code. Once the code has passed this testing, it is moved to the testers to do their regression testing and then onto QA for final validation testing. When all testing has been completed, the code is ready to be released. At any point in time, code can be rejected so that it doesn't accidentally get used in a valid baseline.

The piece of code eventually becomes part of a configuration. That configuration also goes through a workflow that is virtually the same as that shown in Figure 4. Also, the derived products from the build processes of the code units, can have their own workflow. Associated with the workflow are roles, transition conditions, events, and rules for code selection, code visibility and isolation that provide the full semantics of the CM workflow.

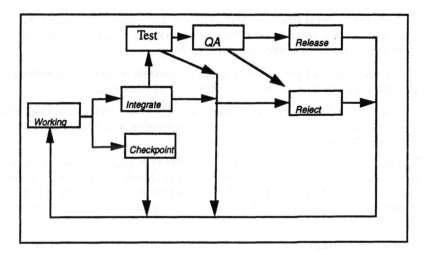

Figure 4: A Typical CM Development Process

9 Conclusion and Lessons Learned

A modern CM solution offers a company many benefits, such as improved productivity and product quality. These help maintain its competitive edge. There are many lessons learned from experiences in developing, selling, procuring and deploying CM solutions which include:

1. The best possible CM solution takes time to achieve, but provides many benefits.

2. Careful procurement and deployment make the best possible CM solution attainable.

3. A company needs to choose whether the CM solution will be an enterprise-wide one or a group-oriented one, and then it needs to commit to that approach.

4. When choosing a tool, short-term and long-term requirements need to be considered.

5. The calibre of people on the Evaluation and Deployment Teams determines the degree of success and speed of it in procuring and deploying a CM solution.

6. Changing to a new and improved CM solution needs to happen in a manner that is conducive to the corporate culture.

7. Training and education of all users about CM, the tool and CM processes are crucial.

8. Using a risk-based adoption strategy is the most cost-effective, painless and successful method for deploying a CM solution.

9. Leveraging knowledge from the vendor (such as by mentoring) is an efficient way of learning from previous CM experiences.

10. All users, regardless of their skill set and including developers and managers, should see a benefit from using the new CM tool. If they don't, there can be insurmountable resistance to change.

11. Automating CM processes as much as possible is vital since automated processes are easier to adopt and to improve than manual processes.

12. Any strategic change for a company, such as deploying a modern CM solution, requires constant management sponsorship and commitment at all levels of the organisation

The quality of the CM tool chosen by a company is generally seen as the key issue in the CM solution. But, if the wrong tool is chosen because the evaluation process was inadequate, or if the tool is poorly deployed due to resistance and lack of strategic planning and sponsorship, no CM tool can effectively fulfil the needs of a company.

9 Acknowledgements

This paper was written while the author worked at Continuus Software Corporation. Special thanks to M. Murphy, E. Soong, J. Warden, M. Johnson, S. Henning, R. Rippy, M. Cagan, D. Weber, C. Eyre, B. Davis and K. Saruwatari for their feedback.

10 References

[1] Burrows, C. , et al, "Ovum Evaluates: Software Configuration Management". Ovum Press. October 1996.

Fully Supported Recursive Workspaces

Lars Bendix[$]

Institute for Electronic Systems, Aalborg University, Denmark
E-mail: bendix@cs.auc.dk

Abstract: Version control deals with support for making changes. The way traditional systems handle this problem is centered around repositories of immutable versions. However, little or no support is given for controlling change outside of said repositories. We develop a conceptual model which places workspaces on an equal footing of repositories and thus we extend traditional version control support to apply to workspaces too. We show how this model was implemented and report on some of the experiences from its actual use.

1 Introduction

In this position paper we take a closer look at how version control support can be supplied throughout the whole programming process. The task of version control is to trace and control changes made to documents. During the life-time of such documents they may be changed and modified many times and thus many versions will be created. Version control tools should facilitate the controlled development of new versions and make it possible to access not just the latest version but also all past versions.

In traditional tools for version control such support is obtained through the use of a central repository. In this repository all versions are kept and anything which resides in the repository is considered immutable. Therefore, all versions which are entered into the repository will be stable and can always be retrieved in the form they had when they were entered. As nothing can ever be changed in the repository, the workspace is the necessary dual to the repository. In the workspace anything can be changed freely as there is no notion of immutability.

Workspaces are used as the place where changes are carried out while the repositories are data bases where immutable documents are kept for posterity. Traditional repositories support version control through many concepts. Immutability ensures that past versions will always be present. Structural mechanisms trace how versions develop from each other. Delta mechanisms represent the actual changes between versions both in conceptual and technical terms.

All this gives good support for managing changes - at the level of repositories. At the level of the workspaces, where we have to actually carry out our changes, all this support vanishes. There is no concept of immutability, no structural support, and no mechanism to represent change. We see no reason why the programmer should be deprived of such proper version control support also in his workspace.

In the next section we carefully analyse version control and change. We look at it from the point of view of traditional tools with a distinct division between the repository and the workspace. This analysis points out the problems in this

---

[$] This research was supported, in part, by grant no. 9400911 from the Danish Natural Science Research Council.

unbalanced distinction where version control is supported only for one of the concepts. In section three we design a model where the repository and the workspace are treated on an equal footing. This extends full version control support to cover also the workspace concept. How this model was implemented and the experiences made during practical use of our implementation is described in section four, while the last section sums up the conclusions from this work.

2 Analysis

The heart and core of version control is to deal with changes. It is a fact of life that documents, whether in the context of software development or in a larger context, are changed more or less frequently. The reasons for such changes are many, but in almost all cases we want changes to be performed in a controlled way. For this purpose we use tools which support version control.

The most basic things to be represented in a version control tool are documents and differences. As can be seen from figure 1, the change of a document can be represented as a history step [ABC90], modelling the difference between the original document and the modified document. The history step can be used at the conceptual level to show us what was actually done in the change process. But it can also be used at the technical level to reclaim storage space when conserving multiple versions. Furthermore, the history steps, when put in sequence, model the whole development structure of a series of changes.

Figure 1. A history step.

The history steps can also be considered a relationship which groups documents which have something in common. What they have in common is that they represent the same document in various versions. The transitive closure of the history step relation is called a version group. This is a very convenient abstraction in order to be able to handle all versions of a document in a larger context where we are not interested in the individual version themselves. For this reason the internal structure of a version group, represented by the history steps, can often be left out as they have been in figure 2.

A very important basic principle in version control is that of immutability. We want to be able to conserve information such that we can always return to it at some later point in time. This means that every version which was once created must be conserved for posterity such that it can be retrieved later if needed. During time this will cause the number of version in a version group to grow. The principle of immutability has had the effect of creating two concepts in traditional approaches to version control. One concept is that of a repository where all the immutable versions are kept. In the repository history steps and version group abstractions are used to model structure and to create clarity. The other concept is that of a workspace where documents are mutable and changes can be carried out.

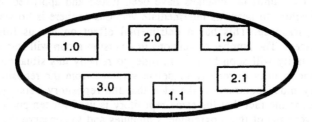

Figure 2. A version group.

These concepts can be seen in figure 3, as can the way in which they are used to exercise version control when carrying out changes. It is not possible to directly make changes to documents which reside in the repository as they must be immutable. Therefore, they are copied from the repository and into the workspace area using a checkout operation on the repository. In the workspace there are no limitations on what can be done as we are here outside of the control of the version control tool. The necessary changes can be carried out in one or more steps until a satisfactory result is obtained. Finally, the repository is updated with the changed document which is inserted using the checkin operation on the repository.

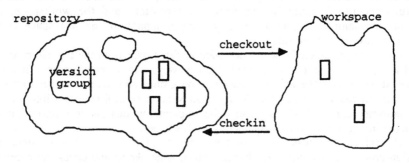

Figure 3. Version control concepts.

This way of supporting version control is used in all traditional systems which have a functionality similar to that of RCS [Tichy85]. It gives a copy-modify-update paradigm for working with changes, in which a solid distinction is made between the immutable repository and the mutable workspace. In itself this is a natural and conceptually sound distinction which causes few or no problems. Much research and effort has gone into giving effective support for the repository concept [Reichenberger89] [Berliner90].

However, all systems support only the repository concept, or at most also the interchange aspects between the repository and the workspace. The workspace itself remains an orphan which is, although recognized as a concept in the way the tool must be used, outside of the control and support of the version control tool. As a consequence there is no version control support for the part of the work which is carried out in the workspace. Neither is there an integration between the two concepts.

The effect of this lack of version control support in the workspace is that the repository is often used for many different purposes which can be in conflict with each other. The project which uses the repository wants to conserve versions which are important to the project - for instance tested and approved versions of program modules. The programmer, on the other hand, would like to keep also intermediate versions - at least until his changes have been tested and approved. So he starts using the repository to keep his intermediate versions as there is no way for doing this in the workspace. This has a detrimental effect on the usefulness of the repository concept. The number of versions in a version group will start to grow out of hand and clarity will soon be lost. In order to remedy this situation, traditional tools have functionality to remove or delete versions from the repository. This is, however, very much contrary to the idea that the repository versions should be immutable. As is the fact that the same repository is used for temporarily keep the intermediate versions of the programmer's modules and to conserve the modules of a whole project.

We find that mixing these concepts is very dangerous. In our opinion the problem is caused by the fact that there is no support for version control in the workspaces where programmers have to carry out their work. And that the problem should be solved by supplying such support instead of abusing of the valid and valuable distinction between immutability and mutability.

3 Design

In the previous section we saw that conceptual confusion was created by the absence of version control support in the workspace. We want to maintain the useful conceptual distinction between the repository and the workspace, but provide the same - or almost - version control support in the workspace as we presently have in the repository.

The principle concepts which we want to carry over from the repository to the workspace are those of component, history step, and version group. First and foremost we want to be able to create version groups and have more versions of a document in the workspace too. Many other version control concepts like locking mechanisms, attribute schema, and delta implementations are less important for the experiment which we are conducting in this paper.

The initial idea was to mirror the concepts of document, history step, and version group directly in the workspace. Thus, when we should check out a certain version from a version group in the repository a new version group would be created in the workspace and the designated version would be copied into this version group. In this version group in the workspace we could carry out our changes in a series of successive edit sessions with the possibility to save intermediate versions along the way. Versions which we could later return to in case we wanted to "undo" some of our changes or in case we wanted to branch off some experimental development. When we had successfully finished making our changes the designated result would be checked back into the version group of the repository as representing the compound result of our changes.

This approach solves the problems mentioned at the end of section two. We would no more need to clutter the repository with temporary versions as there were version control support in the workspace. Furthermore, the contents of all version groups - both in the repository and in the workspace - would be immutable giving a clean conceptual understanding. The only difference is that in the workspace the version groups would have a limited life-time whereafter they - and their contents - would disappear. This is, however, not different from applying the same principle to the version groups of the repository which will have very long life-times.

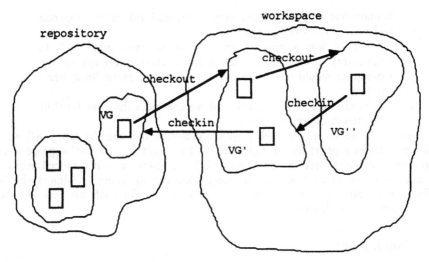

Figure 4. Recursive version groups.

Along the way we generalized the concept of version groups in the workspace into recursive version groups, as can be seen from figure 4. The idea is that if checking out a version from a version group in the repository would create a new version group in the workspace, then it should also be possible to check something out from this version group. Otherwise it would be a different version group concept from the one used in the repository. Thus, all version groups are equal in capability, just that the version groups in the repository have longer life-times. The concept of recursive version groups allows us to check something out from a version group VG' in the workspace, creating the version group VG". This could be done to carry out an experiment or to obtain a coarser granularity between versions in VG'. Exactly as VG' will cause a larger granularity, and thus fewer versions, in the version group VG.

4 Implementation and experiences

The proposed model of recursive version groups to give full support for version control was implemented as part of a larger environment [Bendix95]. This environment is object-based, that is, all artifacts and concepts are modelled by objects. An object consists of a set of attributes and some actions, a part of which are accessible to the user. One of the attributes for a version group is its origin, telling which version caused the version group to be created. For version groups in the repository this attribute has the value NONE. Important attributes for module objects are history_step and father, relating a module to its predecessor and version group respectively.

We implemented our model as part of a system to support integrated version control and configuration management. This system was developed by rapid prototyping as a successive line of generations where one generation was actively used in the development of the next generation. During this practical use several lessons were learned:

> • we experienced a significantly lower number of versions in
> the version groups of the repository. Some version groups would

contain one or two versions only at the end, others between one and two versions per generation.

    • there was a much higher desire to experiment and do exploratory programming. Sometimes version groups in the workspace would have as many as a dozen or more "temporary' versions.

    • only on a few occasions did we use more than one level of recursion in the version groups.

We know of no previous work which addresses this specific topic. All work addresses either support for the repository or for facilitating the exchange between repository and workspace. It should be said that in many cases it is indeed possible to use a version control tool in the workspace too to obtain an almost similar effect. It is, however, outside of the mental model for such systems and the application is manual, cumbersome and error prone.

5 Conclusions

In this paper we have presented a model for version control which gives the same support in the workspace as in the repository. Indeed we have removed the misconception of mixing immutable and mutable aspects in the same abstraction. Our version groups - whether used in a repository or a workspace - contains only immutable elements. It is the version group as a whole which might have a limited life-time if used in the traditional workspace.

The results we have obtained are very promising. Both with regards to the need for support in the workspace situation and with respect to the clarity it brings in the repository version groups by bringing down the effective number of versions. Using the recursive version group approach we can have several levels of version control with each its own granularity of versions: released/in test/under development/experimental.

References

[ABC90]: Vincenzo Ambriola, Lars Bendix, Paolo Ciancarini: *The Evolution of Configuration Management and Version Control*, Software Engineering Journal, Volume 5, Number 6, November 1990.

[Bendix95]: Lars Bendix: Configuration Management and Version Control Revisited, PhD dissertation, Institute for Electronic Systems, Aalborg University, Denmark, December 1995.

[Berliner90]: Brian Berliner: *CVS II: Parallelizing Software Development*, in proceedings of USENIX Winter 1990, Washington D.C.

[Reichenberger89]: Christoph Reichenberger: *Orthogonal Version Management*, in Proceedings of the 2nd International Workshop on Software Configuration Management, Princeton, New Jersey, October 1989.

[Tichy85]: Walter F. Tichy: *RCS - A System for Version Control*, Software - Practice and Experience, Vol. 15 (7), July 1985.

Experience of Using a Simple SCM Tool in a Complex Development Environment

Ivica Crnkovic

ABB Industrial Systems AB, 721 67 Västerås
ivica@sw.seisy.abb.se

SCM Tool used in ABB Industrial Systems

Background

Five years ago our organization started the development of a new generation of real-time systems for process control. The new process supervision systems were based on Unix and Motif. The new development process has required a new, modern and efficient Software Configuration Management (SCM) tool. After the investigation of SCM tools on the market, and some unsuccessful tests of different commercial products, it was decided to start with a simple tool, well integrated in Unix. RCS (Revision Control System) was chosen.

As the number of programmers grew and development projects became larger and more complex, the need for a support beyond pure RCS became apparent. At that time we did not find a CM tool that fulfilled our requirements, so we have started building new functions based on RCS. This development resulted in a product called SDE (Software Development Environment) that is used today by several hundreds of programmers.

This paper gives a brief description of the tool and summarizes the experience of its usage.

SDE basic characteristics

SDE is a software package based on RCS and adjusted for the development of large systems. It includes functions that define working environments for projects and structures of repositories where versioned files are saved. Hierarchical structures of repositories are divided into configurations which makes it possible to develop different versions of software in parallel.

Using slightly modified RCS commands and some new commands related to RCS files, SDE enables easier and faster browsing through the versioned files. In a project environment, users always have a view to a specific configuration of file versions.

SDE includes support for Change Management. Every logical change that has to be done in a development/maintenance session, is described in a Change Request (CR). When a modified file is checked in, it is registered in a CR. A CR is implemented as a versioned file, so it automatically gets RCS file attributes, like state, author, and change date.

SDE uses make for building systems. Makefiles that are automatically generated, use definitions of configurations of all used components, both internal and external.

The Product Management part includes support for the generation of products. A release specification, which is automatically generated, describes changes made in the product.

All SDE functions are available as shell commands. On top of them there are several applications with graphical user interface.

Experience of the SDE usage

Positive experience

The four-year experience of SDE usage shows the importance of having a CM tool that is simple, flexible and efficient. RCS is both simple and flexible and it offers wide possibilities to develop methods that can support different development processes.

SDE functionality has grown as the development projects have grown so SDE has lived up to the new requirements. The SDE basic functions, related to project management and check-in/check-out procedures, are introduced in the organization smoothly without big problems. The new functions of SDE, dealing with formal methods for managing development processes, were added after the basic part was widely used. These more complex parts were fast accepted by some projects, while it took more time for other projects. Some projects have simply stayed with the basic functionality. The experience has shown that it is good to have the possibility of using different levels of complexity.

Change Management is a facility that helps both programmers and project managers to organize and follow their activities. CRs are used as a "to do" list and as formal descriptions of changes made in a product version.

Two kinds of SDE users exist today: Those, experienced Unix users, which mostly use SDE shell commands, and those, with a MS-Windows background or less experienced Unix users, which are using only GUI-applications. It seems that it is important to offer both types of user interfaces - at least on Unix platforms.

Negative experience

Problems which SDE users meet, are in the area of security and performance. When a number of programmers are involved in the same project, the Unix security, which is the base for the SDE security, is not sufficient. There is always a risk that a programmer removes, not only his/her working files, but also the versioned files.

The performance problem becomes serious when creating or merging very large software configurations where a large number of files are checked out and in.

SDE also uses RCS files for saving non-ascii files. The format of versioned files is not optimized for binary files - they occupy a large space, and the check-in/check-out procedures are slow.

Makefiles, automatically generated, look very complicated and manual modifications require a lot of efforts. Files created by make do not have a version identity, so a lot of unnecessary building is done.

SDE is missing support for propagating of a change done in one version of software to other versions.

Conclusion

Using a base tool like RCS is not sufficient for large software systems, but such a tool is very good for building more complex tools on top of it.

The experience has shown that it is very important to have an SCM tool that is a general enough and flexible enough for adjusting to development processes.

Configuration Management as 'Glueware' for Development of Client/Server-Applications in Heterogeneous and Distributed Environments

Peter Eilfeld

sd&m GmbH & Co.KG, software design & management,
Thomas-Dehler-Str. 27, D-81737 Munich, Germany.
E-mail: Peter.Eilfeld@sdm.de

Abstract. This position paper discusses the application of configuration management in distributed and heterogeneous development environments. Essential key is a central repository and the usage of triggers and check in/out mechanisms. These mechanisms establish the interaction of repository and processing sites and are governed by specific attributes of the items stored in the repository. An example is presented and experiences are discussed in terms of benefits and problems.

1 Introduction

The development of client/server (c/s) applications using dedicated tools is state of the art. The resulting applications typically are constructed from a SQL-database on a server with a frontend based on a windows system. The development of other types of c/s-applications is suffering from different shortcomings, however. Only few tools support development independent from platforms and vendors or offer high bandwidth in supporting different programming languages and architectures. Under these circumstances developers are forced to implement their own development environment. This task is complicated by some serious problems, especially c/s-software being located at multiple sites. If development is based upon a PC-/UNIX-architecture, at least two physically different computers with entirely different operating systems are involved, in general a lot of PCs and a few UNIX-servers, which is illustrated on top of Figure 1. The situation becomes even worse, if several teams are working together in a WAN.

The key questions dealing with such a development environment are [1] [2]:

- Where is a source located at the moment for development ?

- Who is working upon it ?

- What should be done with the source and which changes have already been incorporated ?

- Have changes been synchronized, since in general it is necessary to introduce changes both to client- and server-site ?

These questions can be derived from Figure 1 (top), in which any computer is able to act autonomously and independently. Without a coordinating tool it cannot be guaranteed that sources under development only reside on the server labelled with "development server". They may also be distributed on the "build"-server. Application of a configuration management (CM) is a means to avoid such problems. If CM is suitably designed, it can help to manage distributed environment and projects by acting as some kind of glueware by supervising and coordinating all actions at any site. In this position paper a simple model in handling these environments is presented and an example for MS-Windows and UNIX-systems is given.

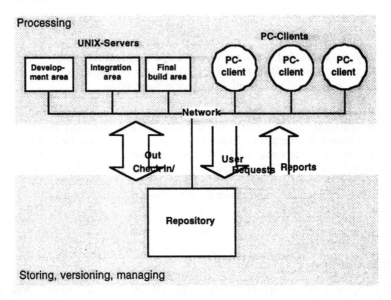

Figure 1: Topology of a typical client-/server-development environment

2 Theoretical Considerations

Repository

One essential point is the usage of a repository or some kind of archive at a central site [3] (bottom of Figure 1). The properties of an ideal repository are described in literature [4]. Basic functions of a repository similar to databases are security, integrity and concurrent access by multiple users. Other important features regarding development environments are [4]:

- handling of complex structures,
- handling of versions,
- views upon versions,
- nested transactions, and
- complex triggers.

These properties will be now dealt with in more detail.

Check In/ Out

In a repository items and versions are stored and managed. In general, editing, processing and testing takes place outside the repository. Thus, developers are requesting check outs from repository to a target location, where processing takes place. This is depicted in Figure 1. In this model check in/out are initiated from the user by accessing the repository from it's frontend (usually at client site). These target locations are different regarding their types, quality and function:

- working area(s) of the developer. From this location edited and tested sources(module test) are checked in back to the repository.

- integration area of the developer's team (integation test).

- building area of the project for building the final release (system test).

Further these areas differ with respect to

- computers, residing in a LAN or even WAN,

- operating systems,

- directories,

- settings of ownerships, access controls, etc.

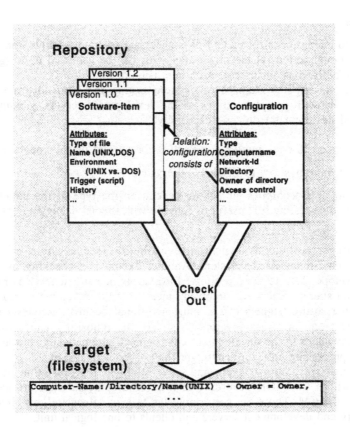

Figure 2   Partial meta-model for attributes in a repository and their conversion to filenames

In the presented model configurations (for definitions see [4], [5], [6]) are used to describe the contents of any target area, by assigning versions of items. For their usage in a c/s-environment, configurations have to contain additional informations regarding the properties of the area. A general 'meta-meta-model' of a repository is defined by [7]. Any objects, especially configurations, are qualified by specific attributes to be used in a c/s-environment, as depicted in the meta-model in Figure. 2. As these informations are stored within the repository, complete and up-to-date reports are possible.

Check in/ out operations as well as exports from repository, e.g. for final release build, are qualified by these attributes. During development, transfers of items are necessary from one area to another. A typical scenario is checking out sources in specific versions from repository into the working area by a developer. This is correlated with an assignment of these versions to the configuration describing the developer area which is of the respective type. Further, the properties, i.e. attributes of this configuration, describe precisely, where to place these sources and their processing after copying out of the repository. Finally, after finishing editing and testing, sources are checked in and a new version is created (and frozen). Thus, version control is involved in check in/ out, too. For team-integration or release build, items are exported to the respective areas, which is described in the same fashion as above.

Triggers

In order to increase control by CM, it is necessary to couple simple transfer of files with additional actions at the target area. This can be achieved by triggers, which are easily defined as attribute of each item (Figure 2).

Thus, via triggers changes of versions within the repository are correlated automatically with complex actions on the development servers, yielding a highly automated development process, especially:

- assignment to configurations, reflecting the current developmental state,

- copy from repository to UNIX/PC filesystem,

- starting (pre-)compiles etc.; these depend on the type of the target area, e.g. for module-testing it is useful to compile with special debugging options.

These triggers efficiently synchronize c/s-builds (see example below), which ensures consistency of the system. Another example is checking in a C-source from developer area to the repository: for reasons of consistency it is necessary to remove all source, object and archived object from the developer's area.

Further, using triggers offers some additional benefits. Requests need to be submitted from only one developer's site to the repository and actions can be started anywhere in the development environment automatically. It's also possible to delay processing until further triggers have been activated etc.

Summarizing, both triggers and a well-defined representation of repository objects within filesystem according to their developmental state are an important aspect of the CM. Those are performing the task of 'glueware', e.g. integration of repository and development servers and clients to one logical unit.

Complex transactions

Checking in a source results in creating a new version and start of triggers, etc . This is already a complex transaction itself. If some error occurs, the system has to be rolled-back automatically to it's initial state both within repository and filesystem. This has to be ensured even, if a lot of items are processed, e.g. for building a final release. Transaction control of the repository now has to be extended to include actions on operating system level und has a wider scope than "two-phase-commits" of SQL-databases. It requires well-defined exit codes of any command and responding to it in a correct and consistent way.

3 Practical Experiences

Due to lack of ideal repositories available, usually versioning and handling additional data of items are managed by different tools, which have to interact intimately. Some different approaches are possible:

1. Versioning is done based on UNIX-filesystem using appropiate tools (e.g. sccs, rcs, PVCS ® ...). A relational database is used for storing additional data. Database and version tool have to be synchronized by implementing control software. This control software also is starting triggers on the operational system level (sd&m, unpublished results).

2. Some CASE-Tools (e.g. MAESTRO-II [8], ShapeTools [9]) offer both versioning and storing attributes within their database (OMS-Database with PCMS-versioning as add-on [8]). Additionally, these CASE-Tools themselves offer abilities to start triggers.

An integrated development environment based upon 2. has been presented recently [10]. It is consisting of an ensemble of individual components providing the above mentioned different tasks:

• Repository:
  MAESTRO-II by Softlab, Inc. with it's "object management system" (OMS) as repository and PCMS for version- and CM; the object classes have been extended according to Figure 2.

• Check In/Out:
  Items are checked in/out to separate UNIX development servers and PC clients using TCP/IP-based communication services (ARPA services, NFS etc.).

• Triggers:
  Changes of versions are controlled by a state automaton, which is part of PCMS. Changes of states initiate configuration de-/assignments and remote build management operations using UNIX-make and similar tools via ARPA services.

Extensive use of triggers providing efficient support of client/server development is shown in an example. Processing a dialog script (dialog manager of ISA GmbH, Stuttgart) involves several steps (Figure 3):

- checking out a dialog file to a working area within the repository and editing,

- export from repository to PC client,

- simultaneous export to UNIX server,

- generation, compiling and archiving of stubcode at UNIX site (COBOL-copies, C-programs and -objects),

- generation of headerfiles.

The individual properties of each step are governed by the properties of the configuration, which is assigned to the working version. It should be noted, that creating a new version, editing and check out both are performed by accessing only the repository via the MAESTRO-II-workstation.

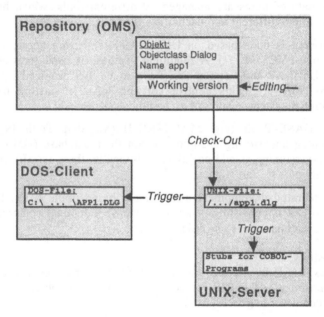

Figure 3   Example for check out and triggers

4 Conclusions

The problems and benefits of CM in a distributed environment will be summarized in the following paragraphs. It has to be stated that the problems arise from the distributed environment itself and are not a property of CM.

Problems

- *Synchronisation*
  Due to management of data and processes by different tools, serious problems concerning synchronizing these data arise. Significant implementation work is necessary to overcome.

- *Standards*
  Since the standardized DCE-package with transparent access to remote sites via RPC and DFS is not well established yet, one has to use some proprietary tools and a lot of customizing.

- *Networks*
  Further problems arise from networks itself and solutions have to be provided, concerning performance, security, reliability etc.

- *Client operating systems*
  Some problems result from operating systems at the client site. Since MS-Windows 3.11 isn't really a multitasking operating system, it is rather difficult to implement makes and triggers running on a PC but started on a UNIX server. This situation becomes better with Windows NT or OS/2. Performance of applications are worse than at UNIX-sites, e.g. operations dealing with the repository.

Benefits

The features of such an development environment are fulfilling the requirements stated in the beginning and can be summarized as follows:

- *Technical flexibility*
  Support of many different platforms (hardware, operating systems, programming languages, tools) is possible, since it is only necessary to get access to remote files and to launch remote procedures. At least for UNIX, ARPA-services are easily available.

- *Team support*
  CM handles large teams at even widely different locations.

- *Consistency*
  Triggers synchroneously yield interface descriptions for client- and server-software etc. Within a common repository relations between client- and server-software can easily be managed.

- *Uniformity*
  Only one common user frontend for client- as well as for server-files and operations is required. The user is not forced to switch to a UNIX-emulation for CM-operations, but is accessing only the repository.

Since the benefits are overriding the problems, one takes advantage of implementing the presented ideas [10]. Further, the technical problems will be solved in the near future due to rapid technical improvements.

References

[1] International Standards Organisation, "ISO Standard 9001. Quality Systems: Assurance of Design/Development, Production, Installation and Servicing Capability". 1987, Switzerland.

[2] Tichy, W.F., "Software-Konfigurationsmanagement: Wie,wann,was,warum?", in *Softwaretechnik '95.*, E.-E. Doberkat and U. Kelter, Editors. 1995, Braunschweig.

[3] Denert, E., "The project library - a tool for software development". *Proc. 4th JCSE München* , IEE Cat. CH 1479-5/79.

[4] Whitgift, D., "Methods and Tools for Software Configuration Management", 1991, John Wiley and Sons:Chichester, New York .

[5] Winkler, F.H., "International Workshop on Software Version and Configuration Control". 1988, Teubner, Stuttgart.

[6] Ben-Menachem, Mordechai, "Software Configuration Management Guidebook". 1994, McGrawHill, London.

[7] American National Standard Institute, "ANSI American National Standard X3.138-1988: Information Resource Dictionary System (IRDS)". 1989, New York.

[8] Softlab, Inc., "MAESTRO-II Administrator- and User-Documentation". 1995, Munich, Germany.

[9] Lampen, A., "Attributierte Softwareobjekte als Basis zur Datenmodellierung in Software-Entwicklungsumgebungen", Ph.D. Thesis. 1994, Technical University Berlin.
see also ShapeTools as free software

[10]   Kh.Zettl and P.Eilfeld, "Verteilte Entwicklungsumgebungen in der Münchener Rück", to be published, Computerwoche FOCUS April/1996.

Post-Deployment Configuration Management

Dennis Heimbigner and Alexander L. Wolf

University of Colorado, Boulder, CO 80309-0430, USA

Abstract. Configuration management must move beyond its traditional development-time concerns with source files. Future software systems will be delivered in binary form and will be composed from pre-existing systems. The term Post-Deployment Configuration Management is proposed to address the problems introduced in managing these new kinds of versioned configurations.

1 Introduction

Traditionally, configuration management (CM) research has supported the management of development-time configurations. As a rule, these are configurations of the source and binary files comprising a software system as it is developed. A tacit assumption here is that the development configuration covers the whole of the deliverable system.

Increasingly, however, delivered software systems only cover a small portion of the software that must be composed in order to construct the total system and make it ready for use. For example, a given piece of software is often only partially instantiated at delivery and must be completed by combining it with such things as shared libraries. Further, even a relatively self-contained piece of software must be parameterized to meet local conditions. In the Unix world, for example, it is common to have to establish pointers to appropriate local file paths by either recompiling pieces of the software or defining environment variables with those file paths.

We use the term **post-deployment configuration management** (PDCM) to refer to the process of taking a delivered, but incomplete system and installing, configuring, parameterizing and instantiating it for actual deployment in the field. We believe that PDCM is sufficiently important to bring it out of the shadow of the broader term "maintenance", where it is often hidden.

As distributed object technology takes hold, there will be an additional problem in establishing connections between various distributed objects Although, PDCM is an issue for almost any kind of deployed software system, we have been focusing on its role in distributed object systems, so we generalize it somewhat to include specifically the managing and installation of remote (networked) component-based, versioned software across heterogeneous environments.

2 Post-Deployment Tasks

The post-deployment configuration process is surprisingly complex. In outline, it covers the following high level tasks:

- *Installation* refers to the problem of installing the source and/or binaries of a software system into the local file system. This includes the problem of managing the dependencies between installed systems.
- *Parameterization* refers to the modification of a software system to take into account the local site context. This includes such things as the location of libraries, various file system paths, and hardware.
- *Instantiation* refers to the process of taking the system binaries instantiating them as, for example, Unix processes, interconnecting them appropriately, and starting the system into execution.
- *Re-configuration* refers to the problem of statically and dynamically reconfiguring the system to evolve it over time. This process may involve reinstallation, re-parameterization, and re-instantiation.

We are addressing specific problems within each of these areas.

3   Installation

Installing a software system can be a difficult task. Not even the physical placement of the files into the proper locations in the file system is always simple because various sites will have quite different local standards about where software should be placed. To further complicate things, if the site is heterogeneous with respect to operating systems and hardware, then there is often a conflict between the assumptions built into the software and the assumptions at the local site. Examples include handling of shared files (i.e., those common across all hardware platforms) and the proper locations for libraries versus executable binaries.

Most major software systems are dependent on many other related software resources. This seems especially true for software available over the internet. These dependencies can take several forms. Consider, for example, building the system from the source. This can require a variety of tools, and often specific versions of tools (gcc version 2.6.2 versus gcc version 2.7.1, for example). Or, consider run-time dependencies where a software system depends on the availability of other software resources in order to execute. Examples might include dynamic libraries, various operating system files, and compute servers.

Thus to build any one system, it may be necessary to build a number of supporting systems, which in turn need other systems. In other words, the support structure *cascades*. Managing, or even determining the resulting dependent software can become a major overhead on the original installation task . We also note that the problem is complicated if (1) the local site already has some of the dependent software installed, and (2) if ranges of versions of dependent software can be used (i.e., version 3.1 through version 3.3 of Q [3]).

We are addressing this problem by constructing a release manager on top of NUCM [6]. This release manager can maintain dependency information and help bring in proper versions of all required software.

4 Parameterization

Software is usually parameterized to take local context into account. Parameterization can encompass almost any site-dependent modification. We try to separate parameterization from the version dependency problem and from the specification of structural elements, which we intend to be part of instantiation. But of course we recognize the fuzziness of these separations.

The current state of the art in parameterization (at least for Unix) is such things as environment variables, *X* resource files, and *Autoconf* [2].

Environment variables essentially define a simple database of (name,value) pairs where both the name and value are strings. Programs can query this database to pick out local values for such things as file paths, hardware (i.e, display names) and such. Attempting to encode any form of complex information into an environment variable is a frustrating experience.

X resource files improve on environment variables in a couple of ways. *X* resources provide a tree structure for parametric information and provide a primitive abstraction mechanism (called, unfortunately, "classes"). The *X* server serves as the database for storing resource information. Basically, the *X* server stores a forest of trees where the leaves are values and can be tagged with a limited set of types. The interior nodes of the trees have no necessary semantics, but by convention at least the top node represents the name or "class" of a particular program. Again, programs can query the database, but the queries are somewhat complex in allowing, in effect, use of the regular expression "*" operator to specify values independent of their depth in a given tree.

The *X* mechanism is a clear improvement over environment variables, but we believe that it has some deficiencies.

- The abstraction mechanism seems to be woefully underpowered, and in practice, it seems like each class ends up having only one member.
- It would be desirable to compute resource values on the fly. For example, there might be a unique identifier resource that changes every time it is read.

Autoconf is a program used by most Gnu software systems, and occasionally by other systems, to parameterize software sources before compilation. One typically brings in a tar file and expands it. Then one goes into the subtree and executes a *config* script that interrogates the local system for information and produces a *Makefile* [1] for building the software system and taking the local context into account. The *config* scripts do all sorts of amazing things to find out local information: they may run the local C compiler with various test programs, for example. *Autoconf* is actually the program that is used by the software developer to construct the *config* script. *Autoconf* uses a specification of parameters taken from the fixed set known to *Autoconf*. For each specification element, it inserts a corresponding test into the *config* file to be executed at installation time.

We believe that the important idea hiding in *Autoconf* and *X* resources is that of database about the local system. We view, for instance, the Microsoft Win95

Registry system as a rudimentary form of the desired capability. In effect, every machine should be running a server that can be interrogated to extract the kinds of information now known to X servers and to config scripts. Additionally, this server should be dynamically programmable to handle such cases as the unique id example.

5 Instantiation

Instantiation is the process of taking the system binaries instantiating them as, for example, Unix processes, interconnecting them appropriately, and starting the system into execution. We also include the shut-down problem as part of this as well.

Instantiation is where our assumption that we are dealing with collections of distributed objects really has consequences. In the case of a simple, single binary executable, the instantiation process is not particularly difficult. But when one needs to instantiate a number of servers, in the correct sequence, and correctly interconnect them, and connect them to previously instantiated servers, the problem becomes much more difficult.

This problem has been addressed in the case of what we would call "distributed computations." Polylith [5] is perhaps the canonical example here. By the term "distributed computation" we mean that there is a program that happens to be decomposed into distributed subpieces and whose purpose is to start up, complete some computation, and shut down. We distinguish the distributed computation case from our case in which we are setting up services that are accessed by other anonymous programs that might not even be running at the time the services are instantiated. Again, we recognize the overlap and that many of the solutions used in the distributed computation case can apply in our target situation.

Instantiation is most clearly a configuration problem in which one specifies the components to be instantiated and the ways they are interconnected. But there are complexities to be dealt with. The number of servers may need to be computed at start-up time based on various local resources such as performance or available instances of certain kinds of hardware. Additionally, the interconnections may need to be dynamically computed, and moreover, some connections may need to reach to presumed pre-existing services that need to be named in some way. An example might be the assumption of the existence of a database server in the environment to be used by the services being instantiated.

One surprising way that this kind of information has been handled is using X resource files again. Instead of using the resource trees to specify parameters, they have been used to specify structural information. Thus, a program might start up, read the resource file and use information there to instantiate and connect subcomponents. While X resources are not particularly good for this kind of specification, the capability does indicate a close relationship between parameterization and instantiation.

Most existing configuration specifications are static in the sense that they are embodied in text files that are processed at instantiation time. As with parameters, we believe that this information need to be kept as a service where it can be queried and modified dynamically. The OMG CORBA [4] model includes a simple instance of such a server. But again, we believe that this server must allow for programmable specifications which, so far as we are aware, is a capability not currently provided anywhere.

6 Re-Configuration

One a system is instantiated and executed, it will evolve over time. This evolution will be both dynamic and "static" (not perhaps the best term). In the dynamic case, one may need to may limited changes in the instantiated configuration while the software system is executing. These kinds of changes might include upgrading some particular server or changing the number of instances of some server or modifying the interconnections. The static case involves taking down the system and looping back to some previous step to change the installation, parameterization, or instantiation of the system. We are just beginning to address the re-configuration area and hope to build on the technology we develop for installation, parameterization, and instantiation, as well as enhancing our own distributed object technology (Q [3]) to support dynamic reconfiguration.

Acknowledgements. This material is based upon work sponsored by the Air Force Materiel Command, Rome Laboratory, and the Advanced Research Projects Agency under Contract Number F30602-94-C-0253. The content of the information does not necessarily reflect the position or the policy of the Government and no official endorsement should be inferred.

References

1. Stuart I. Feldman. Make – a program for maintaining computer programs. *Software – Practice and Experience*, 9:255 – 265, 1979.
2. D. Mackenzie, R. McGrath, and N. Friedman. *Autoconf: Generating Automatic Configuration Scripts*. Free Software Foundation, Inc, April 1994.
3. Mark Maybee, Dennis Heimbigner, and Leon J. Osterweil. Multilanguage Interoperability in Distributed Systems. In *Proceedings of the 18th International Conference on Software Engineering*. IEEE Computer Society, March 1996.
4. Object Management Group. *The Common Object Request Broker: Architecture and Specification*, 26 August 1991.
5. J.M. Purtilo. The polylith software bus. Technical Report CS–TR–2469, Department of Computer Science, University of Maryland, College Park, MD 20742, 1990.
6. André van der Hoek, Dennis Heimbigner, and Alexander L. Wolf. A Generic, Peer-to-Peer Repository for Distributed Configuration Management. In *Proceedings of the 18th International Conference on Software Engineering*. IEEE Computer Society, March 1996.

Change Sets Revisited and Configuration Management of Complex Documents

Stephen A. MacKay

Institute for Information Technology—Software Engineering, National Research Council
of Canada, Ottawa, Ontario, Canada K1A 0R6
MacKay@iit.nrc.ca   http://wwwsel.iit.nrc.ca/

1   Introduction

The SCM-5 workshop in Seattle provided a forum for software configuration management (SCM) researchers, tool developers and users to come together and discuss relevant problems in the field. The workshop concluded with a number of unsolved problem areas. This position statement summarizes those areas and—drawing from our research experiences—discusses a few of the challenges in greater detail.

2   What are the Problems?

SCM models Feiler's models of configuration management (check-out/check-in, composition, long transaction and change set) [Feil91] no longer adequately represent the current generation of commercial configuration management tools or the emerging tools and research systems. Are there better or expanded models to represent workspace concepts? Do we need new models for concurrent development in a widely distributed environment, or can we adapt the existing ones? Are there graphic representations and visualization methods better than the overworked version graphs? Is modelling just an irrelevant academic exercise?

SCM architecture Software projects involving multiple companies benefit from common configuration management tools. However, each group is reluctant to change its own culture. Similarly, customers obtaining updates and patches from development tool vendors are not likely to use the same CM tools as the vendors. There is a clear need to separate the architecture of CM tools from the implementations. Can we define a common architecture for commercial CM tools that would allow software teams to interact even if they are using CM tools from different vendors? Are there existing relevant standards?

SCM and process The popularity of ISO 9000 and CMM certification has made companies more aware of software development processes. What is the relationship between SCM and the overall software process? Is CM merely one part of the software process or is CM itself the process? How do the various standards on software processes view CM?

Distributed, concurrent development Commercial CM tool vendors are beginning to provide support for widely distributed, concurrent software development, but there is little agreement on the mechanisms. Are there models or appropriate graphic representations of distributed, concurrent development that would aid in user understanding and acceptance of this powerful paradigm? What are the significant problem areas (scale, merging, group dynamics, etc.)?

CM of complex documents

Most current CM systems store non-textual configuration items in the repository as frozen "binary" entities (possibly compressed). This is unsatisfactory in 1995. How can we do proper CM of word processor produced documentation; multimedia documents; databases; project files for advanced graphical user interface generators; and "source code" for non-textual languages? How can we determine what has changed in a non-textual configuration item? Can we represent or determine the differences between products composed of more complex components?

The remainder of this position statement begins by looking at CM models for widely distributed, concurrent, software development projects. It then continues the discussion of change sets begun in Seattle. It concludes with a brief discussion of some of our preliminary thoughts on configuration management of non-textual components.

3 Models for Concurrent, Distributed Development

Today's new culture of software development relies on teams of developers equipped with desktop workstations or personal computers. The teams are frequently distributed worldwide and may not be reliably networked. This environment brings special problems, particularly in areas such as: distribution across time zones; access to the repository by intermittently connected developers; and sharing the repository across company boundaries.

Version-oriented CM
Version-oriented configuration management focuses on defining and managing product versions through the handling of revisions and variants at the individual component level. The component and product versions are the first-class entities, managed by the developer. One of the common features among version-oriented models is the use of the directed acyclic version graph. Each node in the graph represents a version of the component or product and each edge between nodes represents the transition between versions (an *is-version-of* relationship or the "delta" between the versions) [vand95].

At the component level, version graphs quickly prove inadequate. While they can easily represent the migration path for a short time, they do not scale for longer projects nor do they handle components that are undergoing significant concurrent modification [MacK95]. Trying to study relationships between components using their individual or combined version graphs is difficult. The pictures provide a clear history of each individual component, but are of little help in determining which version of one is related to which version of the other.

Product-level version graphs usually result in a simpler picture, but they do not convey enough information. For example, when analyzing product migration, it is difficult to determine what constitutes a change between versions or how two arbitrary versions are related because the deltas (edges) are not first-class entities. For highly portable products with many active versions, it is difficult to express the application of a single change to a variety of versions.

For concurrent development, version graphs introduce artificial branches that have little to do with the structure of the product, making the model more difficult to understand and maintain. Commercial CM systems implementing version-oriented models, usually discourage branching for full concurrency, even though it is the only mechanism they provide for development to proceed simultaneously on a single configuration item [MacK95].

Change-oriented CM

Change-oriented configuration management focuses on managing logical changes to a baselined product. Here, the description of the change—known as a change set—is a first-class entity, managed by the developer. The versions are derived by applying relevant change sets to the baseline. Developers therefore work with product-level deltas, collecting all those individual components that are relevant to the particular change, excluding other groupings that made sense in other situations (like initial product design). This structure reduces considerably the difficulty of managing the revision and release process [Wein95].

Feiler notes that concurrency control is outside the change set model, but he goes on to state:

> Change sets can also be used to support distributed concurrent change without centralized coordination. Each site generates change sets independently. Once the changes sets are exchanged between sites, each site can, at its leisure, combine change sets. The result is that the system evolves at both sites. If assignment of changes to sites is planned carefully, conflicts in change sets can be kept to a minimum. [Feil91, pg. 43]

Managed carefully and supported with appropriate CM tools, change sets provide exactly the concurrency management required in the widely distributed development environment. Importantly, the mechanism scales down to smaller teams as well.

The *workspace* mechanism [Dart90, Dart92]—where developers can get and modify components from the repository independently of other developers—is a natural way of implementing change sets. Augmented with Dart's *transparent view* and *transaction* mechanisms, the change set model becomes a powerful and complete method for describing configuration management in widely distributed environments.

Change sets have often been viewed unfavourably, characterized as a *Chinese menu* approach in which individual revisions are tracked and then collected into logical groups to define a version. Often a check-out/check-in methodology is used to manage the revisions. This approach represents a limited view of change sets, trying to superimpose a version graph on the change set model. The research community needs to find representations and visualizations that free us from version graphs.

Two visualization techniques, described at SCM-5, provide a starting point. The *Database and Selectors Cel (DaSC)* approach, developed in our laboratories at the National Research Council of Canada, characterizes change sets as groups of layers stacked on top of a known baseline [Gent89, MacK95]. Tandem Computers' *Fully Populated Paths* mechanism uses *Railroad Diagrams* (resembling DaSC laid on its side) to show the relationships among change sets [Schw95]. Railroad diagrams look familiar to people comfortable with version graphs, but they convey significantly more information. One of the useful outputs from SCM-6 would be progress towards a uniform graphical notation for change-oriented configuration management.

4   CM of Complex Documents

The future of software development will not remain focused on managing changes to files containing only ASCII text. Already developers—even in traditional environments—are faced with revisions of: documentation produced by word processors or page layout programs; test case data stored in databases; soft-copies of design drawings; and binary resource descriptions. We are now beginning to add to the mix: multimedia and hypertext documentation (e.g., HTML, Hypercard, etc., with embedded sound and video); data maintained in personal or shared productivity tools (e.g., Lotus Notes); project files for advanced graphical user interface generators (e.g., XVT) and compilation environments; and even full visual programming languages (e.g., Prograph CPX). Full configuration management of these components is difficult, so little commercial CM tool support is available. Most tools only permit storage of a complete, compressed copy of the component in the repository. A few, like Voodoo, store a compact delta of the binary files.

We believe change-oriented methodologies, particularly DaSC, will support a number of these new application areas. We have recently begun exploring some of them, but it is too early to publish results. Two clear issues have emerged. Managing revisions while editing documents stored in proprietary formats is extremely difficult. The vendors of the tools that create these documents must provide: a powerful document editor with appropriate calls to manage a change set methodology; a document editor with sufficient hooks to allow the addition of extra functionality; or enough information about the document formats to allow companion tools to be written. If they fail to meet this challenge, customers will migrate to competing vendors. There is a great challenge for the CM research community to investigate ways to bring the variety of documents under common configuration management. Another challenge is in representing the differences between products composed of more complex components. Whether we are looking for tools to automatically generate differences between two known versions, or for representations of the differences that the software developer can visualize and manipulate, the problem is equally challenging. There are many opportunities for discussion and further research on this topic alone.

Acknowledgments

I would like to thank my colleagues, past and present, in the Software Engineering Group for their many contributions to our DaSC project and for reviewing this position statement. I would like to thank especially Charles Gauthier, Morven Gentleman, Anatol Kark, Darlene Stewart and Marceli Wein for their efforts and support.

References

[Dart90]   Susan Dart. Spectrum of functionality in configuration management systems. *Carnegie Mellon* University, *Software Engineering Institute Technical Report: CMU/SEI-90-TR-11*, De.r 1990. 38 pages.

[Dart92]   Susan Dart. The past, present, and future of configuration management. *Carnegie Mellon University, Software Engineering Institute Technical Report: CMU/SEI-92-TR-8*, Jul. 1992. 28 pages.

[Feil91]   Peter Feiler. Configuration management models in commercial environments. *Carnegie Mellon University, Software Engineering Institute Technical Report: CMU/SEI-91-TR-7*, Mar. 1991. 54 pages.

[Gent89]   W.M. Gentleman, S.A. MacKay, D.A. Stewart, and M. Wein. Commercial realtime software needs different configuration management. *Proceedings of 2nd International Workshop on Software Configuration Management (SCM)*, Princeton, NJ. Oct. 24-27, 1989. Published as *Software Eng. Notes*, 17(7): 152-161; 1989. NRC 30695.

[MacK95]   Stephen A. MacKay. The State of the Art in Concurrent, Distributed Configuration Management. *Proceedings of 5th International Workshop on Software Configuration Management (SCM-5)*, Seattle, WA. Apr. 24–25, 1995.

[Schw95]   Bill Schweitzer. Fully Populated Paths: A Conservative, Simple Model for Parallel Development. *Proceedings of 5th International Workshop on Software Configuration Management (SCM-5)*, Seattle, WA. Apr. 24–25, 1995.

[vand95]   André van der Hoek, Dennis Heimbigner, and Alexander Wolf. Does Configuration Management Research Have a Future? *Proceedings of 5th International Workshop on Software Configuration Management (SCM-5)*, Seattle, WA. Apr. 24-25, 1995.

[Wein95]   M. Wein, S. A. MacKay, D. A. Stewart, C.-A. Gauthier and W. M. Gentleman. Evolution Is Essential for Software Tool Development. *Proceedings of the 1995 International Workshop on Computer-Aided Software Engineering (CASE-95)*, Toronto, Ontario, Jul. 9-14, 1995.

Modeling the Sharing of Versions

Alan Dix[†], Tom Rodden[‡] and Ian Sommerville[‡]

[†]The HCI Research Centre, School of Computing and Mathematics, Huddersfield University,
Huddersfield, HD1 3DH, UK
[‡]Collaborative Systems Engineering Group, Computing, Department, Lancaster University,
Lancaster, LA1 4YR, UK
email: alan@zeus.hud.ac.uk, {tam,is}@comp.lancs.ac.uk

1 Introduction

As prototype cooperative systems mature into products they face a growing set of commercially based demands. However, the current view of use exhibit by prototype CSCW systems has limited the growth of groupware products. In essence, existing cooperative applications assume that they are to be used in research labs and seldom consider other settings. Limited effort has been applied in establishing an understanding of the relationship between flexible and open cooperative systems and the managed commercial domains within which they are to be placed. One place where this mismatch is most evident is in the lack of support for the evolution, management and co-ordination of the products of collaborative endeavours. Surprisingly little effort has been expended in developing a generic model of version management for cooperative applications. However, significant personnel are invested in the establishment and co-ordination of procedure to manage just this activity within most commercial projects. In this paper we wish to consider a generic version model suitable for application within cooperative settings.

To achieve our object of a generic model we will build a model, of how users might share a version set. The intent here is to promote the representation of users and how they might share a version set. Thus our approach is distinct from existing models of versions in that we wish to represent the sharing of information and the relationship between users sharing this information. The work presented in this paper introduces a model of how versions can be shared and this sharing made explicit to users.

2 Background

The core of our consideration of versions is the problem of version management and its role in configuration management. Most existing work on configuration management focuses on the control of large software projects. To support the configuration management process, many different software tools have been produced. Tools such as SCCS (1), and RCS (2) support version management by optimising the storage requirements of multiple versions and providing check-in and check-out facilities which ensure that only a single copy of a controlled item may be modified by one person at one time.

Both SCCS and RCS are limited by a very simple model of version identification. When a version is to be retrieved, this record must be consulted to find the version name. This is an error-prone process once there are more than a few versions. To counter this problem, version management systems have been developed which support attribute-based version identification and which link versions with the software process activities responsible for their creation (3,4,5). Rather than forcing the retrieval of a specific version using some arbitrary name, these systems allow the characteristics of the version to be used to identify it.

The focus on all of this work on version management has been prescriptive with an onus on controlling and centralising the version management process. There has been remarkably little research into the problems of versioning in shared settings where the demands of more than one user need to be addressed. Work that has occurred to date focuses on the merging of versions produced by different members of a group (6) which has been concerned with merging independently made changes to software components. The version models adopted by most existing version management systems has also sought to preserve the illusion of a single-user virtual machine. This illusion is, however, problematic to most approaches supporting collaborative work.

It may at first sight seem attractive to maintain an individualistic model from a control point of view, it means that many parallel group activities need to be serialised when mediated by such systems. This often forces users to work outwith the system causing the underlying version model to be compromised. Where versions have been important in CSCW systems application developers have been forced to develop their own model of versions. For example, a version model has been developed as part of a hypertext co-authoring system(7). The developed model is closely bound with the supporting application and focuses on supporting cooperative document production, rather than a generic approach to version management

Likewise, a number of researchers have developed pragmatic solutions to the shortcomings of existing version management models. For example, Garg and Scattchi (8) have successfully integrated a hypertext system with RCS to control software documents. Similarly, Pendergast and Beranek (9) have addressed the problem in collaborative workstation design and Beaudouin-Lafon (10) has included a simple version model in a shared editing system.

In this paper we wish to move beyond these specific approaches to consider a general model of versions that takes into account the fact versions will be used by a number of users. The model focuses on representing the relationship between users and the dependency graph representing the version. The starting point for our consideration is a representation of how a collection of objects may be shared .

3   Sharing a pool of information?

In this section we wish to consider a general model suitable for representing the cooperative sharing of information. The starting point for a general model is the representation of a collection of objects shared by a number of users. This shared information space is represented by the simple pair

SS(U, O)

The shared space SS(U,O) associates a set of objects O (determining the space) with a set of users U. The set of users U is a heterogeneous collection of objects that may represent users, groups of users or any object capable of exerting an active presence. This association between users and objects in the space takes the form of a number of mappings that are central to reasoning about the relationships between users sharing the set of objects.

3.1   Presence Positions

The presence of user is represented in the general model by the object of particular interest and a surrounding set of adjacent objects. This *presence position* is represented by the simple pair

P(pos, Adj)
where pos ∈ O and Adj ∈ $\wp$ O
note: $\wp$ – powerset.

The mapping of users to an object in the space allows us to model the effect of users in the shared information space. Presence positions have a *position object* and an *adjacency set*. Position objects represent one of the heterogeneous forms of object within the space. Adjacency sets are a collection of the other objects in the space. This representation of the presence of users in the space forms the basis for representing both the effect of users. In the most general case we do not consider restrictions on membership of the adjacency set associated with a particular position point.

We shall call the set of all presence positions for a shared space the presence set, PP(O) or *presence space*. Where

$$PP(O) = \{P(o,A)| o \in O, A \in \wp O\}$$

We refer to the particular parts of the pair using a simple bracket notation. Where P is a presence position

pos(P) is the position object
Adj(P) is the adjacency set

3.2   The edit set

A function edit_set exists which maps the set of users to the shared space. This function effectively places a user in the space by returning a presence postition. The function is intended to be used to map a user to many potential presence positions in the space. This reflects the most general case of a user having a number of positions in the space. The general function is of the form

edit_set: U X Id → PP(O)

The linking of users to the space using a this function exploits a label that identifies the different edit sets associated with a user. This is a set of arbitrary labels that can be associated with different instances of the edit set function.

3.3   The focus_set

A function focus_set exists which maps users to a position point in the space. The focus function also uses an arbitrary label to allow a user to have a number of associated foci and is of the form

focus: U X Id → PP(O)

3.4   Location, Aggregate Focus and Edit Set

The focus and edit_set functions map a user to a number of points across the space. It is often important to reason about the collective or aggregate edit_set and focus of users formed by this set of position points. Three functions can be used to reason about a users location, aggregate edit set and aggregate focus.

location: U $\rightarrow$ $\wp$O
location(u) ={ g| g ∈ O and (pos(edit_set(u,id)) = g or pos(focus(u,id)) = g)
}

Agg_edit: U $\rightarrow$ $\wp$ O
agg_edit_set(u) ={g| g ∈ O and (g∈ adj(edit_set(u,id)) }

Agg_focus: U →℘ O
agg_edit_set(u) ={g| g ∈ O and (g∈ adj(focus(u,id)) }

The *location* function returns the set of objects a users exerts an influence on in terms of focus and editing while *agg_edit* and *agg_focus* return the set of all objects within the users collective focus and edit sets.

4 Sharing the effects of others

The principal aim of the model is to allow us to reason about and represent the awareness users have of each other. In doing so we wish to represent some notion of awareness which indicates whether users are strongly or weakly aware of each other. The general model allows this by providing a basic form of awareness and using a function to represent this awareness.

The awareness function is defined to map to a set of values defined from an awareness mode set. Consider the set of modes defined in terms of the placement of users in each others focus and edit_set and the overlap of these sets. We can define 10 arrangements of users in others focus and edit set and 8 overlapping modes.

A = { mode1, mode2, mode3, mode4, mode5, mode6, mode7, mode8, mode9,
mode 10, overlap1, overlap2 overlap3, overlap4, overlap5, overlap6, overlap7, overlap8}

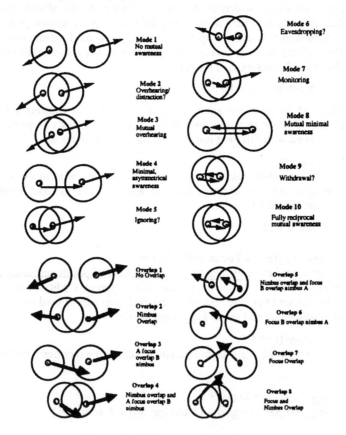

Figure 1 : Different modes of awareness

Each of the elements of the set of awareness A represent the different modes of awareness which represent the overlap of the sets associated with two bodies. These arrangements are briefly reviewed in figure 1. In each figure the edit set is indicated using a circle while the focus is shown as a directed arrow. Each of the modes shows a potential interpretation of each of the arrangements. This work is directly motivated by the spatial model of intertaction suggested by Benford et et, (11).

These general cases of the model maps the presence of users in the space to 18 different modes of awareness. This is achieved using a modal awareness function. A particular awareness function is defined which maps from two users of the shared graph to the awareness set A. This is expressed

awareness_mode: UxU → A

The function uses membership of the aggregate edit set and focus sets to determine the particular mode of awareness. For example, mode 1 in figure 1 corresponds to:

location(u1) $\not\subset$ agg_edit_set (u2) and location (u1) $\not\subset$ agg_focus (u2) and
location(u2) $\not\subset$ agg_edit_set (u1) and location (u2) $\not\subset$ agg_focus (u1)

The consideration presented here has presented abstract definitions for focus, edit_set and awareness. In the following section we wish to examine the effect of the structure of the information forming the space being shared.

5 Sharing Graph Structures

This section introduces a mathematical consideration of graph structures. We then consider how we can model the sharing of these general graph structures using concepts drawn from our model. Finally, we consider an interpretation of this graph based model in terms of versions.

5.1 Graphs and Directed Graphs

In this section we wish to consider the general application of the model across a number of domains. Rather than consider different specific mappings to particular non spatial applications, we wish to develop a view of the spatial model that is generally interpretable across a number of applications. The starting point for this exercise is a consideration of general graph structures and how the model can be mapped to these graphs.

A graph is a discrete structure consisting of sets of vertices (nodes) which may be joined by edges (arcs). A simple graph involving 5 vertices and 5 edges could be of the form shown in Figure 2

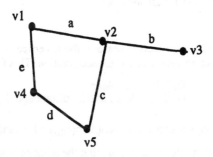

Figure 2: a simple graph

V(G)   is a set of objects called vertices.

E(G) is a multiset of edges. Each element of E can be mapped to a multiset of two vertices from V.

A graph can exploit an incident function *i* which maps edges in E to vertex pairs drawn from V. The incidence function is of the form

$$i: E \rightarrow \{\{u,v\}| \ u,v \in V\}$$

A graph combines each of these elements in a tuple as G(V,E,i). The graph drawn in Figure 3 would be of the form

$$V(G) = \{v1,v2,v3,v4,v5\},$$

$$E(G) = \{a,b,c,d,e\},$$
$$i(a) \ |\rightarrow \{v1,v2\}, \ i(b) \ |\rightarrow \{v2,v3\}, \ i(c) \ |\rightarrow \{v2,v5\},$$
$$i(d) \ |\rightarrow \{v5,v4\}, \ i(e) \ |\rightarrow \{v1,v4\}$$

5.2 Adjacency in Network Structures

The general model for the shared network does not consider the means by which adjacency sets are constructed. This generality allows sets to be constructed for arbitrary collections of the vertices in the network. This freedom allows us to consider non continuous selections and nodes selected from contextual sensitive criteria such as database queries. However, we also wish to consider particular properties to adjacency sets. To allow us to do this for each user we use a range of property functions which test the spatial properties of adjacency sets.

Linked Function

We can define a direct linked function which tests if the nodes in a presence positions adjacent set are directly adjacent to a location. This function can be used to specify the properties of particular focus and edit set. The function is of the form

$$linked: PP(G) \ |\rightarrow Boolean$$
$$linked(pp) = \forall_V \in adj(pp) \text{ and } joined(loc(pp), v)$$

$$\text{Where } joined(v,g) = \exists x \ (x \in E(G) \text{ and } (i(x)|\rightarrow\{v,g\} \text{ or } i(x)|\rightarrow\{g,v\})$$

The linked function allows us to specify that a particular user's focus or edit set is formed from directly linked nodes. For example if we wished to state that all of the foci associated with a user Steve are formed from directly connected vertices we would state

$$\forall_l \in Id \ linked(focus(Steve, l))$$

Sphere Function

This extension of the linked function reasons about vertices that lie within a specified distance from the location vertex of a presence position. This function is of the form

$$sphere: PP(G) \ X \ N \ |\rightarrow Boolean$$
$$sphere(pp, l) = \forall_V \in adj(pp) \text{ and } in\_distance(loc(pp), v, l)$$

$$\text{Where } in\_distance(v,g) = len(path(v,g)) < l \text{ or } len(path(g,v)) <= l$$

The sphere function allows us to state that the adjacency set for a focus or edit_set is formed from the vertices within a given range of the location point. For example if we wished to state that the edit_set associated with a user John is formed from vertices within a range of 4 we would

$$\forall_{l\in} \text{ Id sphere(edit\_set(john,l), 4)}$$

The sphere and linked function can be used to specify adjacency properties for particular foci and edit sets identified by the user, label pair. Altering focus and edit_sets is associated with changing the specified properties of the adjacency sets associated with the focus and edit_sets .

Shared Directed Graphs

Our final consideration is to examine the situation when the edges in the shared graph are directed. In this case the general model can be restricted to exploit the directed nature of the graph. We do this by reconsidering the nature of focus and edit set.

We consider the adjacency sets associated with edit set points to consist of vertices connected to the position point by outgoing vertices. This reflects the nature of edit set as delimiting the range of effects across the space.

Focus on the directed graph is constructed from sets of vertices connected to the location point by incoming vertices. This reflects that focus represents the portion of a space whose effects you are interested in.

These derivative forms of focus and edit set are constructed using alternative forms of the functions for defining the adjacency set. These become

inlinked: $PP(G) \mapsto$ Boolean
inlinked(pp) = $\forall_{v\in}$ adj(pp) and inward(loc(pp), v)

Where inward(v,g) = $\exists x$ (x $\in$ E(G) and i(x)|$\rightarrow$\{g,v\})

outlinked: $PP(G) \mapsto$ Boolean
outlinked(pp) = $\forall_{v\in}$ adj(pp) and outward(loc(pp), v)

Where outward(v,g) = $\exists x$ (x $\in$ E(G) and (i(x)|$\rightarrow$\{v,g\})

Similarly, equivalent forms of the sphere function exist for delimiting the adjacent sets for focus and edit set for vertices that are not directly connected

insphere: $PP(G) \times N \mapsto$ Boolean
insphere(pp, l) = $\forall_{v\in}$ adj(pp) and
input_distance(loc(pp), v, l)

Where input_distance(v,g) = len(path(g,v)) <= l

outsphere: $PP(G) \times N \mapsto$ Boolean
outsphere(pp, l) = $\forall_{v\in}$ adj(pp) and output_distance(loc(pp), v, l)

Where output_distance(v,g) = len(path(v,g)) <= l

6   Sharing a Version Set

The general models used to represent awareness across a shared network can be interpreted in a range of different ways to reflect a number of different potential mappings from the shared graph to users. This sections briefly outline a possible interpretations of the network based for version sets. The aim is to model awareness across a set of versions of information. In this case we rely on the mappings:

- Versions of information entities map to nodes on the network.
- Version dependencies and derivations map onto links.

- The use of particular versions of information map them to locations on the network.

- User of a particular version have a focus and a nimbus at the location on the network associated with that version of the information.

In this interpretation of the model we assume a mapping of focus to incoming nodes and edit_set to outgoing nodes. Consider a user Steve using a version of a software module *dvs_driverV1.4*. This version is derived from merging a previous version *dvs_driverV1.3* with a second module *dive_driverV2.1*. This version has subsequent version *dvs_driverV1.5* and *dive_driverV4.0* In this case Steve's focus and edit set would be

$$\text{focus(steve, prog4)} \mapsto \{\text{dvs\_driverV1.4.}, \{\text{dvs\_driverV1.3, dive\_driverV2.1}\}\}$$

$$\text{edit\_set(steve, prog4)} \mapsto \{\text{dvs\_driverV1.4.}, \{\text{dvs\_driverV1.5, dive\_driverV4.0}\}\}$$

In this case we have decided to exploit the previously arbitrary labels associated with nimbus and focus to assigning them to local mappings to private versions.

7 Conclusions

In this paper we have considered the development of a general model of information sharing in cooperative settings. The development of the model presented here has focused on exploiting the shared nature of a pool of objects. The set of shared objects and the relations between them form a common "space" onto which users project their action. These actions are made publicly available through the objects forming the space. Thus rather than simply represent the objects in the information space we can reason about the awareness users have of others sharing a version set.

In this paper we have also not considered the means by which the model is presented to users. The development of appropriate presentation mechanisms will directly effect how the model is used in practice. For example, how aware are other users of the each other across an application and how are effects propagated across a community of users. Developing the answer to these questions requires us to construct a series of applications that realise the model presented here and to examine the utility and usage of the model in practice. The construction of these applications represents the next stage in the development of the model presented here.

References

1. Rochkind, M.J. (1975), 'The Source Code Control System', *IEEE Trans. on Software Engineering*, SE-1 (4), 255-65.

2. Tichy, W. (1982), 'Design, Implementation and Evaluation of a Revision Control System', *Proc. 6th Int. Conf. on Software Engineering*, Tokyo.

3. Lacroix, M., Roelants, D. and Waroquier, J.E., (1991), 'Flexible Support for Cooperation in Software Development', *Proc. 3rd Int. Workshop on Software Configuration Management*, Trondheim, June 1991.

4. Lie, A., Conradi, R., Didriksen, T.M. and Karlsson, E-A., (1989), 'Change-oriented Versioning in a Software Engineering Database', *Proc. 2nd Int. Workshop on Software Configuration Management*, Princeton, N.J., October 1989.

5.   Bernard, Y. and Lavency, P., (1989), 'A Process Oriented Approach to Configuration Management', *Proc. 11th Int. Conf on Software Engineering*, 320-30.

6.   Reps, T., Horowitz, S., and Prints, J., (1988), 'Support for integrating program variants in an environment for programming in the large', *Proc. 1st Int. Workshop on Software Configuration Management*, Grassau, January 1988.

7.   Haake, A. and J.M. Haake (1993), 'Take CoVer: Exploiting Version Support in Cooperative Systems', *Proc. Conf. on Human Factors in Computing Systems (INTERCHI'93)*, Amsterdam.

8.   Garg, P.K. and Scacchi, W., (1990), 'A Hypertext System to Maintain Software Life-cycle Documents', *IEEE Software*, 7 (3), 90-8.

9.   Pendergast, M. and Beranek, M., (1991), 'Coordination and control for collaborative workstation design', *Proc. INTERACT'90*, Elsevier Science Publishers.

10. Beaudouin-Lafon, M. (1990), 'Collaborative development of software', in *Multiuser Interfaces and Applications,* eds. Gibbs, S. and Verrijn-Stuart, A., Elsevier Science Publishers.

11. Benford, S., Bowers, J., Fahlen, L., Mariani, J, Rodden. T, Supporting Cooperative Work in Virtual Environments. *The Computer Journal*, 1995. 38(1).

Author Index

Springer
and the
environment

At Springer we firmly believe that an
international science publisher has a
special obligation to the environment,
and our corporate policies consistently
reflect this conviction.
We also expect our business partners –
paper mills, printers, packaging
manufacturers, etc. – to commit
themselves to using materials and
production processes that do not harm
the environment. The paper in this
book is made from low- or no-chlorine
pulp and is acid free, in conformance
with international standards for paper
permanency.

 Springer

Lecture Notes in Computer Science

For information about Vols. 1–1091

please contact your bookseller or Springer-Verlag